The Cotswold Village Trail

90 miles of Cotswold History

Nigel Bailey

One comes across the strangest things in walks

IG

Published
by
REARDON PUBLISHING
56, Upper Norwood Street, Leckhampton,
Cheltenham, Glos, GL53 0DU

Written, Researched, Layout and Design
Nigel Bailey

ISBN 1 873877 27 7

Thanks to Liz
whose long sight can spot a waymark
before I see the post it's nailed to.

For anyone who would like
to penetrate the tourist veneer
of the Cotswolds.

Printed by
IN2PRINT
Cheltenham, Glos

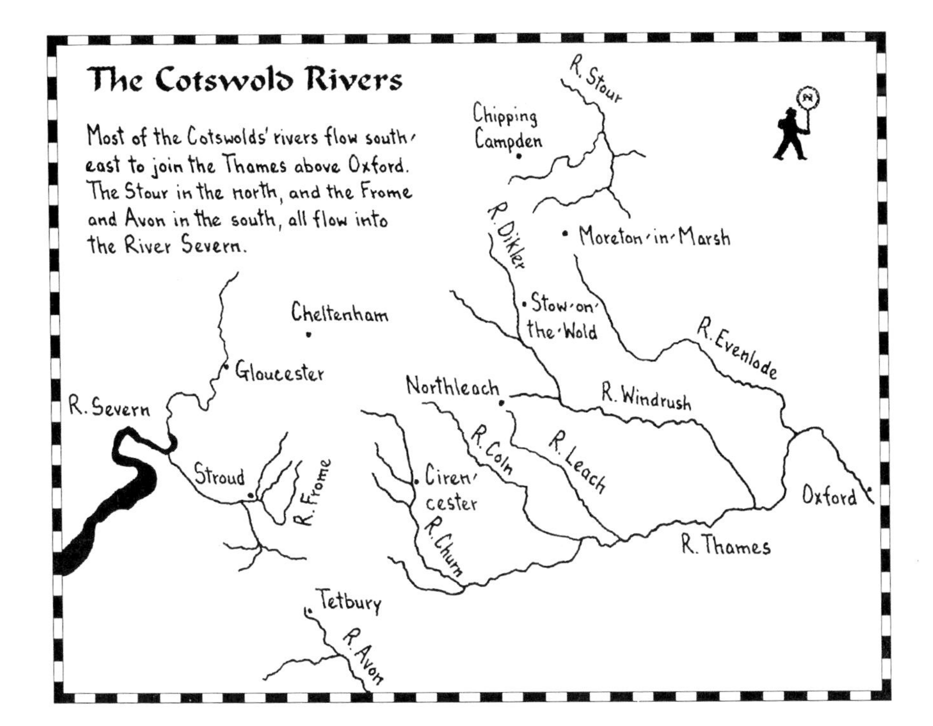

At that time the Cotswolds were on the southern edge of an ice sheet which advanced and retreated about 20 times over two million years. Each time the ice retreated, the meltwater, unable to seep into the frozen ground, formed surface rivers which carved the valleys we see today. Our route follows several of the Cotswolds' rivers and also a number of these charming and curious dry valleys. They were shaped by tributary streams of meltwater and, except in times of very wet weather, they are today completely dry, "hanging" above the main valleys.

The wind and the rain have put the final touches to the landscape we see today. Although at a glance Cotswold stone looks pretty much the same all over the area, there are important variations depending on which of the bands of rock is exposed at the surface.

➤ The oldest group of rocks is the Lias series, some of which are clays - hence the brickworks at Paxford which seem an anomaly in these hills. Any water draining through the limestone is forced to the surface in the form of springs by the barrier of impermeable clay. A chain of towns and villages has grown up where these clays occur at the surface. Many that we meet on our route, such as the Hidcotes, Ebrington and Bourton-on-the-Hill, owe their position to this spring line. In amongst these clays are narrow bands of marlstone, used to build ancient stone clapper bridges, memorial tablets and flagstoned cottage floors.

The Oolites form the main bulk of the Cotswold hills. Above the Inferior Oolite is a narrow band of Fuller's Earth and above this is the youngest of the layers, the Great Oolite, which must originally have capped the whole area. The individual grains that make up the oolite were tiny specks of sand that gained a coating of carbonate of lime to produce a texture reminiscent of fish roes.

➤ The quality of the Inferior Oolite varies considerably. The stone with a high proportion of shells and pebbles was used for road building or lime burning; the ragstones were used for ordinary buildings - cottages and farms; the freestones contain no shells or other debris so they could be finely cut for detailed building work. Many of Cheltenham's finest buildings and a number of Oxford Colleges were built with this freestone.

➤ The Fuller's Earth is a sticky blue clay used in the past for cleaning wool.

➤ The Great Oolite includes a freestone which was the most sought-after of all.

Most of the medieval buildings in Oxford and much of Regency Bath was built with it as was the original St Paul's Cathedral and Windsor Castle. The Great Oolite also produced the area's characteristic stone slates.

The recession and the slump in the housing market have brought hard times to the Cotswolds' remaining stone quarries but one at least, at Farmington, has invested in modern technology and sought new markets. This quarry has reaped the reward of a boom in sales abroad, supplying, for example, stone for a new mosque in the Middle East and all the stone walls and floors for a chain of 40 Winston Churchill theme pubs in California which will have an 1890s Victorian British appearance. Cotswold lads, though, are clearly not what they were: the quarry has had to ship in workers from France to keep up with demand.

A Japanese property developer, Mayagi Kundai, is taking a short-cut: he is having five Cotswold cottages dismantled and shipped to Japan to be reassembled at a cost of some £3-400,000 each.

Footpaths

The area has inherited a dense network of footpaths. While they are a boon to the walker they can be a problem to farmers and estate owners. The cutting or spraying of tracks through crops to leave a clear path can be expensive when the right of way lies straight across a field. Negotiations between landowners, the Ramblers' Association and the local authorities have led to many being diverted to follow field boundaries instead. For example, all but two of the 42 which cross the Misarden Estate have been altered in this way - a useful compromise for both the farmer and the walker.

Gissing wrote in 1924 that *In the old days the word "trespassing" never entered one's mind in wandering about these uplands*. He noticed barbed wire becoming common, paths being blocked and stiles being made insurmountable. He applauded the aims of the Commons and Footpaths Preservation Society and chided the local authorities for their lack of action over footpaths being *filched from the public by being made impassable or quietly hedged in altogether.*

Although we are constrained by keeping to public rights-of-way, the situation today is generally a happier one.

New Age travellers have been a problem. The cost of shifting one convoy from the Misarden Estate amounted to some £2,000. Solutions have been aimed at deterring the parking of buses and caravans by digging deep ditches into grass verges and by dumping hefty tree trunks or stumps in the entrances to lanes. This gives the appearance of Fortress Countryside but hopefully it is a solution to a temporary problem. These measures do not impede our progress on the route.

The Cotswold Warden Service

This magnificent service is provided by 220 or so volunteers organised by the Cotswold AONB Service supported by the Countryside Commission to protect and promote enjoyment of the Cotswolds. They build stiles and footbridges, help maintain the footpaths and sheepwashes, plant trees and clear litter, as well as provide guided walks and information for visitors.

Since the Countryside Act of 1968 local authorities have been required to signpost footpaths where they meet roads. A tribute to the work of the Warden Service is that in the preparation of this book only one footpath was found to be totally blocked, all the rest being in an excellent state of repair and effectively signposted - a very different situation from that found in many other parts of the country. You will recognise wardens by their badges showing the Cotswold Lion Sheep.

Cotswold Tourism

The Cotswolds were opened up to tourists by the bicycle. Both the early 20th century descriptions of the area were the result of bicycle tours which produced Herbert A Evans' "Highways and Byways in Oxford and the Cotswolds" in 1905 and Algernon Gissing's "The Footpath Way in Gloucestershire" in 1924. They found a district within easy reach of London and the Midlands, unspoilt by 18th and 19th century industrialisation; the Cotswolds' own industrial era had been earlier and of a much less disfiguring nature. It was on a smaller scale, more localised, and touched only the valleys of Blockley and the Stroud valleys in the south. The age of the train has left hardly a mark and the motorways bypass the Cotswolds to the south and the west.

Tourism is rapidly becoming one of the major industries in this country and crucial to the economy of the Cotswolds. The old-world appearance of the area has been carefully controlled by planning requirements and, as I write, the Cotswold AONB Service has published draft proposals for managing the area into the 21st century. The report embraces all aspects of protecting this unique environment including the promotion of "green" tourism and the encouragement of visitors away from the main honey-pot villages. Understandably popular with foreign visitors, plans are afoot to build replica Cotswold villages in Malaysia and Houston, Texas.

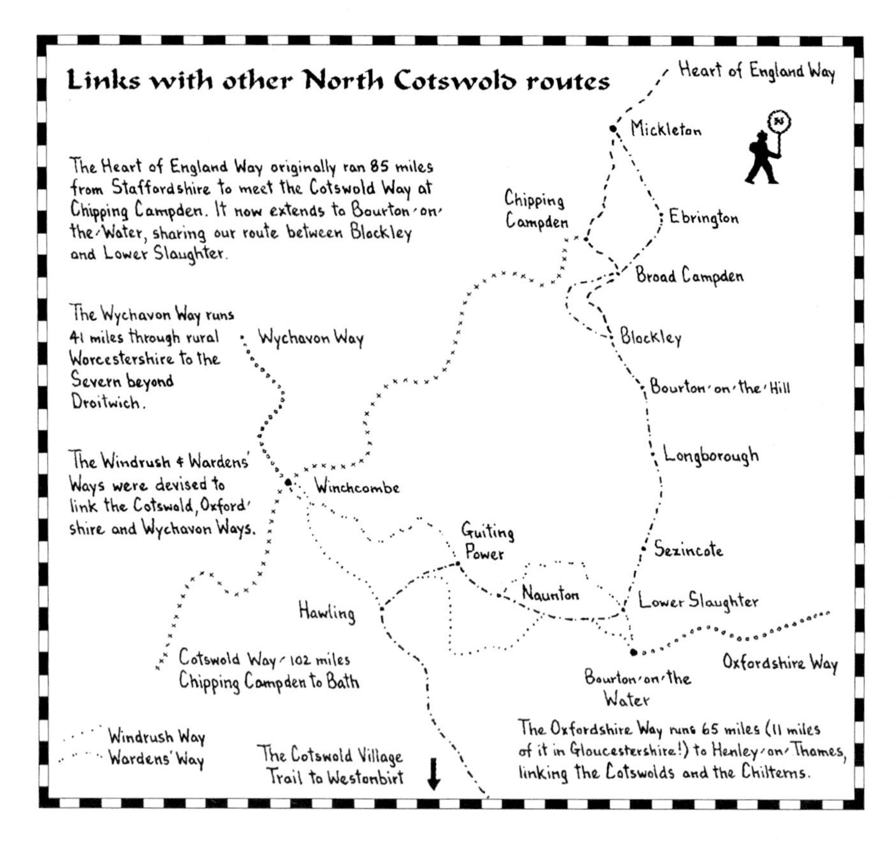

Farming Today

Farming practices play a considerable role in determining the appearance of the landscape. The days of the Cotswolds being dominated by sheep, or even by arable farming, are now long past and today's crops are more varied than ever before. The contemporary agri-business is probably growing oil-seed rape with its alien yellow shriek or flax with its pastel shade of blue, both grown these days for vegetable oil. You will spot many of these blocks of primary colour in high summer, interspersed with the startling scarlet of poppies amongst the corn.

These are certainly strange times for farming - there is a wind turbine near Stroud and even talk of robot tractors. While in parts of the country, farmland is being taken over by golf courses (in the past ten years an area the size of Greater Manchester has been swallowed up, so that they now occupy one in every 200 acres of England) fortunately we only encounter one on our route.

More in evidence on our walk, sadly, is the monstrously crass policy of "set-aside" which requires farmers to leave about 15% of their land out of production. In Gloucestershire alone, farmers are paid almost three million pounds each year, some £140 per acre, as long as they agree to neglect their land and encourage the rat population. Intensive farming since the last war has done lasting damage to the countryside, reducing the diversity of wildlife and leaving the residue of fertilisers and pesticides in the soil, the water and, most worryingly, in our food. With some imagination, though, "set-aside" could be a turning point in our management of the countryside.

The money could be used much more positively to encourage farmers to act as custodians of our heritage by maintaining valued features of the landscape and promoting a variety of wildlife habitats. Longer term "set-aside" arrangements could have a powerful positive outcome, encouraging a reversion to rough grassland and the planting of woodlands.

Fortunately, two schemes have been recently established to help counter the worst aspects of this policy and encourage landowners to adopt practices which will enhance the countryside:

➤ Grant aid and advice are available within the new Cotswold Environmentally Sensitive Area (which includes most of the Gloucestershire Cotswolds) to help maintain historic features of the landscape. Here, too, the Countryside Stewardship scheme aims to improve public access.

➤ The Countryside Commission, based in Cheltenham, offers assistance for the management of "set-aside" land. This can promote the maintenance of important habitats, avoid ploughing the sites of barrows or ancient field systems or even encourage reversion to the farming practices of earlier days.

A recent decision in Brussels will help further by allowing woodlands and land devoted to conservation projects to be counted as part of the farmer's "set-aside". This is welcome news for the appearance of the Cotswolds, enabling more farmers to take part in heritage projects and tree-planting schemes. Good news too for birds such as skylarks, redshank, stonechats and snipe, which have been in decline in recent years, threatened by the changes taking place to their habitats.

So now, any farmer with a bent for jigsaw puzzles and the knack of interpreting the intricacies of domestic and European legislation, can operate as a guardian of the countryside. There does seem to be, though, a glimmer of hope that the interests of farmers and environmentalists can coincide, using "set-aside" positively to regenerate the countryside and encourage a sustainable form of food production that does not lead to long term ecological damage.

Churches

One of the most pleasing features of the route is the number of country churches. Frustratingly, a few of them are kept locked for fear of vandals. If there are no instructions on where to obtain the key and you fail to meet the groundsman or the flower-arranging person, you could always resort to Crockford's Clerical Directory!

The Pre-Reformation world was dominated by the idea of ensuring heavenly protection, so all churches were dedicated to a saint or saints, although the dedication of Paxford church is unknown. Over the centuries many saints have also come to be recognised as the patrons of various groups of people - St Christopher as the patron saint of travellers is probably the best known.

Where a particular individual saint is encountered for the first time on our route, I have included a panel giving details although the lists are not exhaustive. Some of the early British saints such as St Eadburgha (Ebrington) and Kenelm (Sapperton) do not appear to be patrons of anything.

Bulls and the Law

The legal position is that farmers are allowed to keep bulls of some beef breeds together with cows in fields crossed by footpaths. Dairy breed bulls should not be kept where there is footpath access. Anyone with a qualification in Agriculture will have no trouble distinguishing between the two; it's all rather ambiguous for the layman. Having experienced one extremely frightening incident with a bull during a walk, I tend to skirt round any field containing them.

Young bullocks tend to be curious so they may approach you. They are, actually, likely to be more afraid of you than you are of them.

Refreshments en route

The route is well endowed with pubs so on almost every stretch you can plan your day with a break at a pub around lunch time. They all serve at least a "ploughman's lunch" though each pub's conception of what ploughpeople have for lunch is intriguingly varied. Most, though, are good value for money.

All the pubs serve real ale and, in many cases, real cider. CAMRA must be one of the country's most successful pressure groups, in 20 years turning back the flood of warm, flat, keg beers. You will find a wide range of Britain's 1,000-odd different beers on offer including those brewed at the Cotswolds' three independent breweries, Donnington which is on the route, Hook Norton and the Uley Brewery near Dursley with its Gloucester Old Spot pig logo. Look out for its punningly-named range of beers - Hogshead, Pig's Ear, Pigor Mortis and Old Spot Prize Ale (for my money, the best beer you'll find on the route).

Let's wish an equal degree of success to Pipe Down, the Campaign Against Piped Music, formed a few years ago to *restore freedom of choice to all individuals, so they do not have to tolerate another person's choice of music*. Most of the pubs on our route avoid piped music altogether.

What to Carry

On any lengthy walk it is worth taking at least a small rucksack for food and drink (it is surprising how much liquid you will want on a hot day); a first aid kit comprising plasters, a bandage and a tube of antiseptic cream; a phonecard and coin for a telephone and a small piece of plastic sheeting large enough to provide a dry seat on a wet day.

I've never been seriously bothered by dogs while walking but if the prospect concerns you, a Dog Dazer[1] is an electronic dog frightener that will clip to your belt. Its ultrasonic shriek, inaudible to humans, will scare away the fiercest dog.

[1] Available by mail order from Dazer UK, 43 Northcote Road, London SW11 1YY or 0171 228 2360.

Binoculars, though heavy, offer an extra dimension of interest in the countryside and are useful for spotting distant waymarks if you don't have a long-sighted wife.

It is good practice to carry a map, compass and whistle.

"50 ways" to walk this walk "One Way"

It is much more satisfying to be able to tackle a long-distance route walking in one direction only, avoiding the need to backtrack. Local buses are of very limited help so some ways to organise a one-way walk are:

- ➤ carry a fold-up bicycle in the boot (and a padlock and chain)
- ➤ carry a moped on a cycle carrier
- ➤ involve a friend who will take you to your start point, leaving your car at the day's destination
- ➤ involve a friend who will drop you off and pick you up
- ➤ take a taxi to the start point, leaving your car at the day's destination
- ➤ backpack with a tent
- ➤ carry a rucksack and stay at Bed-and-Breakfasts
- ➤ walk one way and hitch-hike back
- ➤ walk with friends; leave one car at your planned destination and drive a car to your start point
- ➤ stay at Youth Hostels; this would involve the Ffyona Campbell technique as the only Youth Hostel actually on our route is at Duntisbourne Abbots; another is just off the route at Stow-on-the-Wold.

If none of these is possible you'll have to retrace your steps or devise a circuit.

Opening Times

Some of the properties we visit on the route are not normally open to the public except through the arrangements of the National Garden Scheme. More than 3,000 gardens throughout the country are members, opening for just a few days each year, raising about £1.5 million annually for charity. Dates vary from year-to-year and are published in a yellow-covered guide, "Gardens of Gloucestershire", available for a few pence from newsagents, WH Smith etc. Many of them are absolute gems and the visitor can feel a real sense of privilege visiting a private garden.

Weather Forecast

You can get a detailed local weather forecast by phoning the Met Office's Weathercall service on 01891-772-275; alternatively, you can use the guidance offered in the following rhymed list of 31 signs of impending rain. It was written in 1821 by Dr Edward Jenner, a Cotswold man, born at Wotton-under-Edge, more famous for discovering the vaccination which has now eradicated smallpox than for his amateur interest in meteorology.

He is said to have based it on local sayings and beliefs about the weather and sent it to a friend as the reason for postponing a proposed outing. It has come to be known as "Twill Surely Rain":

The hollow Winds begin to blow;
The clouds look black, the Glass is low;
The Soot falls down, the Spaniels sleep;
And Spiders from their cobwebs peep.
Last night the sun went pale to bed;
The Moon in haloes hid her head;
The boding Shepherd heaves a sigh,
For see! a Rainbow in the sky.
The Walls are damp, the Ditches smell,
Clos'd is the pink-eyed Pimpernel.
Hark! how the Chairs and Tables crack;
Old Betty's joints are on the rack.
Loud quacks the Ducks; the Peacocks cry;
The distant hills are looming high.
How restless are the snorting Swine;
The busy Flies disturb the Kine.
Low o'er the grass the Swallow wings,
The Cricket, too, how sharp he sings,
Puss on the hearth, with velvet paws
Sits, wiping o'er her whiskered jaws.
Through the clear sea the Fishes rise,
And nimbly catch th' incautious flies
The Glow-Worms, numerous and bright,
Illum'd the dewy dell last night;
At dusk, the squalid Toad was seen,
Hopping and crawling o'er the green;
The Whirling Dust the wind obeys,
And in the rapid eddy plays;
The Frog has changed his yellow vest,
And in a russet coat is drest;
Though June, the air is cold and chill
The mellow Blackbird's voice is still.
My Dog, so alter'd in his taste,
Quits mutton-bones, on grass to feast.
And see yon Rooks, how odd their flight,
They imitate the gliding Kite,
And seem precipitate to fall -
As if they felt the piercing ball.
'Twill surely rain, I see with sorrow,
Our jaunt must be put off till morrow.

How to Use this Book

The book is arranged in 12 sections ranging in length from six to nine miles, a comfortable day's walk, leaving time to visit some of the places described on the way. Each section is a mixture of route instructions and articles linked to features of the route. Each section begins and ends with a quotation from one of the Gloucestershire poets whose lives are briefly sketched in Appendix A.

The page layouts and the arrangement of each section are unconventional. Route instructions are laid out in double columns. The extended articles are interspersed with the route instructions at relevant points - what better than to take a rest and read about the feature when you are in exactly the right spot.

Many paths on the Cotswolds are waymarked with arrows, on yellow circles for footpaths and on blue circles for bridleways. They are frequently used in the instructions but abbreviated to Y↑ and B↑.

(20) This symbol shows the approximate cumulative distance in miles.

And for those of you keen on maps...

The sketch maps and descriptions in the book are sufficient to guide you along the route. If you enjoy looking at maps and the wealth of detail shown on the Ordnance Survey Pathfinder and Outdoor Leisure maps (roughly 2½ inches to a mile), they are well worth the investment. For the whole route you would need the Outdoor Leisure map 45, Cotswolds, and Pathfinder maps 1020, 1113, 1133, and 1152.

The squirrel motif is based on a design for fire dogs by Ernest Gimson, now in the Cheltenham Museum.

1
Mickleton to Broad Campden

7½ miles

I'm homesick for my hills again -
My hills again!
To see above the Severn plain
Unscabbarded against the sky
The blue high blade of Cotswold lie

WH

Mickleton to Broad Campden

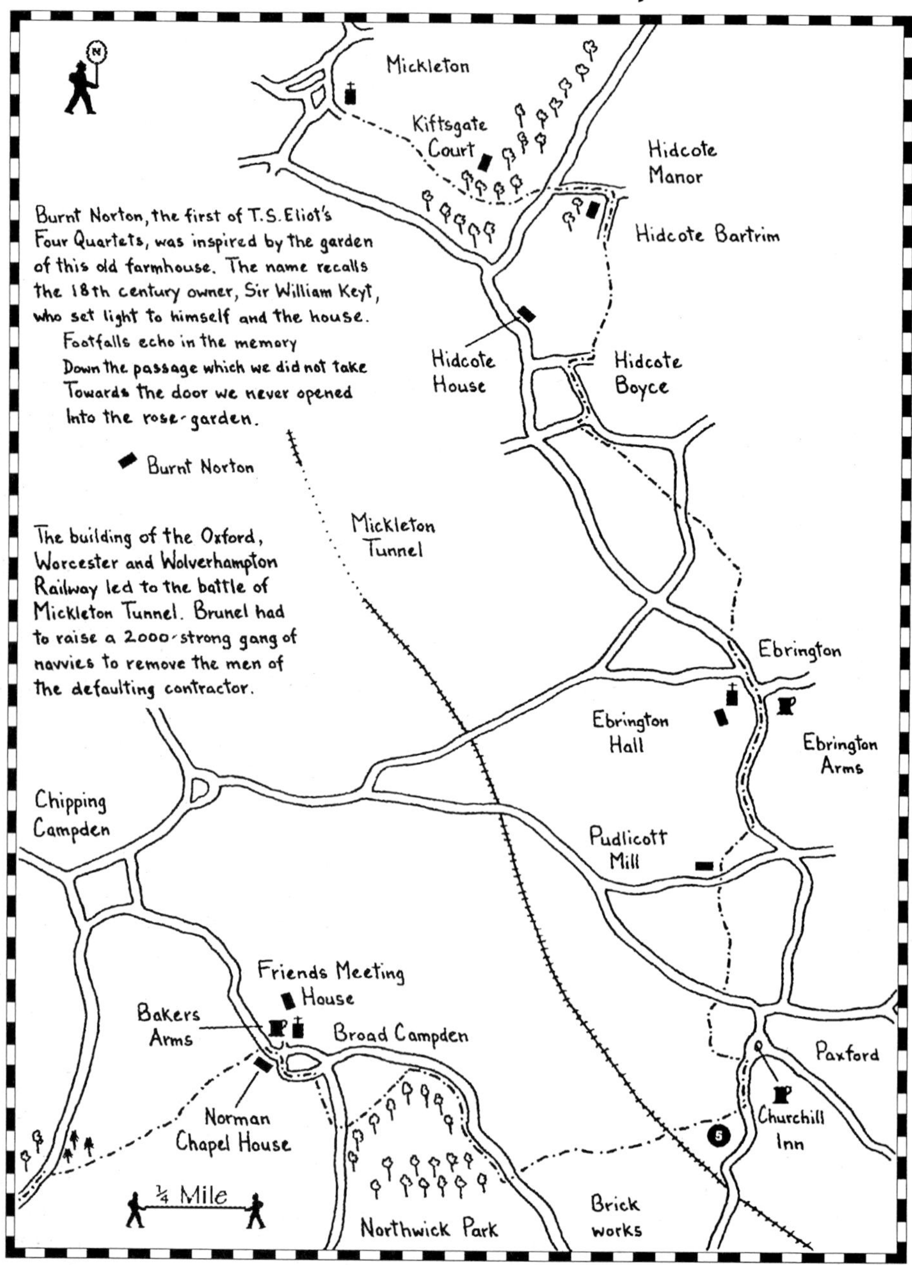

Based on 1981 to 1991 Ordnance Survey mapping with the permission of The Controller of Her Majesty's Stationery Office

Our route begins outside the church at Mickleton. Immediately, the mixture of stonework and brick in the houses tells us we are on the edge of the Cotswolds. Follow the road curving left, pass the gate to the cemetry and go through the gate marked Heart of England Way (HoEW). Swing a little right to aim across the field towards the first oak tree and then straight on to a large and small gate together. The well-worn path then winds beside the little stream. The view to the left confirms that Meon Hill would have made a splendid start point but there is no right of way to the hill fort on the top.

Emerge from the trees, going through a gate with B↑. Follow the hedge and fence, still beside the stream, then curve left to reach another gate with B↑. Follow the grassy track as it curves up and left with the valley. At each step your perspective on the trees changes while Kiftsgate Court, up to the left, moves in and out of view.

Where the trees close in on both sides, pass through a gateway with B↑. Swing a little left to aim for the pillars of the lodge at the top of the field. In spring you will see a mass of bluebells on the wooded slope. You will almost have reached the lodge before you can see the blue gate that is your exit from the field. Looking back down the valley, the hill you see in the distance is Bredon Hill, an outlier of the Cotswolds.

On the road, follow the signpost for Hidcote Gardens. Just before its car park turn right on to a road lined with holly trees.

As you pass Hidcote Manor you see an unusual barn conversion: this one, with the addition of suitable windows, was turned into a chapel. Look up the avenue of beech trees to the left with a statue in the distance. You may well see a large black boar in the field and wonder why he is not advancing towards you. If you investigate you will find a ha-ha or sunken wall keeping him in his place.

Continue past the delightful but untypical cottages with their thatched roofs and timber-clad upper storeys. As the road curves right, around the end of the barn, go straight on through the gateway of Manor Farm into a field.

Follow the clear path straight on between the market garden crops, aiming for a lone pine and eventually spotting the 17th century Hidcote House down to the right. Just before the hedge, curve left to a footbridge leading to an awkward stile with Y↑. Again follow a clear path till a kissing gate brings you on to a track at Hidcote Boyce. Turning right, the track becomes a road with a lovely espallier apple covering the entire end wall of the house.

Turn left to take the road out of the hamlet. After 600 yards, at a T junction, take the gate with Y↑.

Keep to the grassy farm track, roughly following the contour. After a couple of hundred yards an indistinct path branches off left. Follow it, aiming for a group of oaks to the left of two willows. If you come to a barn by an orchard you have dropped down the field too far and a notice tells you so. A gate with Y↑ and simple stile take you into the next field. Cross this keeping just below the hedge to a gate with Y↑ by a woodwormed tree stump. Go straight on to a stile with Y↑ in a triangle of oak trees. Go straight on again to reach a stile that brings you on to a road below the orchard of Cotswold House.

Cross the road to a gate with Y↑ and follow a grassy track to reach the bottom

Contd: page 7

The Pudding Club

The Pudding Club has met at the Three Ways House Hotel in Mickleton since 1985 to enjoy traditional British steamed puddings such as spotted dick and Lord Randall's pudding. The hotel's definition of a pudding is that it should be a substantial dish needing a long cooking time, served hot with custard. There are always seven different puds to try and a standing offer of free wine for coming up with a new recipe.

The Mickleton Hooter

The valley you are climbing up is known as Weeping Hollow and is said to be the haunt of a ghost known as the Mickleton Hooter. Its reported appearance varies from that of a tall white woman to a calf with a man's head. More often it is not seen, just heard, emitting a terrifying wailing or screeching. A possible explanation is an incident said to have happened in Weeping Hollow in the 16th century. Sir Edward Greville, mistaking his son for a robber, accidentally killed him. There may, though, be a natural cause for the moaning sound. The valley is shaped like a narrow funnel so it is possible that the wind distorts everyday sounds to the extent of scaring the locals.

You should manage to climb the valley without encountering the Hooter - the last report mentioned by Mark Turner was 30 years ago.

Kiftsgate Court

Here lies a beautiful three acre garden that sweeps from the house and over the scarp edge of the Cotswolds making the most of the steepening slope and the views across the Severn Valley and to the distant Malverns. Everything you see here was created in the last 75 years.

The house was built in the 1880s and incorporates the entire Georgian facade of Mickleton Manor which was brought up the hill by a specially-built light railway. The gardens were created after the First World War by Heather Muir, extended by her daughter, Diana Binney, and have been open to the public for the last 20 years. They are now in the hands of the third generation, Anne Chambers.

Near the house is a series of rectangular gardens, one splendidly displaying early summer flowering bulbs, one with a pool and melodeous fountain.

The record-breaking Kiftsgate rose

To the east is a group of colour-related borders, the splendid, sunken White Garden and beds of curious old roses, at their peak in mid summer. Two Simon Verity statues catch the eye, a stone seat made from two tombstones and the Mother and Child which stands in a magical little grove of Scotch firs, bright with cyclamen well into the autumn.

Westwards the slope falls away dramatically with steep paths and terraced banks of plants defying gravity. Below the summerhouse, stone steps like grand staircases divide to pass either side of a small pool with the mask of a water god. Everywhere, trees and hedges with archways and hidden doors, shelter a profusion of plants jostling for space. The garden is an enchanted, intimate place to stroll which seems as if it was created long ago. It is still evolving, though: at the foot of the slope is the Bathing Pool with its 1986 Grecian Temple folly hiding a changing room.

The star attraction is what is claimed to be the largest rose in England. The "Kiftsgate" rose is an absolute monster which, despite repeated cutting back, covers a quarter of an acre and has climbed to more than fifty feet. In summer it is covered with millions of small, scented, creamy-white blossoms.

In the early days of opening to the public, a board outside announced the *Home of Rosa Filipes "Kiftsgate"* but too many gullible visitors asked for details of the lady. A newspaper recently advised visits at least twice each month throughout the summer!

Hidcote Manor Garden

Major Lawrence Johnston was an American born in Paris, who took British citizenship in order to fight the Boers in South Africa. Returning from the war and needing an occupation, he took to farming and in 1907 his mother bought him 300 acres of Cotswolds including Hidcote Manor and the hamlet of Hidcote Bartrim. Starting with the bare hillside and without any master plan, he evolved what was to become one of the most important English gardens created this century which now enjoys a world-wide reputation. The ten acre garden is in fact a series of outdoor "rooms" which means that a visit is full of surprises. Each is separated from its neighbours by long walks and hedges of every kind and linked by narrow arched "doorways"; one is a mixture of hornbeam, beech, holly, box and yew which has come to be known as a harlequin hedge. There are four miles of hedges of different sizes and shapes, many of them cut into elegant topiary, so that the whole garden has an architectural feel. While this pioneered a new

The Lily Pool and clipped Portuguese laurels

gardening style, to an extent the "room" idea was forced on Johnston: the site on the exposed Cotswold edge needed shelter if anything was going to survive.

Each "room" is a unique haven with a mood of its own but there is also a sense of humour at work here. The Pine Garden is not a garden of pines but a garden designed around an old Scots Pine. A lawn is edged with shrub roses set off by a backdrop of...rhubarb. My favourite is the original Old Garden beside the house and the huge spreading Cedar of Lebanon. Its wide borders look haphazardly arranged with plants growing in profusion but they repay some time spent admiring the subtle design. Here too is the climbing rose, originally called "Hidcote Yellow", now renamed Rosa "Lawrence Johnston".

Some of the most attractive "rooms" are:

- The Stilt Garden with arrestingly clipped hornbeams and views of Bredon Hill
- The Rose Walk of gloriously scented old French roses
- The Red Borders with their carefully controlled blend of reds and coppers in late summer
- The Pillar Garden with clipped yews like a Classical temple
- The Theatre Lawn with its circular stone-walled stage was for many years used to present open air productions of plays.

Many of the rarities on display came from Johnston's own plant hunting in South Africa, Mexico and China in the '20s and '30s, journeys he undertook accompanied by his valet and his chauffeur. Whilst he was not honoured during his lifetime, Johnston proved to be one of the century's most influential garden designers and half a dozen plants bear his or the garden's name, such as the fuschia "Hidcote Beauty" and "Lavandula Hidcote". Hidcote is regarded as the County's botanical gardens.

In 1948 he put Hidcote in the hands of The National Trust - the first garden it ever acquired. The Trust has maintained it immaculately though it did disperse its collection of Regency garden furniture. He moved to Menton on the French-Italian border where in the winters he had been creating another garden, Serre de la Madonne, clothing former olive terraces with sub-tropical plants to create similar effects to those at Hidcote. He died there ten years later and his French garden rapidly returned to nature.

If you are a frequent garden visitor, don't miss this gem amongst the National Trust properties; if you have never visited a garden before, start now.

If you can possibly arrange to come back here towards the end of the next century you will find another extensive garden. Susan Hill, the novelist, is developing a garden around her 18th century stone farmhouse at Ebrington so that the landscaped garden blends into the 40 acres of surrounding parkland. Already she has planted hedges, ornamental trees and a hawthorn maze, extended an orchard and added to it climbing and rambler roses and installed a large lake, a nut walk and a secret garden.

Perhaps in a hundred years time it will compete for our attention with Hidcote and Kiftsgate Court.

of the orchard, leaving it over a fence with Y↑. The field you now walk on has pretty dramatic ridges and furrows. Drop diagonally down this field, aiming for the hedge that runs past the football pitch. Leave the field by a half-hearted stile with Y↑ and follow the field edge, past the football pitch, to enter **Ebrington** (pronounced Yabberton or, phonetically, more like Yubber'n).

Reaching the road, turn left past some imaginatively designed modern stone houses. You pass attractive houses with colourful front gardens perched on the banks either side of the road to arrive at the village green where the local builders had a couple of aberrations.

➤ Ebrington used to have a unique Cow Charity dating from the 17th century which bequeathed the milk of ten cows to the poor of the village "annually for ever". Milk rationing in the Second World War made the arrangement difficult to administer and in 1952 the bequest was changed to a money trust.

➤ Sir John Fortesque's effigy lies in the church dressed in red robe and ermine cap, the robes of office of Lord Chancellor. A remarkable man, he lived through the reigns of eight kings and reached the age of 90. He fell foul of Edward IV and was exiled to Holland where he wrote the first English law book. At the age of 67 he was fighting at the Battle of Towton with Henry VI. In 1456 he bought the manor which is still in the family today.

➤ The manor has seen so many alterations that it now looks architecturally incoherent. A little of the 13th century original remains on the ground floor of the south wing and some of the interior is Tudor. *.....the tall chimney of the picture parlour was so shook by the violent and twisting winds of the autumn of 1823...it has had to be taken down.*

➤ The church tower has a rare hand-wound clock with no face or hands which chimes the hours.

➤ It is said that hedges are grown high in Ebrington to keep the cuckoos in: *that way summer will last all year.*

➤ A folk song collected by Percy Grainger in the 1900s tells stories of the Yabberton Fools - but then it was collected over the Warwickshire border at Ilmington.

➤ A path runs from the village cross near the green to the church past a lovely row of stone-built former almshouses with dormer windows.

Ebrington Arms
Free House.
Good range of food with the menu chalked on a beam.
Donnington, Hook Norton, real cider and a weekly Guest Beer.
Huge open fireplaces; the one in the dining room retains its oven.

Pass to the right of the Ebrington Arms for the road out of the village. Follow this road, May Lane, for ½ mile, passing three scruffy sheds, and where it bends left take the gravelly lane right at the footpath sign. After following the lane across one field, take the stile left with Y↑ to cross the garden of Pudlicott Mill with its varied species of ducks, geese and injured swans which are often returned to the wild.

Contd: page 10

Drystone Walls

For monument of native skill
In timeless texture living still,
For austere beauty, slowly grown,
Give me a wall of quarried stone.
FM

You've now encountered your first Cotswold stone walls. You're going to encounter lots of Cotswold stone walls. Lots and lots and lots...

Before the 1750s, walls weren't a common feature of these uplands which must have presented a quite different panorama of undivided sheep pastures. The walls which did exist at that time marked parish boundaries and separated ancient fields. From the 18th century the Enclosure Acts gradually required the land to be parcelled into the chequerboard we see today.

Without a ready supply of wood for fencing and with soils too poor for hedge growing, the obvious means was to build walls with the readily available stone. This also had the advantage of potentially standing for ever, the stone expanding and contracting with the weather, bedding ever more snugly into place. And, as long as it was built by a skilled waller, it needed very little maintenance. This, of course, is the key to the problem we see today with many walls collapsed or crumbling. They were not built by skilled craftsmen but by farm labourers. Wall building and repair were generally winter jobs like hedging and ditching, making sound use of the cheap labour force when it was not needed on the land.

Today's farms and estates have very few labourers with spare time in the winter and it is barbed wire that comes very cheap. Landowners no longer need stone walls. Of course, a wall built without mortar also makes an attractive "quarry" so many have been plundered over the years and the stone recycled. Grants are increasingly available and enthusiastic groups such as the British Trust for Conservation Volunteers, do repair at least some stretches of fallen wall.

It looks pretty simple. Choose a stone from the pile, (the one that's the perfect shape is in there somewhere!), place it where it seems to fit best, then move on to the next. Anyone who has tried to build a retaining wall in a garden will know that this is not so.

A Cotswold wall is actually two outer walls and a space between filled with small stones and rubble. From two feet thick at the base it tapers to 16 inches at the top. If you see a wall being built or repaired you'll notice a wooden frame of this shape being used as a guide. Traditionally, the waller placed a bottle of home-made wine in the core of the wall; then, if he was not paid for the work he would return, demolish his wall and retrieve the bottle.

The wall is capped with "toppers" or "combers", large flat stones placed on their edge at a slight slant. The faces were built up in rough courses in staggered rows so that each stone tied the two beneath it into position. Traditionally no mortar was used. The stone is fairly soft, easily shaped and with the skill of the craftsman, only gravity was needed to hold the wall in place. Experienced wallers reckoned to lay about seven yards of wall in a week.

To withstand rain and frost, the stone was laid the same way up as it lay in the quarry. Experienced wallers knew at a glance which way up was correct; the modern rockery builder probably does not and is soon disappointed with his handiwork.

You'll notice some of the oldest walls built with very narrow stones like roofing tiles. A wall densely covered with mosses and litchens is another mark of great age. You'll distinguish between the fairly rough work put into field boundaries and the meticulous use of larger, squared stones in walls bordering a manor or country house, the stones fitted together with hardly a gap like in an Inca temple.

You will also find a variety of stone stiles - upright-standing slabs, squeeze stiles which are gaps in the wall tapering to just a few inches width at ground level, and, my favourites, the wall ladders.

By the time you finish this walk you'll be a connoisseur of drystone walls. You'll have seen gleaming newly-built ones and grey, ivy-clad ancient ones; walls built as if with bricks in regimented layers and others in courses which drunkenly undulate; elegant curves of walls sweeping across a hill and walls that run straight and true for miles; walls slowly being pushed over by the growth of a tree; walls leaning precariously, Pisa-like; large dressed quoins used to neaten the edge where a gate was let into the wall; blocks you'd have trouble lifting and slates as thin as wafers; walls that have caved in where some underground stream has swept away the foundations; gaps where stones have tumbled out and spilled to the ground; and jumbled piles of mossy stones which once-upon-a-time were walls.

You'll find that these walls hold a fascination like waves breaking on a beach or flames licking from a log. The lines between the courses, never as regular as brickwork, will draw your eye and challenge you to speed along the trail.

I'd sooner go hedging than build a stone wall,
All pick up and place it and hope it don't fall;
When east winds blow bitter and keen in the trees,
I'd sooner lay blackthorn than dry-wall and freeze.

FM

Cross the road with care to a stile with Y↑. Turn right to follow the field edge, crossing a wooden footbridge to enter the next field. As you follow the stream's meanderings, notice how it has cut deep into the clay. Cross a farm track and continue to the corner of the field, then drop down right to the road. Turn right, cross the stream and turn left over a simple footbridge at the footpath sign. Walk between stream and fence.

Just past an elaborate modern stone bridge, jig right then left over a stile with Y↑. After 200 yards go left over a wooden sleeper bridge with Y↑. Leave the farm track to follow the hedge, aiming for a stile to the left of **Paxford** village church and school which were combined in one small building.

➤ Up the road by the pub is a small shop under a huge old Hovis advertisement.

Churchill Inn
Free House.
Arkells, Hook Norton & keg cider.
Pleasant village pub. The inn sign shows a remarkably young-looking version of the eponymous Sir Winston.

➤ Beside it a cottage, apparently empty, bears the date 1646.

Turn right along the road, passing a barn with a cow weather vane. Leave the road by a bridleway sign right, by a post box. Go through the wooden gate with B↑ at Pye Mill - the name comes from *pied* so it is likely that this mill was at one time a treadmill rather than a water mill. Cross the yard with its odd collection of buildings, leaving it by a green gate.

Continue straight on for about a mile following the brook. As you cross a series of fields separated by gates with B↑, pause at the railway line for the view back to Paxford. When you reach the road, turn left then right over a stile with Y↑ into the corner of Paxford Business Centre. The buildings you are passing began life as a Second World War American Army Hospital. After the war they were converted to house Polish refugees, some of whom lived there till it was closed in 1970. About a hundred yards up the road beside the wood is a stone monument carved with Polish names.

Turn immediately right over a stile with Y↑ into the belt of trees. Follow the brambly path which improves when it swings left away from the road. Half a mile after swinging left, watch out for a Y↑ right on a post. Drop down to the road by a wooden bench and take a break - you've climbed 80 yards since the Business Centre. The bench gives a lovely view of Broad Campden with Chipping Campden beyond and the Vale of Evesham stretching away in the distance. The church at Chipping Campden is the start, or the end, of the Cotswold Way.

Cross the road at the footpath sign and head down the centre of the field aiming for a stile then a path between two hedges. Drop down some steps and over another stile to the road. Either cross it to continue on a narrow path between hedges or take the road left which shows you more of the smartly kept village of **Broad Campden;** both routes bring you to the church.

➤ The Friends Meeting House: this Quaker meeting room dates from the 1660s, fell into disuse 100 years ago and was restored in the 1960s with a beautifully worded welcome by the door.

➤ The Norman Chapel House hides behind a tall stone wall topped with a hedge opposite the church. It was rescued from dereliction by CR Ashbee and rebuilt as a house for Ananda Coomeraswamy in the early 1900s. Ashbee and his wife lived their last few years in the house. The best view is from the bench on the tall mound by the church.

➤ An American millionaire, Joseph Fels, bought 70 acres of land at Broad Campden for use by the Guild of Handicrafts. The aim was to combine craft work with crop and animal husbandry but the experiment was short lived.

➤ In the village was the studio of the sculptor, Doris Lindner, who modelled the bronze statue of Arkle the racehorse that overlooks the parade ring at Cheltenham racecourse. She also made a 500 limited edition in bone china. All of her china pieces can be seen in the Dyson-Perrins Museum in Worcester.

St Michael, patron of

- the sick
- coopers
- grocers
- paratroopers
- policemen
- battles
- hatters
- swordsmen

Bakers Arms
Fine country pub.
Half a dozen real ales including beers from local brewers Stanway, Donnington and the Wickwar Brewing Company.
The inn sign recalls with ears of wheat, sheaves and dough that this was once a bakery. Try a double or even a triple Ploughman's!

It's Arkle on the stands' side for Ireland and Mill House for England on the far side...and this is it with Arkle just taking the lead as they come to the last fence. It's going to be Arkle if he jumps it.

Arkle coming to the last now and Arkle has a length over Mill House...he's over. Mill House is trying to challenge him again but it's Arkle on the stands' side. Mill House over on the far side coming up towards the line...and Arkle is holding him. Arkle going away from Mill House...this is the champion.

And so the result of probably the greatest Gold Cup run at Cheltenham: first Arkle, second Mill House and third Pas Seul.

Sir Peter O'Sullevan's BBC commentary, 1964

The Tale of a Printing Press

If I were asked to say what is...the most important production of Art...
I should answer, a beautiful house; and if I were further asked to name
the production next in importance...I should answer, a beautiful book. WM

William Morris is the best-known figure of the English Arts and Crafts Movement. During the second half of the last century he established a reputation as a designer of furniture, fabrics and stained glass and as a poet, writer, translator and early Socialist. He aimed to revive the traditions of medieval craftsmen and combine beauty and usefulness in everything he produced. His work became very fashionable: he was commissioned to design wallpaper for Queen Victoria's new house, Balmoral. His connection with the Cotswolds is a little tenuous because, although he was the tenant of Kelmscott Manor, near Lechlade, just over the Oxfordshire border, he used the house more as a retreat than a permanent home.

He loved all aspects of books and had long been interested in early manuscripts. He produced hand-written and illuminated versions of the classics and his own translations of Icelandic sagas. It was not until 1889, though, that he set up his own Kelmscott Press aiming to produce books of a quality rarely seen since the early hand printers like Caxton.

He certainly took the enterprise seriously. The paper was hand-made incorporating Morris's own design of watermark; the bindings were of intricately tooled leather and the typefaces were his own - "Golden", "Troy" and "Chaucer",

The legendary Kelmscott Chaucer and the cabinet designed for it by CSA Voysey

echoing the styles of the earliest printed books. He even collected herbs and bark to prepare his own inks and hand-carved all the wooden blocks.

In the seven years up to 1898 more than 50 titles were printed. His greatest achievement was the beautiful version of the complete works of Chaucer with decorated borders and 87 magnificent woodcut illustrations which took nearly four years to complete.

SALLY GRAY.
Words by R. Anderson, Esq.
Air Cumberland. Traditional.

A page from the Essex House Songbook

Morris' purpose in all this was not to make a profit but to encourage quality of craftsmanship so he would have been pleased that after his death the presses passed into the hands of CR Ashbee's Guild of Handicrafts which a couple of years later moved from Whitechapel to set up as a craft community in Chipping Campden. The early productions of their Essex House Press were the Guild's own songbooks, produced in Ashbee's own typeface design, "Endeavour". He quickly established a very high reputation. The books were decorated with woodcuts and fanciful initial letters and bound elaborately in leather, ebony, rose and holly woods and decorated with silver and enamel. His most ambitious project was the Edward VII Prayer Book.

The Norman Chapel House, Broad Campden

Many of the titles were obscure and competition from commercial presses, like Dent who had introduced vastly improved standards of design and legibility, led to the closing of the Essex House Press but the Cotswold connection continued.

Ananda Coomaraswamy was born in Ceylon (Sri Lanka), spent his early years in Madras and was educated at Wycliffe College. He was a philosopher and the

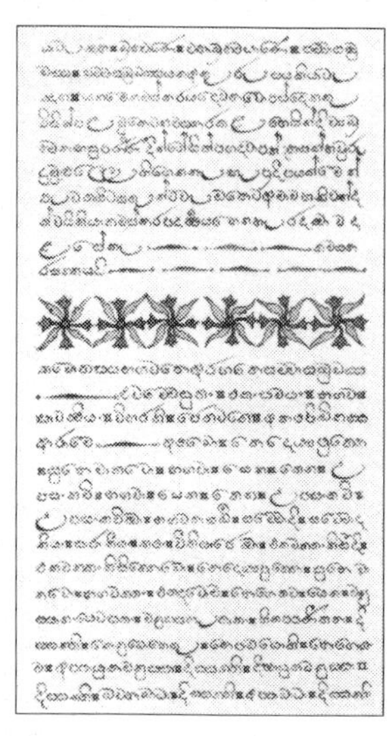

Illustrations from "Mediaeval Sinhalese Art" - an 18th century manuscript and an engraved tobacco box

authority in the West on Indian art and craft. His first wife, Ethel, sister of one of the Guild's jewellers, headed the revival of hand-loom weaving, gravitating from the Ashbee circle to Eric Gill's community at Ditchling in Sussex.

In 1907 they moved into the The Norman Chapel House in Broad Campden and decorated it with a mixture of Eastern treasures and products of both Morris and the Guild. He was the pioneer historian of Indian art and was greatly concerned at the loss of traditional craftsmanship in Ceylon after 100 years of British rule. He bought one of the Guild's presses to print oriental texts and his book, "Mediaeval Sinhalese Art". An aphorism of his is often attributed to others: *An artist is not a special kind of man, but any man is a special kind of artist.* Whilst he was a cult figure in London artistic circles, he must have sounded an altogether discordant note - tall, olive-skinned with flowing black hair or turban, walking the quiet lanes of the north Cotswolds.

The other press was bought by Benjamin Chandler of Hidcote House but as far as I know he never produced any books with it.

Morris, Ashbee and Coomeraswamy would, I am sure, be both saddened and amazed by the very idea of desk-top publishing!

In Gloucestershire where I was bred,
The men get work and the girls get wed;
The beer is brown, but the cider's red,
And there's nought for the law to do.

JH

2
Broad Campden to Longborough

8½ miles

A four hours' tramping
With brisk blood flowing,
And life worth knowing

IG

Broad Campden to Longborough

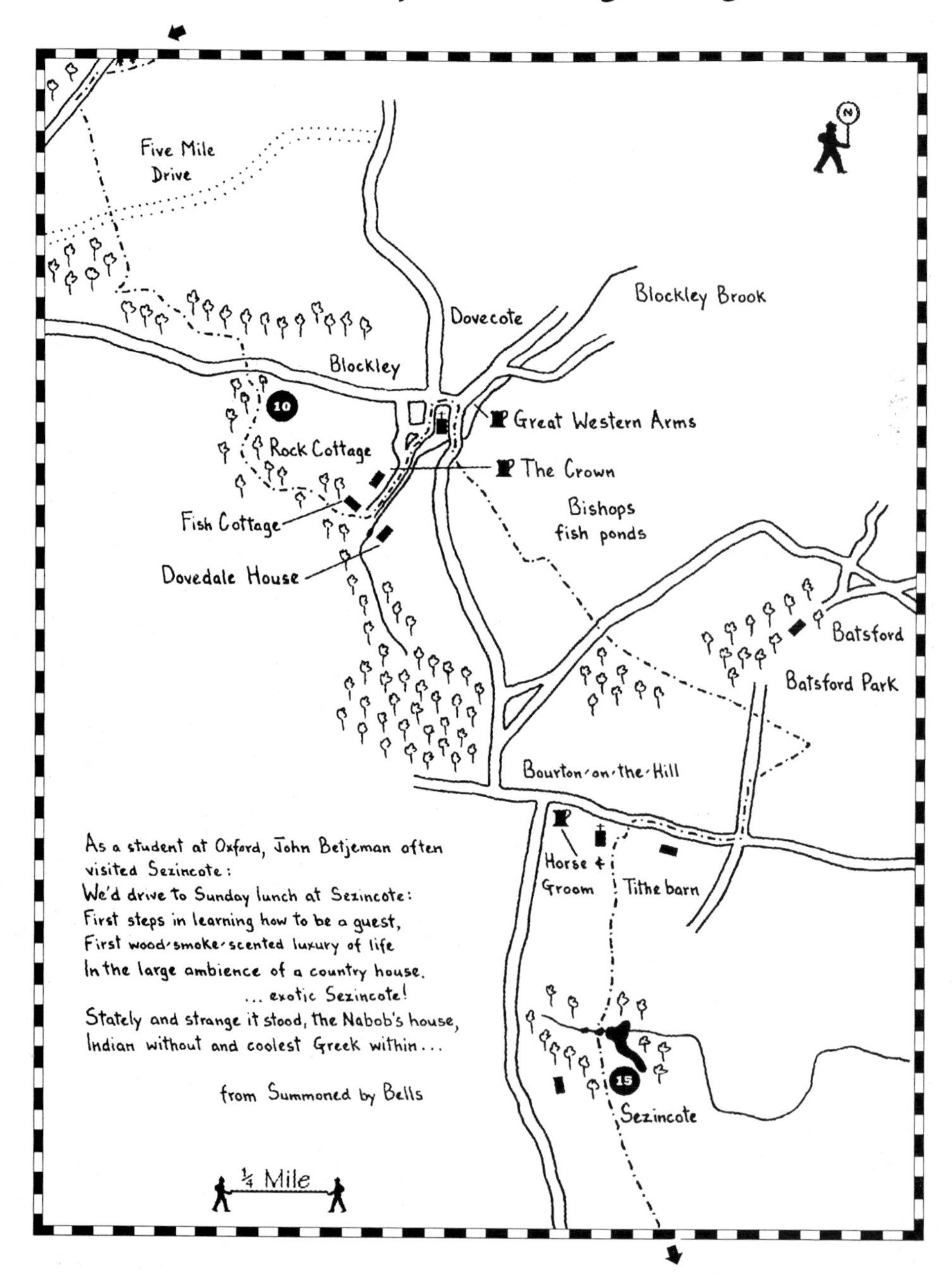

Take the bridleway uphill opposite the Bakers Arms, the track clearly following the boundaries across three fields, climbing all the way. You're likely to be alone with the skylarks. As you reach a small conifer plantation continue on the paved road to the main road and turn left.

After 300 yards turn left at the bridleway sign opposite some new tree planting. Keep to the left of the wall until you reach a wide gap about 100 yards short of a cluster of firs, then cross to the right side. Skirt the fir trees growing in an abandoned quarry and continue by following the field boundary. Where you reach the line of trees a B↑ sends you right for 100 yards where a gate takes you left into Five Mile Drive. This attractive tree-lined drive runs for two miles from Northwick Park to the Cross Hands finger post. If it weren't private we could have shortened our route from Broad Campden.

A second gate leads you out of the Drive. Keep to the distinct path which, by a B↑ on a short post, joins a gravel road taking you down to the right. A little before the valley bottom, take the first lane, sharp left, unmarked. A tunnel of rhododendrons brings you to Northwick Hill farmhouse. A Y↑ points you right. Turn left at the bottom of the pheasant runs. Then go through an unmarked gate, right, and follow the path that drops to the left.

At the valley bottom take a few steps left then take the rightmost of three tracks, up the other side. Notice a beautifully moss-covered wall in the trees to the right. Keep to the track as it bends sharp right. Pass through two gates to cross the road at the footpath sign. The track curves left then right into Shales Coppice, dotted with primrose and wood anemone which I believe is correctly pronounced as a question, "would Anna moan?" Follow the track curving left for the long gradual descent into The Warren.

A gate brings you out of the wood on to a road by a new house and then an oak with an enormous girth. When the path branches, keep left. Turn left on the road which is the main street into **Blockley**.

➤ The first house on the left as you reach the road into Blockley is Fish Cottage. A stone plaque on its wall commemorates a pet trout that died here in 1885:

Under the soil
The Old Fish do lie
20 years he lived
And then did die
He was so tame
You understand
He would come and
Eat out of our hand

➤ The high raised pavement on the left offers good views of Blockley's cottages crammed into all available spaces often separated by intriguing little alleyways. Blockley is unlike other Cotswold villages, perhaps because it grew later with the silk trade endowing it with a number of 19th century houses or because it was heading for the size of a small town until the silk trade ended or maybe because until 1931 it was part of a different County, Worcestershire.

➤ A slate plaque on a gate pillar of Rock Cottage marks the home of the phophetess Joanna Southcott. All but the shell of the cottage was gutted by the fire in 1971 which also destroyed many of the

Southcott relics but it is now rebuilt and can be glimpsed up through the trees.

Continue past the Russell Spring on High Street.

➤ Blockley lies in the deep valley of a Knee Brook tributary. The fast-running stream encouraged corn milling and by the late 17th century silk throwing was making Blockley an industrial village. Silk workers took the raw cocoons and twisted two miles of silken thread from each to supply to the Coventry ribbon-making trade. Pressed for space, the workers' cottages crept in random rows up the hillsides. In 1850 there were six mills employing about 600 but free trade in silk brought total collapse of the industry by 1885. The mills were all turned over temporarily to other trades as varied as piano and shirt-collar making, but all are now private houses.

➤ William Morris didn't set up a craft workshop in Blockley! although in 1880 he viewed an abandoned silk mill with a view to doing just that.

➤ When the Rushout Chapel in the Parish Church was deconsecrated, 2000 skeletons were found in a charnal house beneath. The church also has a chained 1617 Bible.

From The Square branch left up Bell Lane which brings you to the Bowling Green, reckoned to be the only piece of flat ground in the village.

➤ The garage topped with a dovecote was built in 1958.

➤ The railway reached Blockley in 1853 as part of the unpromising-sounding Oxford, Worcester and Wolverhampton line which, soon after completion, sold out to the ubiquitous GWR.

➤ In the coaching era Blockley had 23 inns but now the village boasts just a hotel and a pub.

Crown Inn
is also a hotel.
Offers eight Real Ales.
Smart, crowded, with an extensive menu. Interesting photos of old Blockley.

Great Western Arms
Hook Norton tied house.
The inn sign shows the arms of the Great Western Railway.
Pleasant views over recently converted silk mills.

Dovedale House

A short way up the road to the right, by Fish Cottage, up the valley known as Dovedale, lies Dovedale House, the site of Blockley's claim to be the first village in the country to have electric lighting.
In about 1887 Lord Edward Spencer-Churchill used water power to light the house, a shop and the church. It is difficult now to appreciate the novelty of the “moonlight glow” of the lamp on top of the church tower which was said to be visible from four counties.

Contd: page 23

Joanna Southcott, Prophetess

Joanna Southcott was born near Exeter in 1750, the daughter of a tenant farmer, and worked until she was 42 as a domestic servant. She built a local reputation as a prophetess, successfully predicting imminent deaths, successes and setbacks in the French Wars and the quality of the harvest. She then began experiencing voices and visions which convinced her she was the Woman from the Book of Revelation, the bride of the Lamb, chosen by God to announce the Second Coming. She believed she was receiving messages from the Holy Spirit, usually in verse, which she transcribed to eventually fill 65 books and pamphlets published from 1801, with a lot more in manuscript.

Her verses, known as Communications, mainly prophesied the coming of the Millennium or explained Bible passages in the English of ordinary people. In those harsh economic times and with the constant threat of a French invasion, her preaching gripped the public imagination. The source of her writings was hotly contested because, although she was not illiterate, she had received very little formal education beyond Bible study and her handwriting was almost illegible.

Rejected by the established Churches, she began to found her own chapels and from 1802 travelled the country in order to reach a larger following, mainly amongst the poor but with a smattering of clerics, notably the Rev TP Foley, a fervent follower who devoted a great deal of time to her cause. She developed her own form of service and both she and her preachers gave the sacrament, distributing wine and cakes. Hymns fashioned from her writings became enormously popular.

Joanna Southcott

In 1804 she settled with two companions, a Miss Townley who had a substantial private income and her servant, Ann Underwood, at Rock Cottage, Blockley. The two acted as secretaries although it took Underwood a year and a half to learn to decipher Southcott's writing!

Each "Believer" who could prove familiarity with Southcott's writings was given a "seal" which would protect them from danger and, some believed, enable them to live for a thousand years. Many soldiers carried seals at the battle of Waterloo. She referred to these Believers as Friends and claimed that 6-700 were sealed in a single meeting. Estimates of her following are hard to establish but they range from tens to hundreds of thousands, forming a very considerable popular movement.

In 1814, at the age of 65, she astonished her followers by announcing she was pregnant with God's child, Shiloh, who would be the second Messiah. Her followers, impatient with the non-arrival of the millennium, wanted proof. Close women friends confirmed they could feel the child move and 17 doctors were convinced the pregnancy was genuine. To provide an earthly father for the child she secretly married a Blockley man, John Smith, the owner of Rock Cottage.

During the next few months hundreds of Believers travelled to London to witness the birth and thousands more flocked to be sealed, many of them inundating the prospective mother with lavish gifts. Much of the country was in a frenzy of anticipation with various Southcott imposters roaming London. A hymn composed to greet the birth of her son began:

Shiloh to our faith is given,
On this bright auspicious morn;
Shiloh, choicest gift of heaven,
For a faithless world is born.

In late December 1814, in the fourteenth month of her "pregnancy", Southcott died. The autopsy found no sign of a child but also failed to establish a cause of death. John Smith died in 1829 and is buried in the churchyard to the south of the tower beside George Troup, another Believer.

With no appointed successor, the cult soon disintegrated, and of course Southcott had her detractors: in 1822 M Aiken wrote *she held in mental bonds an amazing proportion of the stupid part of the English nation*[1].

Encouraged, though, by the hope that Shiloh had been born spiritually, if not physically, a number remained firm Southcottian Believers. The movement did continue within a fairly close-knit group and a century after her death Alice Seymour created something of a revival of interest in Southcott's Communications. She had retired as a Head Teacher to devote her time to writing prophetic works and promoting the writings of Southcott. She maintained the tradition of "sealing" Believers and sent seals to protect soldiers fighting in the First World War. In 1917 she managed to buy Rock Cottage. She moved there in 1919 and continued re-assembling a vast collection of Southcott Communications, documents and memorabilia.

The sealed of the Lord
the Elect and precious
Man's Redemption to Inherit
The Tree of Life.
To be made Heirs of God and
Joint Heirs with Jesus Christ.

Joanna Southcott

Seals were handwritten, signed by Southcott, folded and sealed with wax

With the cottage as the "Southcott Centre" she reprinted much of the previously published writings and together with Mary Robertson she released a considerable stream of further Southcott commentaries. Southcott followers could still be numbered in the hundreds, some retaining the Southcott rituals, and could be found in strength in New Zealand, Australia and USA.

[1] Aiken includes Southcott in a book of famous religious "Imposters". Ironically, Professor Derrett can trace no one of that name entitled to the degree he claims, which makes Aiken himself an imposter.

They published a monthly newsletter, the Southcott Despatch and even ran the The Olive League Branch, an international "school" for young Southcottians. New Believers continued to be "sealed" right up till 1934.

Seymour and Robertson also made public what had been known in Blockley folk-memory all along: that Southcott had lived during the last ten years of her life at Rock Cottage. At the time it had been a carefully kept secret, providing a place of retreat. In Southcott's final book in 1814 she wrote that she had been obliged to conceal her refuge and identity

...to preserve my life from malicious and inveterate enemies, who threatened to set the house on fire where I lived...

Alice Seymour, in a photograph rescued from the fire

Much of the Southcott mystique today focuses on the Great Box said to contain a huge collection of Southcott artefacts. Originally her prophecies were sealed in a box and examined a year or so later to test the predictions. Eventually the Box was sealed with instructions that it should not be opened for 120 years (1924 at the earliest) and then only in the presence of 24 Bishops. Exell traces the Box through the hands of a chain of Believers through to 1898 but its current whereabouts is not known, except presumably by the Panacea Society, founded before the First World War by Helen Exeter. It seems improbable that the conditions for its opening will ever be satisfied.

Ironically, Rock Cottage was gutted by a fire in 1971 in which Mrs Annie Veysey Stitt, who had succeeded Alice Seymour as secretary, died. Many relics perished. Many of those that were rescued are now in the hands of the Blockley Antiquarian Society. Dr Exell has carried out some fascinating detective work on these Rock Cottage relics establishing many points which confirm Southcott's residence at Blockley. He estimates that 9000 pages of Communications remain unpublished.

At the time Joanna Southcott was leading her sect there were plenty of other cult leaders and prophets within or on the fringes of the Christian church - leaders such as Richard Brothers, Elias Carpenter and the bizarre-sounding Rabbit Woman. All made a mark in their day but Southcott maintains a modest following even at the close of the 20th century and the Panacea Society, based in Bedford, continues to distribute her writings.

Batsford Park Arboretum

The Arboretum of more than a thousand tree species has been created since the 1920s, based around a garden laid out in the late nineteenth century by the first Lord Redesdale, Algernon "Bertie" Mitford, who built the house. Wishing to avoid Victorian formality, he developed a "wild" garden, carefully enhancing the features of the site. He also gave it a strong oriental influence in the arrangements of pools, streams and rock, a legacy of his time spent in the east; he had travelled extensively, his diplomatic career taking him to St Petersburg, Peking and then Tokyo as attaché at the British Embassy. The natural groupings of trees he had seen in Asia influenced the siting of trees he introduced to Batsford.

A splendid Buddha...

Other eastern touches are the Japanese garden with its charming Rest House, a splendid Buddha, bronze Japanese deer and a fierce-looking Chinese lion. The collection of bamboos is still impressive and at one time was one of the best in the country.

For a decade after the last war the gardens fell into decay but from 1956 Lord Dulverton developed the Arboretum we see today, now administered by The Batsford Foundation.

The trees include a fine mixture of the beautiful, the rare and the strange. Amongst the beautiful are the autumn leaf colours, vivid against a foil of conifers, the forty or so species of magnolia and the thousands of spring bulbs.

Rarities include the Davidia, the handkerchief tree, which in May displays huge pairs of white bracts reminiscent of paper tissues or white doves. It was introduced into this country by Ernest "Chinese" Wilson, the most successful of all the turn-of-the-century plant hunters. There is a tulip tree with cup shaped flowers and scented bark and South American snowdrop trees. There is even a scion of a mulberry taken from Shakespeare's own tree in Stratford in 1923.

...and a fierce-looking Chinese lion

The Ginkgo Biloba, or maidenhair tree, is not particularly rare but has a strange history. Millions of years ago it was common in Europe but it disappeared. It survived only in central China where it is known, delightfully, as "yinxing", and was reintroduced to Britain in the 18th century. It is in fact the earliest tree we know of and may be the missing evolutionary link between ferns and flowering plants. Its fan-shaped leaves are unlike those of any other existing tree so we can only see their likeness in fossilised leaves like the one recently found in a quarry at Naunton. Tablets made from the leaf are sold as a cure for fading memory.

Spring or autumn, Batsford is a fascinating place for anyone with an interest in trees and discovering the sites of the various pieces of sculpture is pure delight.

Continue up Churchill Close, turn right into St George's Terrace, and right again into Lower Street to leave the village. A little beyond Rose Cottage, leave Blockley by turning off the road, left, at the HoEW sign - and a more enigmatic one reading "The Duck Paddle". At the end of the lane a stile with Y↑ leads into a field. Cross the field, keeping to the boundary, to reach another stile with Y↑. Turn right and climb the embankment which marks the remains of the medieval Bishops Fish Ponds.

Aim for a stile to the right of Park Farm's blue B&B sign, noticing the collection of ploughs in the drive. A stiff climb up the left edge of the field takes you to a stile at the top of the field just above a spring.

Turning left brings you on to a lovely tree-lined bridleway which we follow for only 200 yards giving you your final views back over Blockley. Pass through a gate and immediately turn right through another with Y↑ which almost qualifies as an Intriguing Gate Fastening Mechanism.

Follow a fine line of trees - beech, horse chestnut, ash and sycamore, crossing one stile with Y↑ and take the gate into the copse. Cross the road and squeeze beside the gate with Y↑ by a neatly curved high stone wall. The wall accompanies you for more than half a mile as you continue on the woodland track at the edge of Park and Century Plantations. The track drops, steepening gradually, and can be slippery.

Turn sharp right with the track and after a few yards turn left on to an unsurfaced road. Follow the road beside a handsome high wall until it curves left. Go straight on over a stile marked HoEW to walk across very distinct ridge and furrow. A double gate brings you to the lodge at the entrance to Batsford Park beside a lovely young magnolia. Strictly, cross the next field noticing how the ridge and furrow changes direction. The lone pine in this field looks like an escapee from the Arboretum. Turn sharp right to gain the drive out to the main road (not all of the drive is a right of way). At the main road turn right for **Bourton-on-the-Hill.**

➤ On the left as you enter the village, the splendidly restored stone barn in the grounds of Bourton House, dated 1570, is reckoned to be one of the largest and finest in the Cotswolds. The beautiful roof beams are original and climbing roses wander up the walls. It can be visited on request.

➤ Bourton House includes some 16th century remains - cellars, stables and a brewhouse. Most of the house, though, is an outstanding 18th century Queen Anne rebuild. The grounds include a formal white rose garden, low box hedges and a small knot garden designed around a medieval fountain set in cobblestones.

➤ In the bus shelter, plaques commemorate winning the Bledisloe Cup in 1991 and 1993.

➤ Two prisoner-of-war camps stood here on the Stow to Broadway road during the last war. For a time one became a camp for Polish refugees then both were demolished and the site was planted with conifers.

➤ The village has some wonderful houses ranging from 17th to 19th centuries - the School, Ivydene with its summerhouse, the Retreat almshouses, Porch House,

Contd: page 27

"The Mitford Girls! The Mitford Girls!"

Batsford Park was a childhood home of the Mitfords, the seven offspring of the second Lord and Lady Redesdale, known as "Farve" and "Muv". Nancy, Pamela (Tante Femme), Tom, Diana, Unity (Bobo), Jessica (Decca), and Deborah (Debo) grew up in the eccentric world of the English upper classes and must be the most extraordinary set of siblings born this century. A Betjeman poem about them coined the phrase "The Mitford Girls" and Ned Sherrin borrowed it as the title for his West End musical. Both portray their debutante lifestyle in the glittering social whirl of the '30s but their later lives were to take them in astonishingly different directions.

Nancy settled in Paris working as a very successful comic novelist and biographer, best known for her witty novels of British upper class life such as "Love in a Cold Climate" and "The Pursuit of Love". Batsford can be taken as their setting and many of the Redesdale family were models for the characters. Her "Noblesse Oblige", published in the '50s, started the debate about U and non-U language and manners - a way to distinguish the aristocracy from the masses.

The Mitfords and their parents in 1928. Back row from left: Nancy, Diana, Tom, Pam. Front: Unity, Jessica, Deborah

Pamela accompanied her father on a gold-prospecting trip to Northern Ontario and in 1935 she drove to Czechoslovakia in a Morris 8. She married a successful Oxford physicist, National Hunt jockey, and airman, Derek Jackson, the second of his six wives. They moved to Ireland, took to farming and horse breeding, but eventually separated. She returned to a house at Caudle Green in the '50s where she lived a life surrounded by poultry, animals and vegetables till her death in 1994. The unpublished Betjeman poem, "The Mitford Girls! The Mitford Girls!" ends: *Miss Pamela, most rural of them all.*

Tom was an accomplished musician and a qualified barrister. He served in the army throughout the last war, volunteering to fight the Japanese rather than the Germans. He was killed by a sniper in Burma in 1945.

Diana fell under the spell of the charismatic Sir Oswald Mosley, a brilliant political thinker who belonged in turn to all three British political parties. Dissatisfied with them all, he founded two of his own, first the New Party and then the British Union of Fascists. Diana divorced her first husband, which was definitely not a U thing to do, and married Mosley secretly in Berlin in 1936, with both Hitler and Goebbels attending the reception.

He was interned through most of the war in Brixton and she too spent three and a half years in prison, firstly in Holloway, regularly receiving letters threatening death to her children. For the final two years they were imprisoned together and released in 1944 when Mosley became ill. Although banned by the BBC and most newspapers, and no longer holding any political sway, he founded the anti-immigrant Union Movement in 1948. Most people would be surprised to learn that he lived till 1980. The Hon Lady Mosley has remained exiled near Paris but returns for the annual dinner of the Friends of Oswald Mosley.

Unity became for four years a frequent companion of Hitler who called her the *perfect specimen of Aryan womanhood.* She supported the increasingly anti-semitic Nazi beliefs, enjoying their Jew-baiting and speaking at party rallies. When war was declared she shot herself in a Munich park but lived on for nine years in a child-like condition with the bullet still lodged in her brain, cared for by her mother.

Jessica, to family disapproval, ran away and married Winston Churchill's nephew, Esmond Romilly. A Communist subversive from an early age, he had absconded from Wellington public school to produce a rabble-rousing magazine, "Out of Bounds", and later fought for the Republicans in the Spanish Civil War. The couple decamped to the USA and he died bombing Germany, serving with the Canadian Air Force. She joined the Communist Party, was active in the Civil Rights movement and in the '50s began a writing career with "Hons and Rebels" based on her upbringing - *our childhood surroundings, through which ran a rich vein of lunacy...*

Pamela in a 1938 portrait by William Acton

Her best-known campaign writing was "The American Way of Death" which paints a distasteful picture of the Californian funeral industry. In her mid seventies she released a pop record as Decca and the Dectones. She died in Oakland, California in 1996.

Deborah married Lord Andrew Cavendish who became the Duke of Devonshire. Since 1959 their jet-set life has been modified by the responsibility of running Chatsworth in Derbyshire. With its £250 million of art treasures and 70,000 acres, it is one of the most magnificent of stately homes. As the owner of its farm shop she likes to describe herself as *a shopkeeper.*

Their later childhood was spent just over the Oxfordshire border at Swinbrook where Nancy, Pamela and Unity are buried.

The Bledisloe Cup

Gloucestershire's Best Kept Village competition in 1938 was the first of its kind anywhere in the country. Organised by the Gloucestershire branch of the Council for the Protection of Rural England, the Bledisloe Cup is awarded annually to the winner in each of three categories, large, medium and small. The winning villages receive £100, a plaque, a heraldic sign to display on the village green and the Bledisloe Cup itself, engraved with the village name. The trophy is named after the agriculturalist, the first Viscount Bledisloe. On our route, Mickleton, Bourton-on-the-Hill, Longborough and Daglingworth proudly display their winners' plaques. Oddly, the Bledisloe Plate is competed for between the previous year's three successful villages.

One of Mickleton's three plaques

The winners are not necessarily the villages that appear on the postcards because the organisers are not seeking chocolate-box cottages in manicured gardens. The notes for judges insist the aim is *not to find the most beautiful village, nor the most ancient, nor the most picturesque*. Instead, they are looking for villages which appear cared for by their inhabitants, where young and old show a pride in their community and where, in places, the nettles and the cow parsley are allowed to grow and provide a home for wildlife - just the way things should be in the country.

I'm sure, though, as late May approaches and entries have to be in, the bedding plants will be in place in the borders, the hanging baskets will have been hung and the mowers will have smartened up the village greens. I'm also sure that the villages which become finalists will keep things in trim through August to pass the unannounced inspection by the mystery judge.

The sign on display in Cherington

next to the church, with its rather drunken-looking windows and a gazebo beside the churchyard.

➤ Enter the churchyard by the iron gate opposite Sundial Cottage. There are splendid gargoyles and a curiosity in the form of the Winchester Bushel and Peck. Measures for corn were very important at a time when tax was paid as a tithe and these bell-metal measures[1] were used as a standard for the whole country during the reign of Elizabeth I.

➤ As you walk along this main street the ground floors of the cottages are sometimes above head level and sometimes well below your feet. The Old Bakery has a free-standing bakehouse and chimney.

Cross the churchyard and leave by the gate and steps. Turn right on the road, bend right and leave it, left, at the footpath sign with HoEW Y↑ into a lane. A spring is marked with a stone inscribed Deo Gratis AD 1919.

A gate with Y↑ leads into a field. Cross this to another gate and keep straight to cross the next field to another gate. Follow the hedge towards the far side of the field but note the stile is about 50 yards in from the hedge. Keep going towards the line of windbreak trees. Two kissing gates with Y↑ take you through the trees into the parkland of Sezincote - pronounced Seezincote.

Keep straight, crossing an access road and guided by yellow arrows on fallen trees and intriguing glimpses of the house through the trees of its gardens. As you reach the edge of the wood keep beside the fence to be funnelled towards a pair of gates with Y↑ on a bridge over a stream.

You are now in view of the astonishing house up to the right. A large tree stump provides a good point to sit and take a look up to the house and down to the lake.

Resume the line you were following, up hill towards a gateway in the post and rail fence. Continue to the top right corner of the field where a short track leads to a stile with Y↑. Cross the road and follow the hedge. The views to the left are of Moreton-in-Marsh and the wolds stretching into Oxfordshire. A pair of gates with Y↑ lead into another short track beside a small plantation.

Horse & Groom
Pub, restaurant and hotel.
Draught Bass, Old Speckled Hen & Hook Norton.
Horse riding paraphernalia and cricket prints decorate the walls.

St Laurence, patron of

- brewers
- armourers
- glaziers
- students
- cutlers
- confectioners
- cooks
- washerwomen

[1] The use of the word "stone" for a measure of weight has its origin in the Cotswold wool trade of the 14th century, a time when rogue merchants might seek to cheat a farmer by using inaccurate weights. The standard practice was ingenious and could form the basis of a good GCSE Maths question. A good sheep fleece weighed 28lbs. Each travelling merchant carried three weights strapped to his saddle, 7lbs, 4lbs and 3lbs. Each sheep farmer kept a stone weighing exactly 14lbs. First they checked the merchant's weights by placing them on one side of a balance with the stone on the other. Once satisfied they were accurate, all the weights were placed on the same side to weigh the fleeces.

Sezincote

Perhaps the weirdest sight in all the Cotswolds is Sezincote, a 19th century country mansion which, as Betjeman says in "Summoned by Bells", is Indian on its outside and Classical Greek within. Whilst the house is not open to the public, its Indian features can all be seen from the ten-acre garden which can be visited.

Sezincote was built for Sir Charles Cockerell with a fortune made with the East India Company. The Indian influence was assured by employing his brother who had already designed a house for Warren Hastings, the British governor of Bengal, together with the painter Thomas Daniell who was the foremost authority on the architecture of the subcontinent. Wishing to do the entire job properly, Sir Humphrey Repton was consulted for the design of the park and the water garden.

The most striking feature of the house is its great onion-shaped, copper-clad dome. The other external decorations are also Mogul inspired - the peacock windows and even the reproduction of Hyder Ali Khan's mausoleum. If the orange hue of the stone blocks looks odd it is because it was stained that way for greater authenticity.

The eastern motif continues in the garden which maintains a water theme. Nearest the house, the formal garden is enclosed by an Orangery built with elaborately carved almond-white stone which curves away to end in a domed pavillion, the best example of a greenhouse corridor in the country. Nearby is the recently constructed canal bordered by cypresses which mirrors the house and mimmicks the Mogul Paradise Garden.

The informal garden begins at the Temple Pool and shrine with its stone relief figure of the goddess Souriya. Round the pool, grottoes are decorated with enormous giant clam shells. A Kiftsgate rose climbs a yew beside a Himalayan musk. The drive crosses the ravine-like valley on Daniell's Indian bridge, originally decorated with four cast iron Brahmin bulls. The bridge then gives a splendid view over the rest of the water garden tumbling down to the Evenlode and the large bottom lake.

The second pond features a weeping white Mulberry and a Varnish tree, the original source of Japanese laquer. The third with its three-headed serpent fountain is reached by way of an intricately designed bridge over a pavillion where stepping stones lead to a stone seat. Rock outcrops and many varied bamboos lead to the fourth. The fifth has a Weeping Pagoda Tree and a juniper-planted island reached by a zig-zag wooden bridge.

Sezincote is a real curiosity. Its gardens are splendidly different and the house itself inspired the Prince Regent to change the plans for the Brighton Pavilion to make it *more like Sezincote.* It has been called *a good joke but a good house too.*

Gloucester Old Spots

The best-known of the Gloucestershire animal breeds is the Gloucester Old Spot pig which is white with distinctive black spots. If a piglet has the misfortune to be born spotless it cannot be registered as an Old Spot.

It is difficult to establish when Old Spots became a distinctive breed but it was probably the result of 17th century cross-breeding. Traditionally they were kept as orchard pigs, foraging for windfall apples and living on scraps and the whey left over from cheese making. Lady Isobel Angus has one called Josephine who slept for three days after gorging on fermenting apples.

Over-fed 18th century Old Spots

Old Spots are very big, too big for modern large-scale pork production. If you see one full grown you will be struck by its size of up to 270 lbs. They are also an outdoor pig and will not thrive on the concentrated foods nor in the factory conditions used today for pig breeding. Surprisingly for their size, they tend to be docile, even-tempered and have good maternal instincts.

Despite the efforts of enthusiasts and the Gloucestershire Old Spot Pig Breeders' Club, numbers are diminishing despite the efforts of one sow in the County who recently produced a litter of nine. The number of sows has dropped over the last 20 years from 500 to an endangered species level of about 400, so the Princess Royal is to be congratulated for keeping a small herd at Gatcombe. The Prince of Wales is also enthusiastic: he has a sow at Highgrove called Miss Curteis.

Pub sign from Elmstone Hardwicke

The difficulties of keeping the breed alive are compounded by European Community policies: pig breeders receive none of the Government subsidies enjoyed by all other farmers and they have to try to compete against subsidised European pork. There are some encouraging signs that there will again be a demand for the hardy outdoor pig. There is certainly demand for top quality Old Spot boars: "Foston Sambo", an enormous 290 lbs and a former Champion of Champions, was sold recently for a breed record price of £4,200.

The Breeders' Club is successfully promoting the sale of Old Spot pork locally so that keeping the breed can become more than just a hobby. If you would like to try it, you can obtain pork joints from Chesterton Farm Shop near Tetbury. Top chef Simon Hopkinson rates Old Spot pork highly, describing it as *wonderfully fatted.*

It is sad to see this part of the County's heritage classed by the Rare Breeds Survival Trust as "endangered" especially when, in the opinion of Colonel Dugdale's pigman at Sezincote, Old Spots are more intelligent and easier to train than gun dogs. To improve today's rather negative image of pigs, the Breeders' Club recently ran a competition to devise a modern pig "proverb"; the winning suggestion.

beauty is in the sty of the beholder.

Follow the track at the edge of the field heading towards the tower of **Longborough** church. Go through a gate with Y↑ and continue beside a stone wall to a gate leading to a path at the foot of some allotments. A service road leads to a gate on to the main road. The church has good gargoyles and a number of interesting features:

➤ an elaborate early 19th century pew like an opera box with its elbow rests and velvet curtain.

➤ a collection of Jacobean church pewter, a chalice and flagon, which were dug up in the churchyard

➤ the life-size effigy of an early 14th century knight in his armour

➤ a 14th century octagonal stone font - *a beautiful piece of work* comments Verey.

Coach & Horses
Donnington tied house.
Photo of snow in the village in 1916 and a plaque summing up man's accumulated wisdom!

St James, patron of

- pilgrims
- furriers
- porters
- candlemakers
- labourers

Morris Dancing

The earliest reference to morris dancing dates from 1466 and by the 16th century it was a popular rural pursuit all over the country, with almost every Cotswold village having its "side", the one from Ilmington dating back to about 1650. Invariably, a side consisted of six (traditionally male) dancers, a Fool and musicians, most importantly a fiddler. Locally their dress was white with bells strapped to shin pads. Their repertoire comprised named dances, involving precise, elaborate steps, often peculiar to the village, which were performed at traditional times in the village year: on Saints' and Feast days, at Fairs, wakes and revels, during election campaigns and most commonly, at Whitsun.

In the Cotswolds the "Whitsun Ale"[1] was a well-established festival involving singing, processions, feasting, drinking, various competitions like wrestling, bare-knuckle boxing and shin-kicking, and music and dance in the form of the morris. Many of the sides did long tours of their locality at Whitsun receiving, for rural labourers, good money. Their dancing precision was tested in fiercely fought inter-village competitions. In many cases, any excuse was used to dance the morris.

During the 17th century English Revolution, Puritans tried to ban morris dancing on the grounds that it was lewd and suggestive (along with Christmas puddings and dancing round the may-pole).

[1] "Whitsun Ales" were originally organised by the Church; the churchwardens raised funds by brewing and selling ale. Stroud Morris have recently revived the Ale as a two-day morris festival in June. They and visiting sides perform in Stroud and tour south Gloucestershire villages.

> A **Squire** is in charge, chooses the dances and "calls"
>
> A **Bagman** is secretary, treasurer and in charge of the collection bag
>
> A **Foreman** teaches the dances and organises practices
>
> The **Fool** wields a stick with a tail and bladder, both to amuse and to clear space for the dancers.

When the Monarchy was restored much of the traditional Church calendar reappeared and many of its associated revelries were again permitted.
Some which had taken place on Saints' Days or turning points in the year such as Midsummer or Plough Monday, were never reinstated. Morris dancing seems to have survived this early test and may well have been at its most popular in the following hundred years[2].

By the last quarter of the 19th century, though, the traditional morris had died out nationally except for small pockets in the Cotswolds. The Whitsun Ales had disappeared by the mid-century, discouraged by the village authorities because the drinking and annual settling of scores by the young men tended to go beyond the bounds of gentlemanly restraint. A clergyman of Longborough tried in the 1880s to suppress his village morris, like the Puritans, on the grounds of indecency. At a time of rapid material progress few wanted to take part in such an anachronism or to contribute to the collecting bag.

Cecil Sharp's own photograph of Jinky Wells of Bampton, 1911

Just as morris dancing was about to fade into history, a revival began from two distinct directions. Richard D'Arcy Ferris at Bidford-on-Avon, Worcestershire, was in the business of staging pageants. The morris, harking back to an innocent golden past, seemed a promising act to include. He did so in 1886 and promptly began combing the Cotswolds for more dances. He was none too bothered about authenticity as long as it made a good show.

Cecil Sharp, in contrast, aimed to capture and accurately record the folk tradition before it was lost. Drawn to the Cotswolds, seeking songs and traditional tunes, he first visited the Bampton Morris side, led by Billy Wells, in 1899. Wells had been with the side for 20 years and continued for 30 more as either dancer, Fool or musician. Sharp noted some of his tunes and took some fascinating photographs of the ancient, rustic musicians but did not actually note the dances till he returned in 1905. Casting his net wider, he collected more dances from Bledington, Sherborne and from William Kimber of the Headington Quarry Morris.

Probably his most prolific source was the fiddler, John Mason. When Sharp visited him between 1906 and 1909, he was living in the workhouse at Stow-on-the-Wold.

[2] The Royal George Hotel at Birdlip has an anonymous 18th century painting, Dixton Harvesters, an aerial view of a harvest scene with a line of morris men dancing their way out to the fields.

He had played fiddle for the Longborough Morris and probably for Lower Swell and he boosted Sharp's collection with 45 tunes, some of which Sharp found very strange. The dances found their way into his five-volume Morris Book published over the next few years and his manuscripts (he thought the phonograph too inhibiting)[3] found their way to Clare College, Cambridge.

Most village sides were decimated by the First World War so the sides from Bampton and Headington are unique in claiming an unbroken morris tradition. The publishing and teaching of dances by Sharp and others, who in 1911 formed the English Folk Dance Society, sparked a revival which influenced millions of children through at least till my school-days in the 1950s. Ironically, dances rooted in a bawdy and boisterous village tradition lived on, somewhat anaemically, in our national curriculum.

The Gloucestershire Old Spot Morris on tour in the 1970s dancing in their distinctive top hats

Fear not! The bawdy and boisterous aspect is not extinct. Over the last couple of decades many new sides have formed and perform frequently around the Cotswolds, maintaining the strong connection with Whitsun. Gloucestershire Old Spot Morris is a good example, originally formed in 1972, drawing its 28 set dances and ten jug dances (performed by just one or two dancers) strictly from the Longborough repertoire. The English Country Dance Band currently play many of the Longborough dance tunes.

Morris dancing today is best thought of as a form of street theatre presenting, from Whitsun through to September, the traditional dances and constantly creating new ones. There is, though, apparently a pressure group bent on completing the task the Puritans began: the Campaign to Abolish Morris Dancing Absolutely.

In Gloucestershire where I shirked school,
The vale is hot but the hills are cool;
There are dreams for the wise, there is
gold for the fool,
You can choose what you wish to do.
JH

[3] The Australian composer Percy Grainger also collected folk and morris tunes here from 1907-9. He did use a phonograph and recorded perhaps the best-known Cotswold morris tune, Shepherds Hey. He felt that collecting intricate songs without a phonograph *is mad and stupid*. Hearing his recordings of people born in the Cotswolds when Napoleon still ruled Europe is an extraordinary experience.

3
Longborough to Lower Slaughter

7½ miles

The miles go sliding by
Under my steady feet,
That mark a leisurely
And still unbroken beat
IG

Longborough to Lower Slaughter

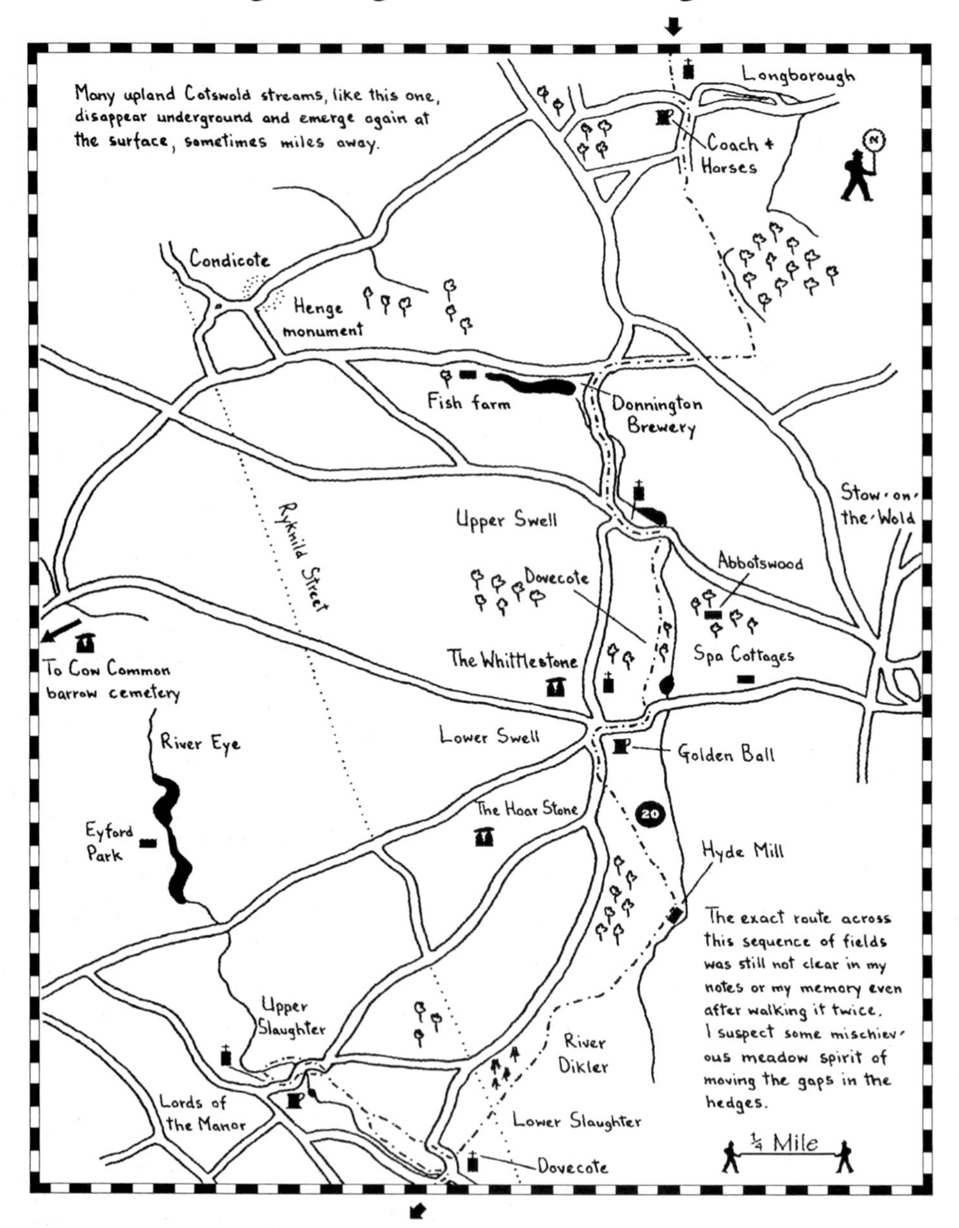

Turn left on the road, pass the pub and take the right turn at the village school. The village is entirely stone-built with houses and farms from the 17th century onwards, with Windyridge, built since the last war, showing that traditional design still has a place. Admire the stone houses as you walk the length of this main street and notice an attractively planted rotted tree stump in a front garden.

At the village green fork left at the Y↑ taking the lower road with a spring gushing from under the road. Turn left at the HoEW sign into a cul-de-sac of tastefully built and converted houses. The road becomes a track at the quixotically named Love Walk. Pass through a gate with Y↑ and fork immediately right off the track to follow the fence. Cross a stile and keep straight on. The house up to the right is Banks Fee, 18th century, with an attractive cupola and a curiously positioned red telephone box.

Follow the indistinct path a little to the right of a line of oaks. Drop down to a stile with Y↑ over a stream, cross a small footbridge and turn left out of the spinney. Follow the edge of the field uphill with a deciduous wood on the left dotted with hazel catkins in February. Strike across the field at a post with Y↑ to reach a pair of stiles on a footbridge.

Keep straight on up the next field to a stile with Y↑ in a hedge. Take a look back at Bourton-on-the-Hill, now well behind you. Turn right on to the path between two lines of trees and some old, delapidated stone walling. Cross the main road and take the road signposted Condicote. After 500 yards take the left forking road, signposted Upper Swell, which drops down steeply to Donnington Brewery.

It is well worth continuing along the road above Donnington Brewery for the extended mill lake, rich with fish and wildlife including Australian Black Swans. Go as far as Donnington Fish Farm, which offers fresh and smoked trout.

From the brewery take the road for **Upper Swell** which follows the course of the River Dikler. The hamlet is an attractive collection of cottages and farms.

St Mary the Virgin
is patron of
the entire human race.

➤ The church looks intriguing at the end of a neat avenue of Irish Yew - but it isn't.

➤ The manor house is 16th century, with beautiful porch and gables, in 18th century landscaped grounds and is one of my favourites. Hutton says *...it is perfection...Who would not ruin himself for such a house?*

➤ By the 18th century bridge the mill still has its water wheel in place and you can glimpse the mill pond behind.

Take the gate and stile at the Lower Swell footpath sign. Note the special instruction for literate horses who are nimble enough to clamber over. Follow the post and rail fencing till you reach the footbridge. Do not cross it. Turn right, uphill, to reach a kissing gate, admiring the matted, exposed roots of the tree to the right. Pass through another kissing gate to gain a path by a wall at the foot of a field to reach a third with Y↑. On this stretch of the walk you will find kissing gates more common than stiles.

Contd: page 38

Condicote

Condicote has been described as the pleasantest of upland Cotswold villages but to my mind it is one of the oddest: you cannot reach it or leave it by any footpath. Yet it has its claims to fame.

The first is in the form of a henge monument, an area of nearly two and a half acres enclosed by an almost circular bank with a ditch either side. The inner ditch was cut six feet down into solid rock and was more than 12 feet wide.

Henge monuments remain mysterious to us because we do not know their purpose. The late stone age or early bronze age people have left us two kinds of monument, henges and stone circles[1], Condicote being the only confirmed henge monument in the County. It was built before 1800 BC in what at the time was a forest clearing. The site must have had considerable significance for the builders to have expended such effort in constructing its outer bank and inner ditch. We know from the design that henge monuments served no defensive purpose, nor were they used for burials. They may have been used to over-winter cattle and seem to have had a ceremonial or ritual function which we are unlikely to ever understand.

The bank stood much higher in the last century but still shows up well from the road which passes through it and even better in aerial photographs.

The village's second claim to fame is that it lies on Ryknild Street which was part of the network of Roman roads. It ran from the Fosse Way near Lower Slaughter, heading north-west into Worcestershire. While most Roman roads have been adopted as modern routes and are surfaced, Ryknild, together with Akeman Street, remain exceptions. Just to the south of the village is a two mile stretch, straight as a crow would fly, still surfaced with crushed stone, barely changed since the last marches of the legions.

Donnington Brewery

One of the most perfect settings in all of the Cotswolds must be that of the Donnington Brewery. Surrounded by low hills, nestling in the valley of the River Dickler, it looks as if it has been there since time began.

There was a corn mill on the site as long ago as 1261. By the 16th century it had converted to fulling cloth and the four acre mill pond had been built. When the Arkell family acquired it in 1827 it had reverted to the role of corn mill together with a malthouse and bakery. Thomas Arkell began brewing as a sideline in 1865 and continued running the malthouse until 1910. Selling first to neighbouring private houses he established a reputation for the reliability of his beers and extended his outlets by buying up local inns.

The brewery passed to his son, John, and since 1952 has been run by grandson, Claude, who was born at the brewery and began work there as soon as

[1] The Cotswolds has a stone circle, the Rollright Stones between Moreton-in-Marsh and Chipping Norton which were recently on sale for £50,000. Legend has it that the stones were a king and his army, turned to stone by a witch.

he left school. At six foot three inches he's a very tall man to have his office in what was once the bread oven.

The recipes for what Claude calls *the family poison* are pretty well unchanged producing two bitters and a dark mild ale. Whilst in Claude's father's day, the barley came from the family's surrounding fields, it now comes from Norfolk and is brewed with Worcestershire hops. The beer used to be sold within the limits imposed by horse transport - no further afield than the horses could travel and return within the day. Even today, most of the 60 to 80 barrels each week is sold through the 15 local Donnington tied houses, four of which lie on our route which will give you a chance to try each of the brews.

Until 1959 the entire enterprise was water powered. Today, water power is still used to hoist sacks, move the beer between vats in the main buildings and to pump the all-important brewing "liquor", Donnington's spring water, under the lake from a surface spring on the far side.

At the time when Thomas Arkell started his brewing enterprise, beer was commonly bought by the barrel twice each year, stored in a cellar and tapped as required. The following prices are recorded for George Garne's Brewery at Burford at about that time:

Superior Stock Ale	@ 1/6d
Superior Bitter Ale	@ 1/4d
Mild Ale	@ 8d

Note, though, that the prices are *per gallon!* Apart from the prices little has changed in 130 years - even the bottle labels are still stuck on by hand.

The Brewery unfortunately cannot open to visitors but take the time to admire this wonderful anachronism from the many different perspectives offered by walking the length of the mill pond.

Cow Common Cemetery

On the bleak wolds above you to the right are the remains of the Bronze Age cemetery of Cow Common. The ten round barrows, each with cremated human remains, date from about 3500 years ago. Presumably the site had a powerful sacred significance because the barrows were arranged around a much older long barrow and one seems to have been built on an even older passage grave of the Neolithic period. So this site was a very special place for our ancestors over a period of at least 2000 years.

Keep beside the electric fence admiring the varied trees of Abbotswood, over to the left. Your path gradually converges with the post and rail fence and leads you to a kissing gate to reach Abbotswood's access road. Turn right on the road passing through Bowl Farm.

➤ The farm is mainly 19th century, built on the site of Sir Robert Atkyn's manor house which he'd built in 1671, having demolished the previous one.

➤ The oddly tall building on the right is a four-gabled dovecote but it was rebuilt in 1917 and no longer has nesting holes.

➤ The red brick walled garden up to the right seems incongruous.

Continue along the access road to what looks like a stone seat on the left. Sit on it. It is actually Lady's Well, a medieval well that gave the Swells their name and it makes a very comfortable spot for a break. Continue to the main road and turn right to enter **Lower Swell**.

De tour

Spa Cottages

Approaching Lower Swell, turn left up the hill towards Stow-on-the-Wold, reaching a row of cottages after 300 yards. In 1807 a chalybeate spring (with iron compounds in the water) was discovered here and the most elaborate of the four cottages was built in the hope of developing a spa resort.

Clearly the enterprise failed but it left us this echo of Sezincote with its honeysuckle and fir cone decorations, its front door beneath a stone pineapple (still a novelty at the time) and Hindu-influenced canopy.

In 1993 the spring was persuaded to flow once again.

Golden Ball

Donnington tied house.
A map shows the territories of the UK's foxhounds, staghounds, draghounds and harriers.

➤ The Old Smithy is one of the few still working traditionally in the Cotswolds. Take a look at the showroom and the fascinating wind dial: the weather vane on the roof is connected to a pointer on a Saxton pictorial map which includes the eight points of the compass. In this way you can "read" the wind directions from indoors.

➤ Look out for an old milepost near the pub with its odd abbreviations for Gloucester and Cheltenham.

➤ Hutton dismisses the church as *...a ridiculous building run up in 1851...* But it has a fascinating 12th century carving above the chancel arch which includes three linked rings, a stylised hare, a fish, a stag, a large-headed man, a beast with a horn, a wolf lying on its back and what seem to be hot cross buns. It is thought this might represent Adam naming the creatures.

➤ The war memorial is disappointing although it was designed by Sir Edwin (hard to think of as a Ned!) Lutyens, architect of Abbotswood. Perhaps this

The Hoar Stone

This is in a field ½ mile south-south-west of the church. It is almost six feet long and three feet high. Sullivan recounts that a gardener from the vicarage claims it extends eight feet into the ground and that when they tried to move it their tackle broke.

Contd: page 42

The Puzzle of the Long Barrows

The neolithic long barrows are a haunting presence on these wolds, providing us with an enigmatic echo of death 5000 years ago. These people were the first of our ancestors to build in stone so these long barrows are the earliest buildings we have inherited. The County has about 70 which are of sufficient importance for a particular type to be named the "Cotswold-Severn" family of tombs. Gatcombe Lodge barrow, the one with the Tinglestone, and the Avening burial chambers are all of this type.

There is great variety in the size, shape and the arrangement of chambers but this family of barrows has a number of features in common:

- they are built on ridges but avoid actual hill tops
- they are roughly rectangular stone mounds, between 30 and 60 yards long and up to 15 feet high
- one end is higher and broader with projecting horn shapes which partially enclose a forecourt
- many, like the Gatcombe barrow, have false entrances, presumably as a deterrent to grave robbers.

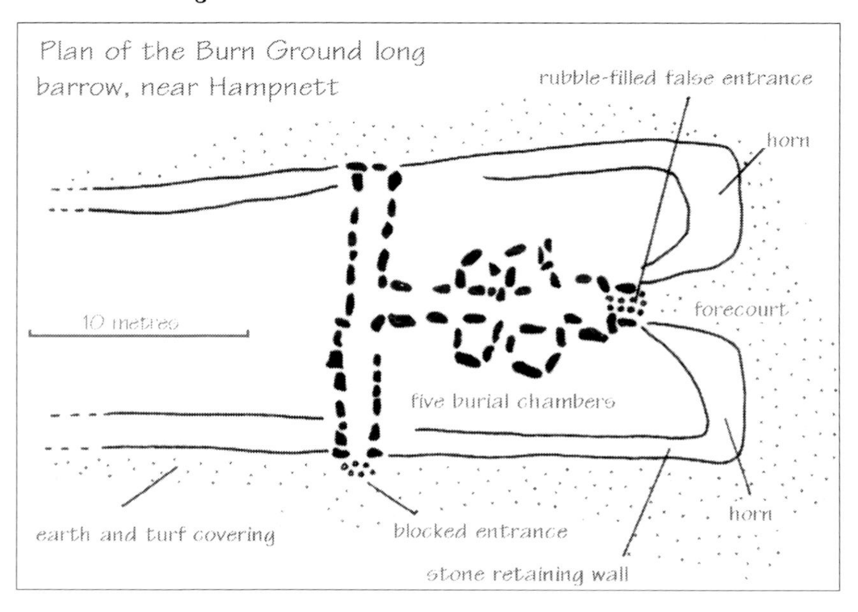

Long barrows all have a passage leading to one or more chambers. These were walled and roofed with great slabs of stone and each chamber was sealed off with another stone slab. The structure was then covered over with smaller rocks to complete the barrow shape. A stone retaining wall around the perimeter helped to keep it all in place. At the time, the bare stone barrows would have stood out more starkly against the wooded background than they do today.

Inside we find anything up to 45 inhumations, usually of incomplete bodies. These were not left to rest because over the three or four hundred years that the barrow was in use, more bodies were added and the larger bones and the skulls were moved and collected in piles against the walls.

The inhumations were not all human: we find the bones of red and roe deer, horse, boar, wolf and wild cat treated in a similar way. Along with the bones there are limited grave goods: pottery, cups, beads and pendants.

The archaeological remains pose more questions than they answer:

- Why was such physical effort put into building these burial chambers? An average sized long barrow required about 16,000 man-hours of labour, much of it for quarrying stone with primitive antler picks.
- How were the incumbents chosen? The whole population was certainly not buried in this way.
- Why were the bodies dismembered or left to decompose before being interred? Some were buried in the passages and even the forecourts rather than in the chambers.
- What strange rituals with fires and feasting took place in the forecourts to necessitate moving the remains?

We can only speculate. Clearly the long barrows were seen as a home for ancestral spirits or perhaps as a source of fertility. There may have been a cult of the dead. The biggest question of all is why, after about 400 years of long barrow burials, did our ancestors switch to cremating their dead and placing them in the much smaller round barrows?

Dovecotes

We tend to think of pigeons today as something of a nuisance. If we live in the city they are a hazard in large railway stations; if in the country, they are a pest causing damage to gardens and farm crops, with a particular penchant for the young shoots of oilseed rape.

The EC classifies them as game birds requiring a nine month close season when they cannot be shot; ironically, many of the farming community want to blast all 20 million of them out of our skies at every opportunity so, each year during the shooting season, the pigeon population roughly halves.

Up until the recent past, though, woodpigeons and various doves were a valuable source of food and we have a

Lower Slaughter's enormous 16th century dovecote with six gables

number of the dovecotes in which they lived to remind us of the part they played in the diet of the country landowner. Olivier de Serres wrote in 1600, *No man need ever have an ill-provisioned house if there be but attached to it a dovecot, a warren and a fishpond wherein meat may be found as readily at hand as if it were stored in a larder* which conjures up a wonderful image of rural self-sufficiency, at least for the landed gentry. Until 1761 only the church and the lord of the manor were permitted to keep pigeons and if a tenant should kill one, the result was imprisonment. Pigeons, easily trapped in the nesting box, provided not only a source of meat during the winter, but also a delicious egg supply and a valuable addition to the stock of manure.

Circular dovecotes at Daglingworth and Little Badminton

Dovecotes or pigeon houses came in all shapes and sizes. The Normans built the earliest ones and the 13th century circular one at Quenington was built by the Knights Hospitaller.

Small ones were often incorporated into the gable of a house or a farm building but the most splendid were stand-alone buildings associated with a manor house or ecclesiastical buildings. Around the country dovecotes took on all sorts of bizarre designs. The one typical of the Cotswolds is square or rectangular, stone-built with four or sometimes six gables and crowned with a cupola or lantern which gave easy access for the birds and kept out the rain.

Inside there is little to see except for the nest holes, sometimes more than a thousand of them, let into the upper parts of the wall and the interior of the roof. Many are now deserted but watch the one at Daglingworth and you will see the comings and goings of the flock of white doves.

Pigeons were a very economical source of food because, once the flock was established, the birds found their own grain in the countryside (up to a hundredweight for each pair each year) and the only labour needed was for cleaning. They breed prolifically: each pair of birds, which mate for life, produce about 16 squabs every year for about seven years - a constant, self-financing protein supply. Their homing instinct, of course, ensured that they returned to the dovecote every night.

A dovecot in the loft
at Duntisbourne Leer

The only real difficulty must have been establishing a flock in a newly-built dovecote. You would purchase the required number of squabs from some neighbouring pigeon keeper, put them into their new home and then, next morning...

The Whittlestone

This stone now stands on the green beside the village hall. It is probably the remnant of a barrow which was moved 200 yards to the vicarage and then moved again to its present site. The story goes that when the Stow church clock strikes midnight the stone goes to Lady's Well to drink.

obelisk wasn't much of a challenge after designing the colossal Viceroy's House in New Delhi, now the home of the Indian President, or the stunning but unbuilt Catholic Cathedral of Christ the King for Liverpool.

Keeping the village green on the right, bend right with the road and turn left at the road sign to Lower Slaughter. At the edge of the village leave the road, left, at the HoEW sign. The lane changes to a post and wire fenced route that guides you towards the corner of Slaughter Woods. Just before the woods Nether Swell Manor comes into view across the wide valley. Continue beside the wood and take the gate with B↑ to the right, cross the footbridge and aim for the buildings at Hyde Mill.

Pass through gates to the former mill where a couple of Lower Slaughter footpath signs lead you around to the right of the house and its extensive garden. After 100 yards take the kissing gate left into the pasture that can completely flood after long spells of rain.

Where the path brushes the River Dikler cross a stile with Y↑ and continue across the field to a gate. Aim for a "lollipop" with Y↑ at a gap in the fence, then aim for a gap with Y↑ at the far right hand corner of the next field. Aim across the next field a little to the left of the lone tree and you will spot a gateway. Turn slightly left to follow the signpost to Lower Slaughter, aiming for a gate with a lollipop in the far hedge.

Swing right to aim for a lollipop by a sleeper over a stream. Go right to follow the field edge beside the wood. Continue straight ahead till, 100 yards before the end of the field, a gate takes you, right, through a hedge. Turn left to reach a stile leading on to the edge of the cricket pitch. Then aim for the gate behind the cricket pavillion without missing the wonderful old roller.

The path leads you past some carefully designed modern housing. Turn right at the road, then turn left to enter Lower Slaughter churchyard. Last time I visited, a fox scuttled out of the scruffy chuchyard corner.

➤ *Be warned*: in summer both the Slaughters teem with tourists, "doing" the Cotswolds.

➤ The name Slaughter sounds gruesome but probably derives from the name of the 12th century Lord of the Manor, de Soletres or de Sclotre.

➤ The mill which had a bakery attached is early 19th century and incongruously built in red brick. Though the mill last ground flour 40 years ago, the water wheel still turns and the mill machinery is virtually intact. Bread was baked up to 1989 and the mill has now opened as the Mill Museum.

➤ In the grounds of the Manor is an unusual 16th century, stone-built double dovecote, visible from the churchyard, and with its six-gabled roof, one of the biggest in the County.

➤ The cottages which line the River Eye with its many small bridges are picture-postcard Cotswolds. Many are 16th and 17th century but others have been altered to give them period features.

Leave the churchyard and turn right, retracing your steps. Follow the road around to the left noticing that some architects still make provision for doves. Where the road turns right, pass through the kissing gate on to the fenced path through the Cotswold Stud. Pass through another kissing gate and veer a little left towards a gap with a post and Y↑. Again veer a little left to a third kissing gate. Follow the well-worn path the length of the field. At the gap with Y↑ swing right and walk uphill to a gate on to the corner of the road.

Turn left, downhill, and right into **Upper Slaughter** at the sign which seems to instruct children to drive with care. You almost complete an anticlockwise circle of the village, crossing a footbridge by the ford in the River Eye, and climbing up past the front of the church.

Continue round the village and turn right at the Warden's Way sign.

➤ The eight Elizabethan cottages in Baghot's Square were rebuilt early this century by Lutyens and no new houses have been built in the village since then.

➤ The Old Manor House is a beautiful example of the Cotswold style, partly dating from the 15th century.

St Peter,
patron of

- butchers
- carpenters
- cobblers
- bakers
- clockmakers
- glaziers
- bridge builders
- potters

Its approach is a long avenue leading to a twelve-gabled Tudor front with transomed and dormer windows and a two storey Jacobean porch. The stone vaulted basement has been used as a farm dairy.

➤ The Castle Mound was a Norman motte and bailey castle which has not been fully excavated.

Drop down to the stone footbridge and kissing gate. Climb up to the right to regain your outward route. Retrace your steps across the long field to the gap marked with Y↑.

The Lords of the Manor
Ruddles
Formerly the Rectory and the home of the Rev FE Witts who wrote "Diary of a Cotswold Parson", extracted from the diaries he kept between 1820 and 1852.
Here your ploughman's lunch will come with a Michelin star!

Now leave your outward journey route by swinging right to a kissing gate leading to the mill leet. Follow this to the village noticing the sluice gate controlling the water level, the variety of trees on the hill to the left and the row of beehives on the right.

Then two more kissing gates, one with an unfortunate dedication, bring you back into Lower Slaughter. On meeting the road turn right to arrive at the mill.

Cotswold Lions

Gloucestershire must be unique in having its own breeds of cattle, pig and sheep and it was the Cotswold sheep that brought prosperity to these hills in the Middle Ages. At that time exports of wool, much of it being reared on the Cotswolds, accounted for half of England's net income.

The Romans introduced long-woolled sheep to Britain. Crosses with native breeds gradually produced the Cotswold or Cotswold Lion, characterised by the whiteness of its fleece and the length of each strand of wool - more than 12 inches.

Then in the Middle Ages, before the drystone walls snaked across the hills, the Cotswolds were virtually a vast sheep ranch owned by the Church. Gloucester Abbey boasted a flock of 10,000 and Winchcombe had at least 8,000. In the mid 18th century there were nearly ½ million sheep on these hills, their coarse wool in great demand to make worsteds for the East India Company.

One of the Garne family's Aldsworth lions

By the 19th century the Cotswold Lions were in decline in favour of smaller, lighter breeds producing a much finer fleece. William Garne of Aldsworth did a limited amount of crossing with Leicesters to improve their quality and from 1832 he exported sheep so that the Cotswold became one of the main breeds farmed in the USA. In each of the four years from 1849 he won first prize for long-woolled sheep at the Royal Agricultural Society of England's Royal Show. Proud of his sheep, he commissioned oil paintings of some of his favourites.

Breeding Cotswold sheep had become something of a gentleman's hobby - Lord Eldon of Stowell Park had flocks at Compton Abdale and Chedworth, James Taylor of Rendcomb Park had flocks on three different farms and HJ Elwes kept one at Colesbourne Park.

Shepherd Hall of Colesbourne

Elwes had decided in the 1880s to improve the flock of Cotswold sheep started by his grandfather, *determined to show people what the breed could do.* His interest was no sentimental one. Aiming to develop a sheep best suited to the bleak Cotswold uplands, he even tried crossing Lions with other breeds. Bringing his scientific background to the task, he experimented with all manner of feeds, mixing vetch and clover, mangles, carrots and swedes, old hay, new hay, oats, peas, beans...anything that would tempt the lambs to put on weight. And it gained him some success, winning first prize at the Smithfield Show for his fattened Cotswold lambs and more awards at fairs in Hanover and Hamburg.

Generally, though, by this time the Cotswold Lion was out of favour. It produced too fatty a meat for the changing popular taste and Elwes writes of breeders bidding against each other at sales to try to prevent the price from falling. The Cotswold Sheep Society, formed in 1892, registered just 15 flocks remaining at the turn of the century.

The Garne family had kept a flock at Aldsworth for 300 years. Early in this century Will Garne persevered while nearly all around him abandoned the local breed. For 30 years his was the only substantial flock of Cotswolds remaining and inevitably it was becoming weakened by inbreeding.

Interest in preserving an ancient breed revived in the 1960s so that the "flockbook" was re-started with Will as President at the age of 86. In the early' 70s the sheep's status was still "endangered" with only 250 ewes but numbers are now up to about 900. The breed's future seems safe in the hands of the Cotswold Sheep Society which now has some 150 members. The Rare Breeds Survival Trust has played its part, improving the quality of the wool by breeding with the descendants of sheep exported to Canada at the turn of the century. It is heartening that this wool is still used by the Cotswold Woollen Weavers at Filkins who turn it into a sumptuous array of garments in their mill in a converted stone barn.

A Three Counties Show champion yearling ewe bred at the Cotswold Farm Park

You should spot some Cotswold Lions en route, recognising them from the length of their wool. They are easiest to spot in early summer when they have been shorn of their 25 lb coat[1] but are left with their long white forelocks, *their beautiful topknots of wool hanging over their faces.*

The Cotswold Sheep Society has recently produced a superbly illustrated book called "The Cotswold Sheep", telling the story of the breed.

[1] Another curiosity of traditional weights and measures emerges from the Cotswold wool trade: fleeces were weighed by the tod, i.e. 28lbs or a quarter hundredweight.

Rattleskull

It's only the hairs on a gooseberry that stop it from being a grape.

In the plum-growing area around Chipping Campden a popular drink was plum jerkum, made in just the same way as cider and, in the past, made in similarly vast quantities. It was said that the very best was made from bullaces which are a wild cross between plums and sloes, producing a drink with a lovely colour ranging from deep purple to claret red.

Somewhere I came across an environmentally-very-unfriendly recipe for Lower Slaughter Cowslip Wine:

1 quart cowslip flowers 1 gallon water 4 lb sugar ½ pennyworth yeast	Put flowers into a bag in stewpan and boil in the water for 1½ hours. Press and add the sugar to the liquid, reheating till the sugar dissolves. Allow to cool to blood heat, then add the lemon juice and yeast. Bottle the following morning.

Apart from the ecological unsoundness of that, a modern country wine maker would throw a fit at some of these instructions and the use of so much sugar would produce an alcoholic syrup.

Instead, I will offer you my own tried-and-frequently-tested recipe for "Rattleskull". This was the local name given, probably for good reason, to home-made gooseberry wine. This recipe makes a green-tinted, crystal-clear wine. After drinking it for many years I actually prefer it to wine made from grapes: the taste is clean and crisp and bone-dry. You will find the recipe in Appendix B.

In Gloucestershire the hills aren't high,
They don't shut out the earth from the sky,
But they feed the Severn, the Thames and the Wye,
Which no other hills can do.

JH

4
Lower Slaughter to Guiting Power

6½ miles

When the fine rain beat on the window,
And the wild wind whirled in the lane,
My love and I would go walking
And sweet was the wind and the rain.

FM

Lower Slaughter to Guiting Power

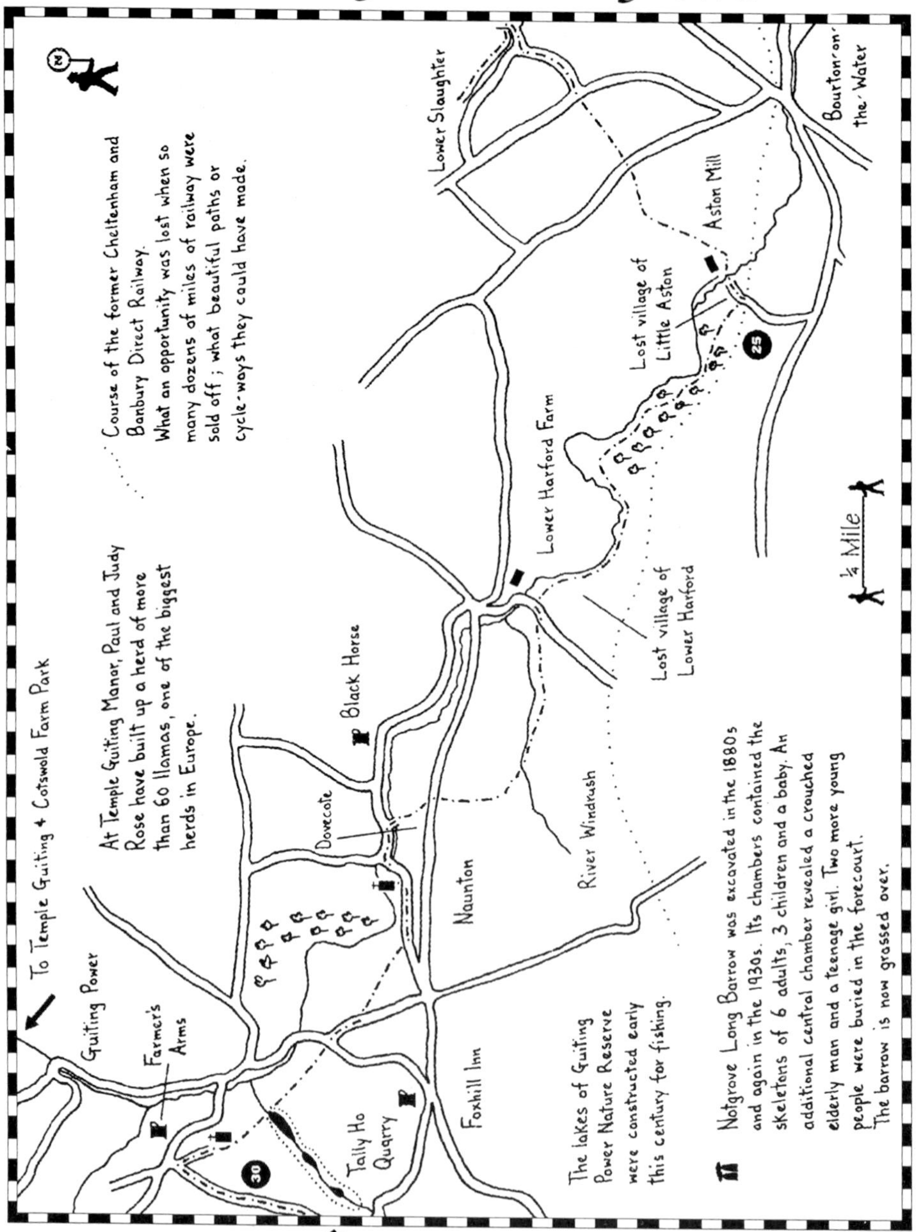

Follow the River Eye with its little footbridges, crossing it at the Washbourne Court Hotel. Turn right, heading back upstream, till a road leaves the village to the left. Climb with the road for nearly ½ mile passing a deep disused quarry on the right, not forgetting to glance back for views of the village.

Cross the road, continuing on the bridleway to cross a second road. Swing a little right to cross the field to its diagonal corner. Pass through a gate with B↑, turn left to pass through another and follow the field edge to reach yet another which leads into a tree-sheltered sunken lane.

At the bottom of the lane turn right to pass the renovated and extended buildings and garden of Aston Mill. The bridge makes a good spot for a rest but if there is even the hint of a breeze don't leave your map untended on the bridge parapet. I certainly won't make that mistake twice.

Climb with the road and where it bends left, go right to Aston Farm. Just above you is the dismantled line of the Cheltenham and Banbury Direct Railway. As you pass through the farm buildings notice the imaginatively placed B↑. Head straight towards the wood, entering it at a post with B↑.

The route through the wood is obvious with several arrows on posts confirming the way. At a steep gulley you pass a railway bridge and a derelict lime kiln. You are close to the Windrush which you will glimpse well below you. At one point, reaching a fork the arrow points you left. A gate with B↑ leads you out of the wood.

Follow the field edge and at another post drop left, steeply, to river level through gorse, its vivid yellow flowers with their coconut scent, bright against their dark green foil.

Go through a green gate to walk beside the meanders of the Windrush and an impressive railway embankment. The bridge was presumably needed to allow the passage of farm traffic.

After two stiles with B↑ you will be walking across the banks and hummocks that are the remains of the medieval village of Lower Harford. To your right, someone has been keenly constructing lakes among the pastures.

Leave this "lost village" by a stile on to the road near Lower Harford Farm. A Windrush Way sign takes you left up the road for 100 yards passing a cattle pen. Leave the road right at another Windrush Way sign, turning immediately left.

You are now heading up the valley of a little Windrush tributary with an encouraging amount of recent tree planting. Keep just below the new trees, dropping to the floor of the valley to pass through a gate with B↑.

When you see Roundhill Farm on the left cross the stile with B↑. Cross the field and go through a small red gate just below a very high stone wall that supports nothing more elaborate than a small field, although the OS map indicates a small building, Lodge's Barn. Follow the obvious track that takes you gently up the hill and then steepens to reach a stile with B↑. The lane takes you through the recently completed Naunton Downs Golf Course. As you approach the road the very long village of Naunton comes into view.

Cross the road and go through an unmarked gate into a sunken lane. Where the lane bends left, keep straight on down the hill. Pass through a gate Y↑ and cross the Windrush noticing the cartwash and the huge stones that

Contd: page 53

Gloucester Cattle

The animals are a dark mahogany red with an irregular line of white along their backs, almost black faces and white tails. Their horns are long, pointed and curved forward, sometimes with a double bend.

It's difficult to say when Gloucester cattle, sometimes known as Old Gloucesters, first emerged as a distinct breed but by the 13th century the County was famed for the cheeses made from their milk. It can be said though, with perfect accuracy, that by 1951 there were only 50 cattle left and the breed faced extinction. Had it not been for the Dukes of Beaufort at Badminton, that would have been their fate.

Possibly descended from the wild ox, or maybe from Norwegian breeds introduced by the Vikings, Gloucester cattle produced the milk which made what was considered 150 years ago to be England's finest cheese, Double Gloucester. The breed's decline began in the mid 18th century when a rinderpest epidemic caused millions to be slaughtered. The vacuum was filled mainly with Longhorns, a breed being improved by Robert Bakewell. Another epidemic in the next century speeded up the switch to the more productive breeds.

A Gloucester from Colesbourne Park in 1935, with George Eddolls, the farm manager

By the end of the 19th century most of the Gloucesters had disappeared into cross-breeds but a few small and dwindling herds lived on in the Severn Vale and on the Cotswolds. The only pure herd left was the one at Badminton. Most of this, though, was sold off in 1896 and broken up into several smaller herds. By 1910, when the breed was finally officially recognised, only 130 animals could be located.

In 1922 Seymour Henry, 7th Earl Bathurst of Cirencester Park, joined the select band of enthusiasts in the Gloucester Cattle Society but foot-and-mouth disease and more cross breeding reduced numbers even more, so that by 1935 even the Society looked like becoming extinct with just six "country gentry" members. Even the remains of the Beaufort herd were suffering from inbreeding with its perils of infertility and the early death of calves. In 1965 interest in Gloucesters had declined so much that the Society disbanded. By 1972 the breed was again down to just one herd and again on the brink of extinction. The Gloucester had become Britain's rarest cattle breed.

This last pure herd of 50 was owned by the Dowdeswell sisters, from Wick Court at Saul on the River Severn. By this time they were in their eighties and no longer able to manage the cattle and many feared that the herd's dispersal would herald the end of the Gloucester.

Interest in the preservation of rare breeds was awakening, though, and the sale received a good deal of national publicity. The whole herd was bought by enthusiasts, including two animals which went to the Rare Breeds Survival Trust at Cotswold Farm Park. Determination to revive the breed led to the re-establishment of the herd Society in the early 1970s. The credit for this must go to Charles and Monica Martell of Laurel Farm, Dymock who encouraged likely buyers to attend the Wick Court sale and gradually built up their own herd with the purpose of making genuine Gloucester cheeses from the milk of genuine Gloucester cattle.

Having faced extinction for 200 years the breed is now doing well, its numbers above 500, but as long as there are fewer than 2000, it remains officially a rare breed.

While historically they were triple purpose animals kept for meat, milk and draught, today they are no longer a commercial proposition at all. It is encouraging that without any real economic incentive, the efforts of a few people have saved the distinctive Gloucester breed.

Its prospects seem more healthy now than for many years. In 1994, 30 of the cattle from nine different herds were entered in their class at the Malvern Three Counties Show; 20 years earlier when the class was first re-introduced, only a dozen appeared. More Gloucesters were sold at a recent Gloucester Cattle Market auction than at any time in the last 100 years and there are now about 30 small herds. It is fitting that a small herd of seven is once again living in Cirencester Park.

You should certainly be able to spot some on your walk or at the breed's annual show which has been held for the last 21 years in early July.

Stone Slatters

Stone slates[1] have been used for roofing Cotswold buildings since Roman times. Church and manor buildings, of course, have long been roofed with slates and we know that the Knights Templar exported stone slates in the 13th century from their land at Temple Guiting but, up until the 17th century, the house of the common man was roofed with thatch.

Cottage at Hawling

[1] If you think of a slate as something dark grey and shiny and used with chalks, or as a roofing material, you would be quite correct. Cotswold slates are not true slates in the geologist's sense, but locally are always referred to in this way. In Oxfordshire they are often called Stonesfield slates.

Suitable stone which will cleave into slender sections occurs in only a few localities, often requiring underground mining rather than quarrying so it has never been particularly easy to win stone slates. Stonesfield Quarry on the Oxfordshire border is the most celebrated and has shafts descending more than 60 feet, just one of which is still open to the public for educational visits. In the South Wolds near Box there are said to be more than 60 miles of underground galleries cut by the quarry men.

The slatters' quarrying season lasted from April to October. The slatter entered the shaft down a rope which was used again to haul the rough stone blocks to the surface. These were dampened and covered with mounds of earth, grass or straw to retain the stone's moisture. Each evening when a frost was due the pile would be uncovered for nature to take its course, expanding the moisture and prising the layers apart. In this way the winter frosts did most of the hard work; a simple blow with a mallet did the rest.

Once split in this way, the slatter's task was to chip the stone into regular shapes and sizes suitable for use as roofing. The finishing touch was made by tapping the peg hole through using a sharp pick. Each slate was held in place with an oak peg or in some cases an iron nail through the hole. Paid a piece rate, the slatter was expected to shape upwards of 250 a day.

You'll have noticed that the size of slate decreases markedly from as much as 24 inches at the eaves up to a mere six inches at the ridge which was made from sawn stone laid on its edge. These subtle gradations in size have been likened to the scales of a fish and have their own arcane names amongst slatters, the names varying from district to district with some of the older slatters reluctant to disclose the local names to strangers. Edward Berryman has worked some of them into his poem, Cotswold Tiles:

> The finest roofs in all the land are made from Cotswold stone,
> And the mason gives each tile a name like children of his own.
> By length and breadth the tally runs, by width and depth and size,
> And the mason knows them all by name, for he is very wise.
> Long Day, Short Day, Moreday and Muffity,
> Lye-byes and Bottomers, each a name receives:
> Wivett, Beck, and Cussomes, Cutting, Third and Batchelor,
> Smallest under roof ridge, largest over eaves.

The mystique of naming slates is now long-gone and a more mundane numbering system is used.

There has been no underground mining of slates since 1909 and today none are quarried or split in the Cotswolds. So few have been produced this century that they command extraordinary prices (about three times the price of alternatives) and derelict buildings have been stripped of slates for repair work or to give an authentic roof to a new house rather than use moulded concrete. Laid carefully on stout roof timbers, a slate roof will last for 3-400 years. Henry Ford's "Cotswold" cottage has recently been re-roofed with Cotswold slates and local newspapers have reported thefts of entire roofs from many an isolated barn.

support the wall where it crosses the river. As the road bends up to the left look for the farmer's ingenuity in recycling railway sleepers! Pass the dovecote to reach the main street, turning left to walk through **Naunton**.

➤ At times the village has been known as Naunton-in-the-Vale and Naunton upon Cotswold.

➤ The restored dovecote of 1460 is all that remains of the Manor House. It follows the familiar Cotswold four-gable design and has 1176 nest holes.

Black Horse
Donnington tied house.
Spoof tale of why golf courses were standardised at 18 holes.
Detour up the side road for a cottage with window sills stacked with fossils

➤ Until 1939 a Mrs Garner operated a horse powered cider mill in the village.

➤ Dale Terrace is a pleasant group of cottages, hidden behind an archway near the mill at the eastern end of village. It was built in the 1860s but imitated 17th century design. Some of the cottages have ammonites on display on their window sills, finds from the local stone quarries.

Just past the Baptist Chapel, the road descends. Fork left to re-cross the river. Fork right at the little village green to reach the churchyard.

➤ The tower has two lovely wrought iron sundials of 1718, the black showing stark against orange paint. The gargoyles are particularly good.

➤ A Saxon cross in white stone is built into the wall near the arch of the tower.

➤ The table of "Kindred and Affinity" inside, based on the Book of Leviticus, reminds you which of your relations you are forbidden to marry by the Church of England. They include, for a man, his sister's son's wife and for a woman, her husband's mother's brother. Useful for budding quizmasters! Perhaps incest has been a particular problem in the parish - the table is displayed twice in this one small church.

- fishermen
- spinsters
- Scotland
- fishmongers

Leave the churchyard via the path up to its top corner, glancing back at the mushroom topiary. This brings you to the road where you turn right. Notice the thickness of the ivy on two trees that has been cut to prevent it killing its host and over to the right horse jumps set out in the field of a stud farm.

After 300 yards take a stile right signposted Warden's Way. Follow the contour to reach a post with Y↑ in a gap in the corner of the field. Go straight ahead over the field ignoring the rutted track that forks gently right. Passing to the right of the little wood, take the gate with Y↑ into the road and turn right.

After 250 yards at the T junction go straight across, up into the field. Walk straight ahead to a post with Y↑ at a gate in the hedge.

Steps take you down in front of the lowest dam of Guiting Power Nature Reserve which stretches more than ½ mile up this little Windrush tributary, above the site of Barton Mill.

The reserve has an otter holt[1] above the large pond and perches for kingfishers.

Take the footbridge over the stream and follow the well-trodden path till two stiles with Y↑ bring you to the church gateway in **Guiting** (pronounced guy-ting) **Power**, formerly Lower Guiting. Follow the copper beech hedge straight ahead to the diminutive village school with its diminutive hockey pitch which survived with just 16 pupils till 1994.

➤ The village Bakery still produces fresh bread every day.

➤ The village boasts two village greens and an attractive collection of cottages. 48 of them are owned by the Guiting Manor Amenity Trust set up by Raymond Cochrane to restore and modernise the buildings inside and out. The letting policy ensures that they benefit local young married couples, the elderly and disabled tenants. This ensures the village is not overrun by commuters and provides a stock of affordable housing, a rare commodity in Cotswold villages.

➤ The Dyers is a 17th century mill on a site mentioned in Domesday Book.

➤ Guiting Woods is one of the few remaining ancient woods in the County with oak, ash, hazel coppice and beech.

➤ The first recorded fulling mill was established by the Knights Templar on the Windrush at Temple Guiting in 1185. All that remains is the remnants of the mill pond. It is hard to imagine the infant Windrush producing enough power to drive the hammers but the water table has been lowered throughout the Cotswolds by extracting our modern water supplies.

➤ The 16th century Manor Farm, built as a summer residence for the Bishops of Oxford, is considered one of the finest Tudor manors in the Cotswolds.

➤ For 25 years the village has held a serious annual music and arts festival.

➤ Peer up into the roof of the church to see a wooden version of the Green Man.

Ye Olde Inne

Free house.
Hook Norton, Jouster,
Bass & Guest beers.
Some Danish food.
The menu shows a suggested
5-mile walk from the pub!

Farmers Arms

Donnington tied house.
Splendid carved model of a beer wagon pulled by 6 horses.
Wins my prize for the most generous ploughman's lunch available on the route.

[1] Absent from the upper Thames valley now for more than 20 years, otters seem to be spreading back to the area - one was spotted in the Windrush valley in 1994. But, unlike foxes, beavers or badgers, otters do not build their own homes.
The Gloucestershire Wildlife Trust is keen to encourage their return so, to supplement hollow trees and holes in the river bank, the Trust has been building holts (or tunnels) with logs or brick-and-pipe, above floodwater level, to encourage a re-colonisation.

Castlett Mill Ice-House

De tour

Take the road opposite the bakery and follow it till it becomes a path. Continue another 200 yards, steeply down hill till you can cross the stream. In the bank opposite you will see the arched stone roof of an ice-house, all that remains of Castlett Mill which stood here till 1900.

Until the 1920s, when refrigeration spread to Europe from the USA, most large country houses had an ice-house to preserve perishable foods through the summer. Alexander the Great had had them built in the 4th century BC to support his campaigns in Asia Minor and at about the same time the Chinese had learned how to manufacture ice. By the 15th century ice had become an essential element of Italian aristocratic entertaining and the court of Charles II adopted the craze for ice from the French.

In about 1800 the philosopher Jeremy Bentham was making calculations for a building he called a Frigidarium, a giant ice-house for meat, vegetables, fruits and fish which he could release on to the London market out of season at enormous profit. His scheme stalled at the planning stage.

The principle of an ice-house, though, is simple and simulates the use of caves for keeping wines and cheeses: fresh-water ice is cut in large blocks from a pond in winter, packed in straw and sawdust for its transport, and stored underground where it will remain as ice for up to two years. This keeps the surrounding air at a constant temperature, sufficient to preserve food.

At its simplest, a hole in the ground lined with straw would preserve the ice for a time but the ice-house proper is usually a series of underground domed rooms lined with stone or brick culminating in a deeper section, like a well, where the ice was packed. The rooms were used for storage, those nearest to the "well" being the coolest. The structure needed insulation so the most convenient method was to tunnel into a hillside as was the case here at Castlett Mill. If that was not possible then reed or grass thatch and earth taken from the pond digging would be heaped over the building.

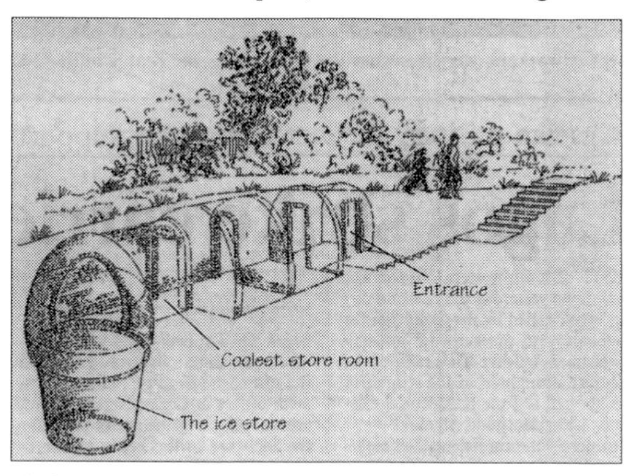

A diagrammatic ice-house built into the slope of the land

So the ice-house was an important complement to the kitchen garden and the orchards of the country house. If greater quantities were needed than the local pond could supply, it was brought in insulated ships from Scotland, the Baltic or even the iceberg-strewn seas around Greenland. Queen Victoria's supplies came from Lake Wenham near Boston.

A far better preserved example dating from the late 18th century is at Northwick Park. The ice-house there might well have been plundered for another purpose: the Victorians adopted the habit of keeping a block standing in the ballroom to cool the perspiring brows of the dancers.

The Mystery of the Templars

In 1118 nine men founded a new monastic Order, The Poor Fellow Soldiers of Jesus Christ. They adopted the three standard monastic vows of poverty, chastity and obedience and they added a fourth - defence of pilgrims travelling to and from the Holy Land, for Europe was in the middle of 200 years of Crusades, trying to wrestle the Middle East from the hands of the Muslims. This new Military Order was given lodgings on the site of the Jewish Temple of Solomon in Jerusalem, hence their more common names of Knights Templar or the Templars[1].

From the start there was more of the soldier than the monk about these Christian brothers. While for most Crusaders the promise was to temporarily lend their hand to a single campaign, the vow taken by brothers in the Military Orders was a permanent one, to protect Christendom.

Their original role was to protect pilgrims in the newly conquered Kingdom of Jerusalem. Travel in the hilly land of Judea and Galilee was dangerous so the Templars organised military convoys to protect the Christians who wanted to visit Bethlehem and Nazareth.

The dull design on the Templars' shields was a reminder of their vows of poverty

Their influence grew swiftly as they established a chain of massively fortified towers and castles along all of the route back to Europe, many of which were never captured by the enemy. They lived in these strongholds rather than in monasteries, much of their life spent in the desert, guarding new recruits to the Crusader armies who often travelled with their families and servants.

The Rules of the Order were drawn up by St Bernard of Clairvaux and included such hardships as rising at dawn, sharing one bowl between two knights, and wearing no decoration except the red cross on the breast of their simple white cloaks. They were forbidden to indulge in the more frivolous pursuits of the medieval knight such as competing in jousting tournaments and dancing.

[1] Lawrence Durrell's "Avignon Quintet" and Umberto Eco's "Foucault's Pendulum" use the Templars as the basis of novels, speculating on a continuing sinister influence for centuries after the suppression.

In 1994/5, 69 members of the Order of the Solar Temple, died in collective suicides (or mass murder) in Switzerland, France and Canada. Initiates of the cult, a weird blend of the occult and Catholicism, wore a white cape with a red cross. Its co-leader, Joseph di Mambro, believed he was the reincarnation of the leader of the Knights Templar while Thierry Huguenin believed he had previously lived as St Bernard of Clairvaux.

Applicants for membership of the Order were warned of the austerity of its life:

for when you wish to be on this side of the sea, you will be beyond it, and vice versa, and when you wish to sleep, you must be awake, and when you wish to eat you must go hungry. Can you bear these things for the honour of god..?

We should perhaps picture them as a medieval equivalent of Desert Rats or French Legionnaires with many of their number joining for adventure rather than religious conviction.

They had rapidly became a very powerful force. Almost every country had a branch of their organisation, a Commandery, which received gifts of money and land and trained new recruits. They were permitted to keep any booty they seized in battle and they multiplied their wealth by acting as bankers to the Crusaders. They grew rich on enormous donations of land and property, insignificant amongst which was a preceptory at Temple Guiting, a small community set up to manage the land they owned around the hamlet. In England there were about 60 of these preceptories, each with a Preceptor, a Knight of the Order, in charge of a priest and a number of serving brothers.

Then in 1308 everything changed. Jerusalem had finally fallen, and with the ending of attempts to reconquer the Holy Lands, the Templars' original purpose disappeared. They returned to their European estates. By this time they had amassed some 9000 manors and titles in Europe, and assumed an aristocratic life, managing their properties and banking operations, a far cry from their vows of hardship and poverty. They had become a clear threat to both the Pope and the monarchs of Europe, many of whom owed money to their Templar bankers.

Their great wealth and exemption from taxation had made them unpopular with their peers; their immunity from secular law meant they were feared by kings. Their internal affairs were veiled in secrecy and a whispering campaign accused them of having secret dealings with Moslem sects, sacrilege, sodomy and usury.

Building on these rumours, Phillippe le Bel of France came up with a brilliant scheme to rid the European monarchs of this huge financial problem: charge the Templars with heresy and abolish their Order.

He persuaded Pope Clement V to act. On a single night their 5000 officers all over Europe were arrested (just 13 escaped) and their property was confiscated. The trials dragged on for seven years.

Eventually, in 1312, the Order was suppressed and the 23rd and last Grand Master of the Temple, Jacques de Molay[2], was burned at the stake. Many died from torture and those who would not confess were sentenced to life imprisonment. Those who did, were pardoned and drifted into other religious Houses.

The secrecy of the Templars, the uncertainty about their guilt and their melting away into other Orders, have aroused continuing speculation about the fate of those who escaped punishment. Some of them managed to spirit away most of the records and valuables from their Paris Treasury.

The Preceptor of the Temple Guiting community was sent to the Tower of London, questioned and tortured, and the Temple Guiting properties passed into the hands of the rival Order of Hospitallers who had a similar House at Quenington.

In time the Knights Hospitallers also became too powerful for Europe's comfort...but that's another story.

The Grand Master of the Templars

In Gloucestershire when girls get bold
They ask for your kisses and not for your gold,
Which is better far as I've been told
Or what would a poor boy do?

JH

---

[2] It has been suggested in a recent book that de Molay was crucified before being burnt and that it is his image that can be seen on the Turin Shroud which, indeed, turns out to date from the right century.

5
Guiting Power to Hazleton

7½ miles

On uplands bleak and bare to wind
Beneath a maze of stars one strode.
Phantoms of fear haunted the road,
Mocking my footsteps close behind

IG

Guiting Power to Hazleton

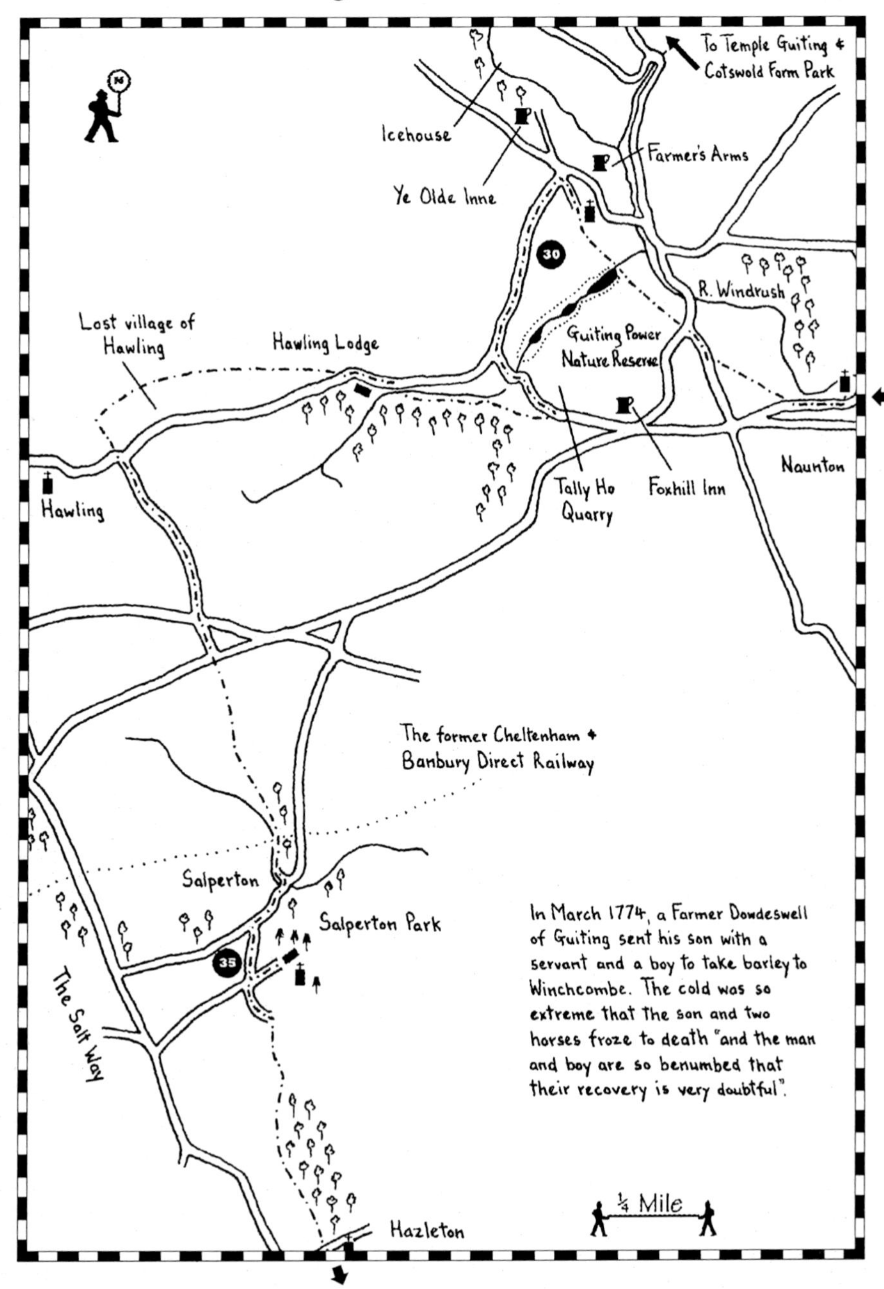

The Railway That Never Was

A proposal was made in 1812 to build the Cheltenham and Cotswolds Hill Railway. It was to run, drawn by horses, from Fox Hill, near Guiting Power to Cheltenham. But what was the motive to build a railway over such difficult terrain to somewhere so obscure?

It was to carry stone pipes. The Stone Pipe Company was digging stone at the Tally Ho Quarry and using Sir George Wright's patented stone cutting machine to cut water pipes out of the stone blocks. The enterprise appeared to be going well and had secured a contract to supply all the pipes needed by the Manchester City Waterworks. The railway would enable the Company to ship out more pipes, more quickly and make more profit.

Cotswold limestone, of course, must be one of the worst possible vessels for water because it is porous and quite brittle. Water very easily seeps through it which is why we see no ponds or streams on these uplands.

The Company went into liquidation and the railway plans remained on paper. Perhaps it won't surprise you to learn that the Stone Pipe Company and the Manchester Waterworks were found to have a number of Directors in common.

A vestige of the enterprise remains: if you walk on the road that runs down from the former Foxhill Inn you will spot the odd pipe and the cores that were cut out of them built into the stone walls. And, further down the hill from the quarry, the terrace of cottages that was built for the stone workers.

The Cheltenham and Banbury Direct

Although it sounds unlikely, in the 1920s the Aberdeen to Penzance express used to thunder through here. Many early proposed lines to link Cheltenham and Oxford were never built; a route was planned through Northleach, another through Shipton-under-Wychwood and yet another through Fairford. The line that was eventually built was completed late because of the difficult terrain: near Salperton, the highest point on the route at 760ft, the gradient of the line was 1 in 60. Not till 1889 were all the links in place which created the through route.

Until 1906 it was really a branch line but once a bridge had been built to cross the Worcester-Oxford railway at Kingham, it became a genuine through route linking the North-East to South Wales with an express train (the Ports-to-Ports Express) each way every weekday. In the same year the completion of the Hatherley Loop meant that through trains could bypass Cheltenham. It also offered a shorter route to London taking two and a half hours compared with three for the route through Stroud, but the switchback stretch over the Cotswolds was painfully slow taking an hour for the 24 miles between Kingham and Cheltenham. Despite the speed, until the First World War there was sufficient business to warrant four passenger trains a day which stopped at all the stations.

The line's chief uses seem to have been taking cattle east to Banbury and iron ore west from Northamptonshire to South Wales. It fell to Dr Beeching's axe in 1962.

➤ As you reach the village you'd be forgiven for thinking you're approaching a small provincial airport: a converted windmill on the right looks like its control tower.

➤ A stone from a cider press stands in the garden of a house called Whistling Down.

Continue on the road to the right of the church, which is only for the dedicated - Norman chevron work on the arches of the door and the nave.

Hazleton perches on a pair of hills. As you climb the road up the second, glance back at the view of Glebe House Farm, the 16th century parsonage, with its dove loft and the church nestling behind. Ignore the first road to the right and at the T junction turn right to pass Priory Farm with its two medieval arched gateways.

Notgrove Long Barrow

This barrow is about 50 yards in length with typical horns. It was excavated in 1881 and again in the 1930s. In its four chambers the remains of six adults, three children and a new-born baby were found.

A cairn in the centre revealed a crouched old man and a teenage girl. Animal bones and the remains of two more young people were found amidst evidence of fire in the forecourt area.

The barrow is now grassed over and open to the public.

Pass the farm and notice at least three houses over to the right which have sprouted, to borrow a Royal metaphor, monstrous carbuncles. Just before a huge modern barn take the unmarked lane left. Keep to the lane which becomes curiously causewayed approaching Thornborough Copse.

As you climb beside the copse notice the walled well on the left and look back towards Priory Farm - the parkland trees give an ancient, hallowed feel. You would not be wrong to think that this place has monastic connections. In the 1140s, Cistercian monks from Kingswood near Wotton-under-Edge set up a community here even though the water supply this high in the Cotswolds was unreliable. They remained for 400 years until the Dissolution, their monastery perhaps on the site of the Coach House of Hazleton Manor about which Verey is uncharacteristically silent.

At the brow of the hill turn right through a gate with Y↑. Follow the rather drunken wall to the stone stile behind The Puesdown Inn.

Continue to the road, turn left past the inn and branch off left on the public path. Take care! There have been two sightings of a coach-and-four emerging from the old road and disappearing into the trees across the main road. Follow this old road for 1¼ miles. It is something of a rabbit warren and includes a bizarre sight - an animal shelter with a huge circular entrance, presumably for housing huge circular animals. For almost the whole way the road is sheltered by a narrow copse.

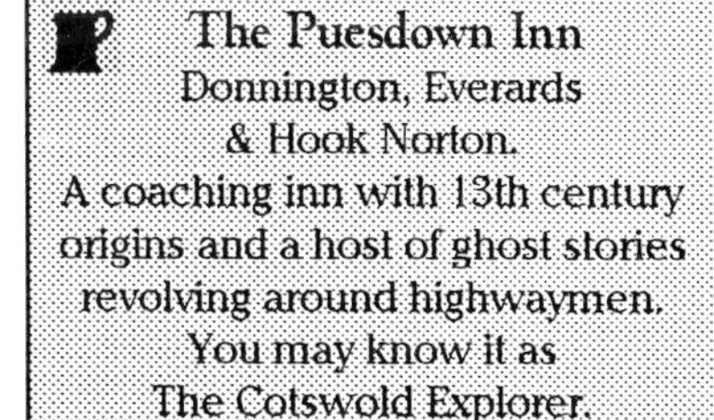

The Puesdown Inn
Donnington, Everards & Hook Norton.
A coaching inn with 13th century origins and a host of ghost stories revolving around highwaymen.
You may know it as The Cotswold Explorer.

Continue on to a road which still uses the line of the turnpike and go straight on for 500 yards. Emerging at a crossroads where the Turkdean road goes left, turn right. The cast iron water pump on the cross makes a pleasant spot for a break.

Cross the busy A40 to join a gated road that leads into **Hampnett** which falls into two parts, one centred around the green which was much more extensive before the Black Death and the other straggling downhill from the church.

➤ With luck you will see some Cotswold sheep as well as some Jacobs and if it's a warm summer day you'll hear birds singing from two aviaries.

➤ The spring that rises on the green is the source of the River Leach which joins the Thames at Lechlade.

➤ There is a large and particularly fine tithe barn with two great cart doors, now converted, opposite the church.

St George,
patron of

- armourers
- cavalrymen
- archers
- saddlers
- soldiers
- farmers
- swordmakers
- Boy Scouts

Contd: page 74

The Glocester Flying Machine

We are so familiar with pictures of stage coaches and coaching inns on Christmas cards, it is surprising to learn that their heyday lasted only about 25 years, from the 1820s to the 1840s.

For 1400 years after the end of the Roman occupation England had managed without a proper road system.

In theory each Parish was meant to keep its roads in good repair; in practice the repair work was shoddy and a cold, wet winter would wash the surface away. So in the early 1700s the journey from Gloucester to London took two days in summer but three in winter. Goods waggons using four or even five horses took as many as five days.

This replica mail coach stands at The Highwayman at Beechpike

The level of comfort on these public coach services was rudimentary. The coaches were large and cumbersome, without any form of suspension. The floors were covered with straw and the only protection from the weather was leather curtains.

Improvements came in the first half of the 18th century with the building of turnpike roads. Turnpike Trusts were permitted to borrow money for road building and to charge tolls for their use. They made a dramatic improvement: roads were widened and straightened, gradients were reduced and bridges built and improved. The impact must have been greater than the opening of a new motorway today.

The first Turnpike road in the Cotswolds was the stretch of the current A419 between Gloucester and Birdlip. The steepness of the hill had long been a problem on the main route from London to Fishguard and Ireland. In some cases the Trust road adopted a new route: between Gloucester and Northleach the old hill-top route through Compton Abdale and Hazleton was abandoned in favour of the route you are now walking, built in 1746.

Corresponding improvements were made to the design of the coaches which allowed full use to be made of the new roads. In 1756 The Glocester Flying Machine started service between Gloucester and London. It was lighter, sprung and used six horses with a postillion riding on one of the leaders. It averaged six mph over the 105 miles achieving a time of 21 hours. It carried eight passengers, each paying 23 shillings for the full journey.

The journey was further speeded up after 1785 with the introduction of light Mail Coaches which took just four passengers. Because they carried the mail, the Post Office provided guards armed with a blunderbuss. As with planes today there was a luggage limit, just twenty lbs.

Pub sign of the Puesdown Inn

To keep up the pace, horses had to be changed every six to eight miles, hence the string of former coaching inns along this road, the Frogmill being the first stop out of Gloucester. The changeover must have been an extraordinary sight, akin to a Grand Prix wheel change, because the fresh horses had to be in harness within one minute. Further south, mid-way between Birdlip and Cirencester, is The Five Mile House, a wonderfully unchanged coaching inn where you can still buy your ale in a genuine tap room.

By the 1820s the journey time was down to 14 hours and 100 coaches a day were passing through Gloucester. Travelling by coach at a few miles per hour sounds a reasonably safe way to travel but, not so. It is surprising how many injuries and deaths were caused by overturning coaches, lost wheels, coachmen falling asleep or falling under their own wheels and rival coachmen obstructing each other.

In July 1817 near the Puesdown Inn, the Gloucester and London Day-Coach was racing with the Cheltenham Day-Coach (at a speed of nearly 12 mph!). The Gloucester coach overturned. Mr Bishop, the coachman was *severely injured about the loins*; a Mr Heath broke his ankle and had to have his foot amputated; other passengers had a cut lip, a dislocated collar bone and *one tooth beaten out*.

Clearly there was strong rivalry between competing coach operators, heightened by instructions given to one coachman to *suffer nothing to pass him on the road, and not to spare horseflesh*.

For 100 years or so from the 1840s the railways became the most common means of transport for lengthy journeys and then we passed into a second age of the road.

Glocester Flying Machine
...On Steel Spring
(in Two Days)...

Sets out from John Turner's, at the Coach Office in the Lower North-gate street, Glocester, every Monday, Wednesday and Friday and on the same days from the Bolt-and-Tun in Fleet Street, London: bothe Coaches lie at the New Inn Oxford, and set out from thence every Tuesday, Thursday and Saturday at five o'clock for Glocester and London.

The price as usual. Each passenger allowed 20 lb Weight: all above to be paid for as usual

Perform'd (if God permit) by

W and J Turner

Extracted from the **Gloucester Journal**

Leaving the church, turn right then take the No Through Road to drop down to the lowest part of the village. At the foot of the hill is a charming row of cottages standing alongside the infant Leach and a pair of weeping willows.

Follow the road around to the left and after 100 yards follow the footpath sign to pass to the right of the large house. The lane is peppered with snow-drops in January. Go through the gate with B↑ and aim for the left end of the stone wall ahead. Follow the fence then drop down to the right to a gate. Walk to the bottom of the attractive dry valley and turn right.

Keep to the gently curving valley bottom until a path swings up left to a gate by a house. Follow the grassy track, keeping beside the stone wall until the track joins the farm access road in front of the stone Furzenhill barn. Follow this road to join the main road.

Turn left and after 250 yards fork right, signposted Fossebridge, although the last time I walked here the signpost had been misleadingly turned to point across open fields.

After 100 yards turn sharp right through a gateway marked Private Road of Stowell Park. After another 100 yards turn left through a double gate. Here is the Hangman's Stone.

Turn immediately left. Turn right and follow the field boundary, an odd mixture of tumbled wall, hedge and fencing, for about ½ mile with the cattle sheds of Oxpens Farm coming into view on the scale of an industrial estate.

A homemade footpath sign and Y↑ point you left towards the farm buildings. After 100 yards go right over a stile with Y↑. Follow the green lane between wall and fence, with pleasant views down to Dean Grove and Cowlease Grove, to a stile leading into a tiny field. Leave by the the gate which takes you on to the farm access road. Turn right.

The road winds down to a Coln tributary passing a woody knoll rich with snowdrops. Just beyond the bridge, notice a neat stone sheepwash to the right. Continue up the road till you meet a barn. Pass to its right, walk its length and go through a gate into **Yanworth** churchyard. The church from this vantage point looks like a miniature with the smallest tower imaginable.

➤ Look to the left of the porch and at eye level you will notice a small hole where the pointer of a scratch dial was fixed and just below, the markings of the hours.

➤ Let your eyes get accustomed to the light inside before you look for the Doom painting; it's on the wall of the west end to the right of the window and shows Father Time as a skeleton wielding a scythe, a constant visual reminder of man's short stay on earth. The church

Hangman's Stone

There are two stones - one is now a part of the stile, the other, seven feet long and up to three feet high lies against the wall with an oval hole near one end.

The name may recall the site of a gibbet or may derive from the story of a sheep-stealer making away from the scene of his crime, the sheep with its legs bound slung around his neck. Trying to make too much haste over the stile he fell, the sheep's bindings caught in the wall and he died slowly by hanging.

Contd: page 76

Hampnett's Controversial Church

Most guidebooks are dismissive of 19th century church restorers and quite rightly, as a great deal of unique historical interest was destroyed. William Morris, visiting Burford in 1876 was so appalled at the alterations being made in the cause of "restoration", that he never again made stained glass and he formed the Society for the Protection of Ancient Buildings.

Hampnett's restoration, though, was of a very different kind. The painting in the church is stunning, with yellows, golds and blues reminiscent of an Eastern Orthodox church, providing a vivid impression of a medieval church interior.

The walls, roofs and arches are all painted, the most impressive part being the vault of the sanctuary, east of the nave. The paintings include angels with blue and gold wings and The Last Supper.

Whether the painting was based on surviving fragments or whether the walls were replastered before decoration is not clear. Either way, we should be grateful to the Rev W Wiggin, the Victorian vicar who commissioned the work. Delderfield most certainly disagrees with me: *The church is ancient but was restored in 1868 at a cost of £700. It was £700 wasted!...but the churchwardens are hoping to remove some of them (the wallpaintings) when funds permit.* Some of the locals seem to disagree with me too: a fund was begun to un-restore the restored church but insufficient money was raised.

If you do crave the genuine, look for the two pairs of charming carved stone doves on the arches of the nave - one pair drinking, the other, preening. Guaranteed, genuine Norman work!

Genuine Norman doves

Some of the best medieval wall-painting in the country is near at hand at Oddington, just east of Stow-on-the-Wold. These Doom figures were painted in the mid 14th century, whitewashed over in the 17th, rediscovered in 1913 and beautifully restored in the '70s.

Some of the curious characters in Oddington's 500 year old Doom painting

The subject of the Doom painting is the Last Judgement, with Christ separating the souls destined for Heaven from those consigned to Hell. These paintings were intended as warnings so the artists went into gruesome detail on the torments to be expected by the damned.

The images include a woman in a pillory, a man hanging from a gallows and a whole group of people being boiled in a cauldron. On a lighter note, the picture shows a preaching fox in a monk's habit.

escaped the ravages of Victorian restorers and retains many Norman features. You may spot up to seven old clocks - scratch dials and sun dials.

➤ Enjoy a rest in the churchyard which used to have, and perhaps will again have, a bench. You are surrounded by a neat cluster of well-maintained farm buildings and cottages. The round hole above the barn door encouraged barn owls to nest and act as a constant guard against the bird and vermin population. The barn is crowned with a cupola.

➤ While you are resting try to guess the Stowell Park estate manager's favourite colour for paint.

Leaving the church, turn right up the main road. Follow it round to the left and turn right into Yanworth's main street. The uniform colour of the woodwork gives a slightly sinister feel. After 250 yards turn left into a broad lane which passes to the right of Yanworth House (painted white!). Note the splendid tree and the ha-ha falling into disrepair.

Cross the stile into the field and aim straight ahead. Before you reach the line of the trees, remnants of the field boundary, turn 90 degrees left and aim for a gate leading on to the road. (Don't try to follow the line of trees as the footpath is blocked with a fence and hedge - a rare phenomenon in the Cotswolds.) Look up to the left to spot unusual accommodation for doves.

Turn right down the road and in 300 yards go left through a signposted gate opposite a farm lane. Swing right to aim directly down to the brook. Cross the stile and bridge and climb straight up the steep wooded slope. Aim for the top right corner of the field.

Pause at the gate on to the road, feeling satisfied that you've climbed 150 feet since crossing the brook.

Take the road down to the right, following it as it turns left to reach a house on a corner. Go through a gate left, just past the house. Just beyond the end of its garden turn left through a gate in the wall - the gateway is astonishingly sited on a spring.

You emerge into the parkland of Stowell Park. Keep the breast of the hill a little to your right, aiming for a fat stunted oak that's been damaged by lightning. At the brow of the hill the house comes into view. Make for the nearest corner of the walled garden and note the colour of the tree house. Keep to the left of the garden passing a couple of gates until you reach stone steps set in the wall. Enter the garden and make for Stowell church which is open to the public.

St Leonard, patron of

- blacksmiths
- domestic pets
- coal merchants
- coopers
- locksmiths
- greengrocers
- the insane
- war prisoners

Leave the garden the way you entered and go back down the hill as far as the gate-on-the-spring, admiring the view of the meandering Coln.

Passing through the gate, walk straight on, to a gate on to the road. Turn left and follow the road to a stone stile on the right just before Stowell Mill. Cross the stile into the field. There is little external evidence left of milling but if you explore behind the building you can see where the water passes under

Stowell Park

Stowell Park is one of the least known of the large Cotswold country houses and deserves to be better known. It lies in a 5000 acre estate replete with a polo ground and edged along its Fosse Way boundary by an impeccable, unusually high, stone wall.

Parts date back to the 16th century. There are two 17th century facades and a dovecote, but much of the house is a Victorian rebuild. Lord Eldon added the battlements to prevent the servants, whose quarters were in the attics, from seeing the family or guests in the garden. Early this century the Eldons, whose family seat was in Dorset, used this house as a mere hunting lodge.

Here in the church is another curious Doom painting, this time from the late 12th century. It was painted directly on to the plaster and has never been retouched or restored. We see Our Lady, flanked by the twelve Apostles, watching the sorting of the souls into the Saved and the Lost in a Trial by Combat.

Walter de la Mare, visiting the church and its paintings, wrote

Scenes from the Doom painting

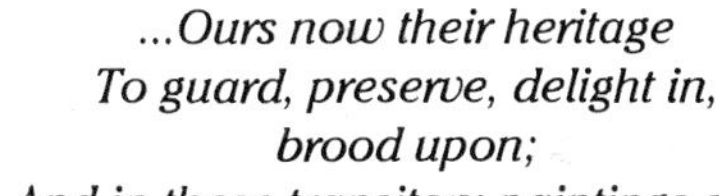

...Ours now their heritage
To guard, preserve, delight in,
brood upon;
And in these transitory paintings scan
The immortal longings in the soul of man

In 1923 the house was bought by the Honorable Samuel Vestey. It still belongs to the Vestey family whose billion pound fortune was based originally on corned beef and now rests on a vast food and shipping empire.

Lady Vestey has reinvigorated the gardens in recent years. On the highest level you enter a walled two acres which is really still a Victorian kitchen garden, producing the full gamut of produce, the air heavy with scent. The restored peach houses with their white peaches, old vines and figs must run along a full 100 yards of wall.

The Dark Walk, on roughly laid stone, leads down to the formal terraces peppered with old and unusual roses and beautiful views over the Coln Valley, Chedworth Woods and beyond.

the mill and the spillway. In fact, the mill machinery is fully working but not open to the public.

You now have to walk away from the stream. Aim for the gateway with a tall signpost on the far side of the field, to the north-north-east. Go through the gate and turn immediately left through another and follow the edge of the field and the Coln for ¾ mile to Yanworth Mill.

Look out for the dogwood tree, known locally as the skiver tree because its wood was used to make skewers. It is recognisable in autumn by its crimson leaves, in winter by its clusters of blue-black berries and in summer by its creamy-white flowers. The view back shows impressive views of Stowell Park. A post with Y↑ leads you through a hawthorn thicket and then beside stark white May blossom to reach a gate on to the road.

Turn left on the road at Yanworth Mill, noting the three millstones set into a wall and further proof that you are still on the Stowell Park estate. After 100 yards follow the road round to the left and just past the house take the sign-posted stile on to the clear woodland path up into Chedworth Woods. Follow several Y↑ on posts which lead you down to the bottom of a shallow valley.

Keep to the rather unattractive forest track as it takes you up the valley. Leaving the woods a signpost points you towards a post on the horizon. From there you see a second post beside what appears to be a lone tree but on closer acquaintance becomes a pair of trees. Continue straight on across the field till you reach the road at a point about 100 yards to the right of a gate you could see silhouetted on the horizon.

Cross a stone stile and continue straight across the next field.

On the far side at a Y↑ drop down through scrubby wood into Listercombe Bottom, following Y↑ posts down to the valley bottom. Start to ascend the other side but turn sharp right to pass through a rather sad, broken gateway.

Turn left and keep to the field edge and then follow a clear path up to a redundant stone stile - you can walk around it. Go straight on till a stile with Y↑ brings you into a lane crossing your path. Turn right. Continue along this sheltered lane that has the feel of a very old route, ignoring a lane off to the left. To the left you see part of Chedworth village which stretches for a good mile on terraces on the steep valley sides. Cross an unmarked stile left into a long narrow muddy field. Cross it and leave by a broken double stile. Drop down to a gate to the right of a house.

Pass between the houses and follow the road down, taking the road right where a stream gushes out beside you. Drop to the bottom of the valley and climb the other side beside a beautifully mossy wall with some neat recent repair work. Admire The Old Farm on your left.

The road turns sharp right to bring you to the main road into **Chedworth** village. Turn right on to this, and pass a deconsecrated chapel where the 110 year old Chedworth Silver Band rehearse - pass by on a Sunday morning and you may hear them practising. At the turn of the century Chedworth boasted six different village bands.

Pass under a former railway bridge and on reaching the main crossroads, take the road to the right which winds around the gardens of the manor and towards the church.

At the church notice:

➤ the gargoyles - a bishop, a man with a horn, an old man with legs crossed and various odd animals;

➤ the splendid assortment of hand-embroidered hassocks;

➤ an extract from Domesday Book displayed on the wall and the chained "Breeches" Bible;

➤ the carved skeleton on the table tomb by the church door.

➤ You may spot, carved in Arabic numerals[1] the dates 1461, 1485 and 1491, a reminder of the Cotswolds' early international importance in the wool trade. At the time, Roman numerals were still the norm.

➤ In the little garden opposite the pub stands a waterwheel. Its millpond is not immediately above the wheel but on the far side of another road, in the Manor garden. The manor had medieval origins. The "church" window in the barn was taken from Cheltenham College.

➤ Church Row and Ballingers Row contain mainly 18th century cottages. Queen Street is a reminder of the visit here of Elizabeth of York, wife of Henry VII.

➤ There is no point looking for Rose Cottage: Henry Ford moved it to the USA in the late '20s! He was so impressed with the cottage that he bought it along with its barn for £500 and had them dismantled. The 500 tons of stone were shipped in a special 67 waggon train to London and on to Mitchigan along with a dovecote and the Old Forge from Broadway. At the Henry Ford Museum at Greenfield Village, near Detroit, the buildings were reassembled in ten weeks by Cotswold craftsmen who, when they had finished the job, were given a free holiday at Niagara. Antiques bought at Broadway completed the transformation. Rose Cottage has recently been re-roofed - with Cotswold stone slates, of course.

Seven Tuns

17th century pub.

John Smith's, Theakston XB and Scrumpy Jack cider. The pub dates from 1610 and the inn sign gives a clue to the meaning of "tuns". Cochin chickens roam the yard.

[1] Puzzle: if Western Europe adopted "Arabic" numerals as an improvement on the Roman system, why is it that most of the modern Arabic characters for the numbers 1 to 10 differ from ours?

Salt of the Earth

Chedworth church holds a copy of a Bible translated by 16th century Englishmen forced to work on it in exile on the Continent; William Tyndale, born in Gloucestershire in 1495 near North Nibley on the Cotswold edge, was put to death for translating and printing his English version. Why did these men undertake such great projects in fear of their lives? How could it be that translating Holy Scripture was a criminal offence?

Europe at the time was like a police state largely controlled by the Catholic Church. The authorities, terrified that Lutheran protestantism would spread into England, maintained their priests' authority by using the 4th century Latin translation of the Bible known as the Vulgate. Although a few copies of an English hand-written version by John Wycliffe, translated in the 1380s from Latin, were in circulation, it was illegal to read them. This ensured that the vast bulk of the population remained dependent on the clergy for interpreting the Scriptures.

Tyndale, a considerable linguist and preacher, wanted a Bible accessible *to every boy that driveth the plough* and he determined to translate it from the original Hebrew and Greek. Failing to get permission for the task from the Bishop of London, he set off for Cologne where, in less than a year, he completed the New Testament and in 1526 printed 3000 copies which were smuggled into England. Living in hiding in the Low Countries he published the first five Books of the Old Testament and the Book of Jonah but before he got much further he was betrayed to the government. He was tried for heresy, half strangled and then burnt at the stake just outside Brussels.

Tyndale's statue on the Embankment

But a revolution was being unleashed. The clamour for Bibles in local languages coupled with the power of the printing press meant there was no going back. Attitudes changed fast and within three years Henry VIII was insisting that every church in the land must have a Bible in English. Associates of Tyndale completed his work and published it in Hamburg in 1537 as Mathew's Bible, after a fictitious Thomas Mathews. Chedworth's Bible was prepared by English exiles in Geneva in 1560, its nickname, the "Breeches Bible", coming from its version of Genesis 3v17: *And they sewed fig tree leaves together, and made themselves breeches.*

> Challenge!
> You would do well to identify which of the following phrases are from Tyndale's Bible and which are from Shakespeare:
>
> 1 ➤ Salt of the earth
> 2 ➤ The scales fell from his eyes
> 3 ➤ In my heart of hearts
> 4 ➤ What a piece of work is man
> 5 ➤ The fat of the land
> 6 ➤ To thine own self be true
> 7 ➤ Tush, ye shall not die
> 8 ➤ Fight the good fight
> 9 ➤ The evil that men do lives after them
> 10 ➤ Eat, drink and be merry
> 11 ➤ The milk of human kindness
> 12 ➤ Blessed are the peacemakers
>
> The answers are in Appendix C.

Various translations followed in quick succession until the King James version of 1611 which we use today[1]. At last the words of the Scriptures were available to everyone without the interpretation of a priest. All of these successors to Tyndale's Bible had one feature in common: they borrowed heavily from his work. About four fifths of the 1611 New Testament is pure Tyndale. His language was down-to-earth and vivid and has been acclaimed as highly as that of Shakespeare, written half a century later. He had the ear for crafting rhythmic and memorable phrases which would lodge in the mind of the listener. Some 500 phrases, familiar to us from the King James Bible are unacknowledged Tyndale. In fact, so many of Tyndale's and Shakespeare's phrases have crept into modern English and its literature, that between them they can be said to have created our language.

Few of the "Breeches" Bibles now remain - one in Bristol was destroyed by bombing in the last war, but you could acquire your own for about £250. So many of Tyndale's Bibles were burnt on the orders of the Bishop of London that only two complete copies remain. One of them was recently bought for £1 million, well below its market price, by the British Library where it was put on display on the quincentennial of its translator's birth.

Tyndale is commemorated with the tower you may have seen from the M5 on the edge of the Cotswolds at North Nibley and a statue on the Thames Embankment. More recently a cantata, "Death of a Martyr" composed by Christopher Boodle, was first performed by the local Tyndale Choral Society who sang it again in Oxford at the request of Tyndale's former college.

The Nibley Monument

[1] Some of these translations of the Bible became famous for their astonishing typographical errors: *Thou shalt commit adultery* - 1631; *Sin on more* - 1653; *The fool hath said in his heart there is a god* - 1653.

In Comes I, Old Father Christmas

In comes I, old Father Christmas, Christmas or not,
I hope old Father Christmas will never be forgot

A local custom you can enjoy at the Seven Tuns on Boxing Day is a performance of one of the Cotswolds' Mummers Plays. These plays seem to date back to a common ancestor, the Elizabethan Richard Johnson's, the "Famous Historie of the Seaven Champions of Christendom". It was written in the late 1590s, possibly to cash-in on the popularity of the Chester and York Miracle plays. Mummers Plays may even stem back to pagan times to some sort of midwinter ritual of birth and death, the old year and the new.

Prince George lies slain:
Is there a doctor to be found
To cure him of his deep and deadly wound?

The plays were passed on as an oral tradition, each village developing its own version with differences in the characters who take part and the lines they speak. Each troupe would travel around their locality at Christmas performing at each village and country house. Perhaps after such a long time the surprising thing is that they have all stayed recognisable as essentially the same play. More than 70 versions have been traced in Gloucestershire.

The play you see here came originally from Longborough, although until the 1880s Chedworth had its own and even close neighbours Yanworth and Stowell had theirs. This revived play has now been performed for 22 consecutive years.

Your first sight of the players is as they march down the hill to the pub's forecourt, faces blackened, jackets and trousers made from strips of brightly coloured rag, their advance accompanied by the exhilarating sound of recorders, melodeon and pipes.

The Doctor arrives - by "horse"

The Doctor removes the tooth:
Once I was dead and now I'm alive,
Blessed be the doctor who made me revive

The music continues while the players clear a space for the performance.

The meagre Good-versus-Evil plot is common to all the plays: Prince George (sometimes King or Saint George) fights at swords with a Turkish Knight and is slain. A doctor is found to revive him which he does by administering a pill and by extracting a tooth! All is played in a boisterous fashion with plenty of word play, horse play and scope for humorous improvisation. The mummers scene in Thomas Hardy's "The Return of the Native" confirms that these plays were performed a century and a half ago in the same rowdy spirit.

In our play Prince George fights the King of Egypt. This version also involves Father Christmas who acts as a sort of narrator and Master of Ceremonies, Bold Slasher, Jack Finney who is an impertinent assistant to the Doctor, Beelzebub or Betsy Bub in a dress with enormous bosoms who doubles up as the Doctor's horse and a witless fiddler (who plays a melodeon!).

In comes I, Fiddler Wit,
With my great yud and little wit;
Me yud so big, me wit so small
I brought my fiddle to please you all

In comes I, Betsy Bub,
On my shoulder I carries a club;
In my hand a dripping pan;
Don't you think I'm a jolly young man?

In the Snowshill version, King George fights four times - with a Dragon (twice), with the Turkish Knight and with a Giant called Bold Turpin. In Kempsford's, Robin Hood has crept in to take the hero's role and the dragon in the Bisley play has recently metamorphosed into a Welshman. In the Waterley Bottom version you'll find Boneypart and a draped figure wearing a cow's skull. Tiddy's book of 1923 collected 33 plays, seven of them from the Cotswolds including this one and the one from Sapperton.

The tin-hatted hero drinking from the wassail bowl at Waterley Bottom

The play ends with a Wassail ("be of good cheer") song, the audience singing along or joining in the chorus while a collection is taken for charity:

Drink unto thee, drink unto thee,
With a Wassailing Bowl
We'll drink unto thee.

I'm sure this band of players would fight hard to prevent this lively link with the past from dying out for a second time. They give three or four performances each Boxing Day at The Frogmill at Andoversford, the Mill Inn at Withington and at Chedworth. Gibbs surely missed the point when he wrote:

Unfortunately the literary quality of the lines is so poor that they are hardly worth reproducing...

Joined by Terry Haines, then Mayor of Gloucester and onetime morris man, for the Boxing Day wassail

In Gloucestershire, when all is said
It's good to live and it's bad to be dead,
You'll not find a pleasanter place instead,
It's more than a man could do.

JH

7
Chedworth to Rendcomb

9 miles

...going as Nature intends
On white ways for discovery of what lay
Unvisited by most...

IG

Chedworth to Rendcomb

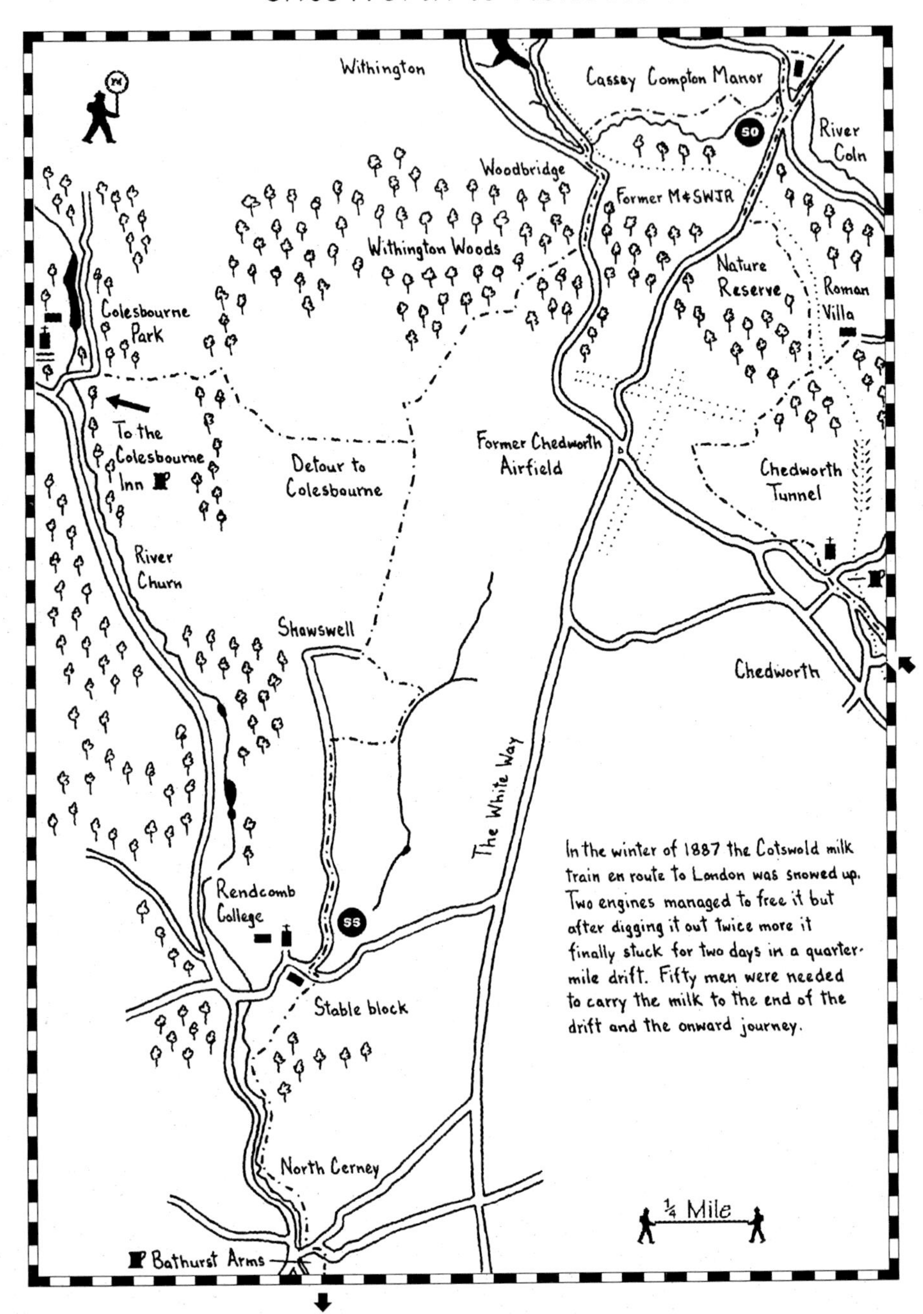

From the church, take a path that leads up to a stile out of the churchyard. Here, just above the Manor in the field called St John's Close, is another connection with the Knights Templars though nothing visible remains of their Preceptory which stood here. The path continues up to a stone stile beside Manor Farm. Take the beech avenue beside the farm's access road. On reaching the main road take the lane right, passing the old and then the new cricket pavillions. Follow the lane for ½ mile passing a small plantation on the right to reach a gateway.

A clear path leads you diagonally right, towards a signpost across the field ahead. When this reaches the airfield perimeter road turn right. From 1942 this airfield was a satellite of Aston Down. Originally it was a base for Spitfires and Wellingtons, then a gunnery squadron which flew Mosquitoes and Martinets and in the closing months of the war it was the home for American Mustangs and Typhoons. Air training ended here in 1945 and the airfield closed in the 1950s. Watch out, though, for the ghost of an airman in full Second World War flying gear who has been seen standing near the airfield by a local vicar.

Continue around the airfield with the road bending left at a spinney. Pass the end of one of the main runways. Leave the perimeter road and continue on a grassy track with Y↑ that leads right, downhill, into Chedworth Woods. Notice the coppiced hazel to your left - at one time all of Chedworth and Withington Woods were hazel; today beech predominates with oak on the areas of clay. These, together with Guiting and Wychwood, are the last of Gloucestershire's ancient woodlands.

When you reach a cross path, go left and, after a few yards, right, steeply downhill. At a crossroads of paths go straight across and under a disused railway bridge. A couple of hundred yards brings you to the Roman Villa. Whichever route you leave by, look out for larger-than-normal snails; often described as a Roman introduction, they actually pre-date the Occupation. The Romans, though, did introduce ornamental pheasants so you may spot the descendants of the ones that escaped into the woods.

Go back up the steep path that brought you to the villa. When you reach the crossroads of paths, turn right. The path is well worn and the route is obvious, through mixed woods and oceans of bluebells in spring until the path curves down to the right to approach the railway embankment. Follow the curve,

Alternative Trust members' route

For ¾ mile you can follow the track of the disused railway on its route through Chedworth woods. At about the ½ mile mark you cross a steep-sided valley on a vertigo-inducing high embankment. Looking down you see the brick arch of the bridge built to cross a woodland track. Looking eastwards you see the tree tops of Compton Wood across the Coln valley. The height of the embankment has placed you on a level with the tree tops.

When the bridge carrying the Compton Abdale to Chedworth road is in sight, leave the railway left through a gateway. A path leads you to the road. Turn right on to the White Way.

Contd: page 91

Chedworth Tunnel

Retrace your steps 100 yards up the bridleway and just before the railway bridge go up the steep flight of steps to the left. The steps are held in place, appropriately enough, with railway sleepers. At the top turn left on to the abandoned railway line which is now part of Chedworth nature reserve looked after by the Gloucestershire Trust for Nature Conservation.

Along the way you will notice how the line was cut through the limestone. Notices ask you not to take samples of rock or hunt for fossils; a more amusing one warns of the presence of adders.

The trees beside the line have grown considerably in the 30 years since it was abandoned. The tunnel entrance is partly bricked up at both ends but, peering over the wall you can see light from the other end, 495 yards away. The tunnel was completed in 1891, quite an achievement with a steam excavator. At least one man lost his life in the endeavour but I prefer to think about his colleagues living in the encampment of huts, looked after by a landlady. Now, she'd be an interesting person to meet...

Chedworth Roman Villa

The story has been told many times before but it bears repeating. In 1864 a gamekeeper on Lord Eldon's estate was digging in a rabbit warren, searching for a lost ferret, when he unearthed cubes from a mosaic. What he had found was the most important Roman villa in the County, preserved by a landslide of Fuller's Earth in the way that Pompeii was protected by volcanic lava. It is now justly famous for its mosaic floors and its baths.

The first thing to strike the modern visitor is the beauty of the setting. The villa lies, cloaked in trees, in a terraced bowl on the hillside, facing east over the wooded valley of the Coln. While this siting might seem inconvenient, losing the sun very early even in summer, it was chosen for its freshwater spring which has never been known to fail.

We can't translate "villa" as simply meaning a house. A villa was the headquarters of a farming estate, the home for the owner, his family and servants and a country retreat for his guests. I like to picture it as a ranch or a South American estancia, equivalent in later centuries to our manor houses. Judging by the number of Roman villas, ten within a ten mile radius of Chedworth, seven on the Coln, and a palatial residence recently uncovered near Swindon, the Cotswolds must have been a rich area in Roman times.

The villa prospered and grew in size over about 250 years up to the end of the Roman Occupation. By that time its rooms, many of them warmed by under-floor heating, had enclosed all four sides of its central garden with verandahs around the inner walls, rather like cloisters, providing sheltered walkways.

Chedworth's most interesting features stem from three major Roman preoccupations: eating, bathing and keeping in favour with the gods.

Many of the rooms had mosaic floors, mainly in blue, white and red using liassic limestone, pure limestone and pieces of clay tile respectively, with occasional variations of purple using Forest of Dean sandstone.

The most opulent floor was in the dining room where the owner could most visibly demonstrate his wealth and his aesthetic sense to his visitors while serving them with the choicest larks' tongues and cocks' combs. Partly destroyed now by tree roots, this mosaic showed a complex scene with Bacchus, the god of wine, in the centre surrounded by his mythical attendants going about their frenzied worship. In the four corners are the panels which give the mosaic its name, "The Four Seasons". This splendid mosaic is one of about 40 made by a "school" of mosaicists based, probably, in Cirencester whose work appears all over Gloucestershire and its adjoinining counties. It is sad that many of the neighbouring villas were excavated by early enthusiasts who kept scant records so that their mosaics have largely been lost.

Just part of the nearby Woodchester mosaic, the largest in northern Europe; Orpheus charms the beasts with his lyre

For the Romans, bathing was a social activity accompanied by conversation and games playing so it is not surprising that at Chedworth sophisticated bathing facilities were developed for the enjoyment of the owner and his guests. Water, readily available from the spring, was used, unusually, to supply two complete suites of baths: the "Spartan" type with dry heat, which we would think of as sauna baths, and Turkish baths with damp heat and plunge pools. The full bathing process was a sequence moving from a warm pool to a hot one where the skin was scraped and perhaps a massage was enjoyed and back again to a cold bath, the effect being a thorough cleansing and an envigorating experience. Over the years the configuration of the rooms containing the baths changed many times confirming that bathing was a central feature of Roman life. The ingenuity of the arrangements for warming both air and water were worthy of any modern central-heating engineer. Most of the villa's other mosaics were placed in these public bathing rooms.

At the north-west corner of the site was an octagonal building that served as a reservoir for the spring water and as a garden feature rather like a summer-house. It also seems to have been a shrine, originally to pagan gods and then in the final days of the villa to the Christian God, the evidence being stones inscribed with the Greek symbol for chi-rho, meaning Christ. Two other aspects of Roman religious life were catered for in the nearby woods with a small temple dedicated to Silvanus, the god of hunting, and a more elaborate building, destroyed when the railway was built, which may have been used for funeral ceremonies.

A reconstruction of the villa viewed from the south-east

Chedworth villa has played a significant role in our understanding of life in Roman Britain so it seems extraordinary that 130 years after its accidental discovery, parts of the site have still not been excavated.

Cassey Compton

Often described as one of the most idyllic of Cotswold manor houses, I find Cassey Compton unnerving. It sits brooding over the wide Coln valley as if sulking for some past wrong.

The house has all the right romantic ingredients: built in the 17th century for the now-extinct Lords of Chedworth; the Coln channelled into a moat, at one time crossed by a drawbridge; we can see the beeches that stand in the former deer park, the bowling green surrounded by clipped yews and a fine line of ancient limes stretching towards Compton Abdale; there are even the remains of medieval fish ponds that suggest an early monastic connection.

Despite all this, Cassey Compton seems an unhappy place. Perhaps it is because one entire wing of the house has been demolished; perhaps because for 40 years the house lay derelict or maybe it is a reaction to its reduced status as estate manager's house for Stowell Park. Whatever the reason, I'm not imagining this uneasy feeling. When workmen tried to install a new fireplace on the ground floor, they repeatedly returned next morning to find it moved out into the centre of the room and eventually gave up the attempt.

now to the left into a little open valley. Almost immediately branch off to the right taking the path that enters the woods. In a couple of hundred yards you emerge on to the White Way, originally a salt road.

Turn right and cross the railway bridge. Follow the road for a third of a mile straight over a crossroads to pass the original front gates of Cassey Compton Manor. Pause at the bridge over the Coln. The main stream flows straight towards you but notice another which joins it from the right. This flows out of what was once the moat which, together with the main stream, surrounded the house. With luck you may spot a heron in the river. Continue up the hill.

Turn very sharp left up an unmarked lane which takes you down to a stone barn with slit windows. Turn left on the road and head towards the house. Just after crossing the river, turn right into a field noticing the Intriguing Gate Fastening Mechanism Number 1.

Go up the field following the slightly sunken track. Just before the first tree turn 90 degrees right. Go over the rise and drop down towards the river. Cross a stile and the wonderful wooden footbridge, fashioned from a single trunk. Keep the fence on your left till you reach a stile with Y↑. Continue ahead, now with a hedge on your right to reach the corner of the field. Go through the gate, turn left and follow the field edge above a wide hedge of dense blackthorn and plenty of catkins early in the year. Take care not to twist an ankle in the many fox holes.

When the hedge ends, keep to the well-worn path on the contour across a steep section of limestone downland with more cowslips than I've ever seen in one place before. From the path you can follow the course of the Coln and, over the valley and level with your path, pick out the course of the disused railway. You will encounter an unnecessary number of Private - Keep Out signs.

Cross a stile of unique design and then a simpler one by the two houses that constitute **Woodbridge**. Follow the garden wall and, just past the beehives, take the stile into a lane. Turn right and pass under the railway bridge.

Turn left on the road towards the house at Colnbrook with its attractive wooded backdrop. Past the house, turn left on the road and follow it uphill for a gruelling ½ mile. Turn right through a gate with a Y↑ into Withington Woods. Follow the woodland path. Go quietly and you may surprise some deer.

If you think of the countryside as a quiet place, Withington Woods may change your opinion. The bird population is pretty noisy. Listen for a while and you may wish you knew more about birdsong so you can picture the sources of the enormously varied calls.

After nearly ½ mile the path curves left to bring you out of the wood at the isolated cottage at Postcombe. Turn right in front of the cottage and follow the lane with a lovely yew to the right.

Take the right-forking path as you approach a clearing. At the posts with B↑ turn left on to a path leading to a stile with Y↑. Follow the edge of the wood and then the barbed wire fence. On reaching the far side of the field jig a little left for a stile on to a farm track. Follow this into the farm yard at Woodlands. If you enjoy the smell of silage you may be in for a treat.

Turn left as you leave the yard to curve round to the farm's concrete access road. Follow this till it turns left.

The M & SWJR - The "Tiddley Dyke"

In France, they say, all roads lead to Paris, in England all railway lines lead to London but it was not always so. Before Dr Beeching's savaging of the railways in the early 1960s it was possible to travel all over the country by rail and the focus was not so strongly on London. You could even travel a practical route from the Midlands to the South Coast.

This was made possible by the Midlands and South West Junction Railway, affectionately known as the "Tiddley Dyke", which, by linking Andoversford with Andover in Hampshire, offered a north-south route to people living in the industrial Midlands.

Plans had been made for such a route as early as the 1840s - even the eminent engineer Robert Stephenson made proposals, but they were all blocked by the strong grip the Great Western Railway held on the West Country. By 1883 the line was completed to the edge of the Cotswolds at Cirencester and the arrival of the first train at Cricklade was heralded by the Town Band and celebrated with an official dinner.

Steaming across the road bridge at Chedworth in 1956, a class of engine which worked the line during the First World War. Notice the second engine, needed to cope with the gradient.

It took eight more years to drive the line across the Cotswolds. The expense was considerable with a great deal of rock to be cut through, as well as the tunnel at Chedworth. Although the company went bankrupt in 1884, the Receiver pressed on with the building so that the through route was opened in 1891 with stations at Foss Cross, Chedworth, Withington and Andoversford. The line was then such a success that in 1897 the Company was able to leave the Receiver's protection.

It is hard now to imagine the impact that the railway had on the rural Cotswolds. J Arthur Gibbs in the 1890s asked a farmer's wife if she had ever been to London. *No*, she replied, *but I've been to Cheltenham.* To her mind the two towns were equally remote and the experience of travelling 16 miles to the "capitol" of the Cotswolds remained a vivid memory.

The line was busy in the summer months promoting holiday excursions to south coast resorts. An express train ran every Saturday morning from Cheltenham to Southampton docks; as well as being the age of the train, for international travel this was the age of the ocean liner and Southampton was one of the world's busiest passenger ports. The nameboard at Cheltenham's Lansdown station even announced, "Change here for Paris".

The enterprising railway company developed an early form of package holiday. A poster of 1888 has a headline "Sea-side excursions" and exhorts *Clergymen, Choirmasters, School Managers, Workmen's Clubs and the Public* to partake of excursions *free of all trouble and expense to promoters* to many south coast resorts including the Isle of Wight. The package could include the train fare, steamer ticket, dinner and hotel accommodation, and even trips around the island.

In the mid 1890s the line was at the forefront of technology: its new dark red coaches, introduced in 1894, had their rape-oil roof lamps converted to electric lighting - the first on any railway. Its most famous loco was a Beyer Peacock 2-6-0, affectionately known as "Galloping Alice" because of the rough ride she provided.

The best year for profit was 1913 and then the war brought the task of carrying armaments down to the military bases on Salisbury Plain and to the south coast for the fighting in France. Canadian, American and Anzac troops were ferried from Liverpool docks to Southampton. Humphry Household remembers as a boy, waving to the troops from the side of the line and wishing he had a camera. On the return journeys, ambulance trains carried wounded soldiers north. The statistics are quite staggering: during the First World War the line carried almost three million men, more than 130,000 horses and 5,700 bicycles. War in those days was a more face-to-face affair than it is today.

In the Second World War the strategic value of the line again proved invaluable. On occasions the traffic was so great that the line ground to a complete halt.

By 1954 England's travellers had entered the age of the car and passengers were so few that it was no longer worthwhile manning Chedworth station. In 1961 the trains were hardly used except by school children and the line was closed.

September 9th 1961, the day before closure, a U class engine near Withington takes the last through train to Southampton

It is curious to think that in the 1880s the route was planned, tunnels dug, embankments raised, sleepers and rails laid in place so that millions of people could enjoy a special outing or be rescued from the battlefield; and that in the 1960s the rails and sleepers were raised and carted away, the stations and signal boxes were removed, leaving the stony bed that you are walking on today. For just 80 years the peace of the ancient Chedworth and Withington Woods was disturbed. Today they are quiet and remote once more.

Note: this section of the route has no pub! so you may wish to try the detour to Colesbourne. If so, turn right here.

Otherwise, follow the footpath sign straight on. Aim across the field for a gate in the wall by a small tree on the left of two larger ones.

Take the obvious track past a Dutch barn and an attractive little valley begins to open up on your left.

Approaching Shawswell, notice the carefully rebuilt stone walls and, just

Colesbourne Inn
200 year old inn.
Wadworth 6X and IPA, Hall & Woodhouse, Tanglefoot & Stowford Press cider. The inn is built, not with Cotswold stone but, oddly enough, with quartz & tufa.

before a barn in the throes of being converted, follow the sign left for the Guest House. Drop left to a gate just before the Guest House entrance. You'll see a variety of ducks enjoying their new pond.

Follow the rutted track downhill. Where a small stream crosses it, go through the gate to the right and cross the field to another gate and continue beside the hedge. Climb over a hunting gate which is topped with an unfriendly strand of barbed wire and keep to the bottom of the next field which is dotted with cowslips.

Go through the oversized gate and turn right, climbing the hill beside the fence. At the top of the field go right for some yards to reach a stile. Don't grab hold of the top rail: it has barbed wire attached.

Turn left on this new road which is the access road to the renovated houses at Shawswell. At the main road turn left for a mile of metalled road to **Rendcomb** with plenty to look out for on the way:

➤ Rendcomb sits on a promontory so you can see the valleys on either side, the splendidly wooded Churn valley to the right.

➤ The line of pines on the left horizon is on a lonely, eerie stretch of the White Way. Further along the same hillside the odd shapes of the stands of trees seem to form letters for a giant Scrabble game.

➤ Look out for an enormous inflatable rabbit that might appear over the left horizon - honestly, there's a photograph to prove it!

➤ Notice the house on your left with the bread oven.

Pass the playing fields of Rendcomb school and, just as the enormous stable block comes into view, turn left, signposted Chedworth.

➤ The village church, completely rebuilt in 1517, is one of the finest in the Cotswolds with a wealth of interest from many different periods: the Norman font, a replica of the one in Hereford Cathedral, shows reliefs of the Apostles - except for Judas, whose space is left blank; the fine wooden rood screen was probably carved by the man who created the one at Fairford, one of the most impressive “wool” churches, financed from wool trading profits; the lock plate shows the date 1527 (or 1517?) in Arabic numerals; some of the stained glass is 16th century; there are three bells dating from the 15th and the 16th centuries, each with its Latin inscription.

➤ Above the village to the east is Rendcomb airfield which was used from 1916 for wartime flying training. It is still used as the base for the three Boeing Stearmans of the Flying Circus, a professional

Contd: page 98

HJ Elwes, Plant Hunter

Henry John Elwes collected trees, but not like you or I might collect trees. He collected hundreds of them from all over the world, many of them totally new to botanists and brought many of them back to grow in the Cotswolds. Most of the ornamental plants and trees we see in this country are not natives: the Romans brought us the sweet chestnut and the tulip was unknown to Europe until the 1560s. Elwes was one of that band of scientific explorers and plant hunters who helped extend the range of plants grown in the British Isles.

Whilst at Eton he studied wildfowl on the Norfolk Broads and in the Hebrides. Retiring from the Scots Guards as a 23 year old captain, he was able to use his time and considerable wealth to develop this early interest into big game hunting, shooting birds and egg collecting. In 1870 he travelled to India and Sikkim, suffering amazing hardships, pursuing his interest in ornithology - always on the look-out for previously unidentified birds, exotic butterflies and moths. Lame from repeated leech bites, he climbed the equivalent of four Everests in ten days and collected birds, plants and more than 200 different ferns. He even entered Tibet which, then as now, was closed to Westerners.

Elwes in sporting kit, 1899

Four years later, travelling in Turkish Anatolia, living on bread, onions and sour milk, he discovered the giant snowdrop, one of the eight plants to be named after him. Finding the specimens was only part of the hazard: many of these bulbs, so carefully gathered, were stolen or lost when changing ships on the trip home.

He travelled incessantly. From the age of 17 to the year before his death, he never spent a continuous year in England, hunting specimens all over the world, on one trip becoming the first Englishman to find yeti footprints.

In 1891 he inherited Colesbourne Park and began to turn 700 acres of frost-prone, shallow soil into a forest. His observations in Asia had made him aware of the importance of the soil, water, nutrients and the microclimate and now he put this understanding to work to show off the specimens he had collected.

He lived here surrounded by hothouses filled with experimental plantings of rare and exotic species, including 87 new introductions. Colesbourne Park testifies to his success with many rare trees such as the Japanese Wingnut, the Californian Nutmeg and Golden Western Red Cedars which are among the biggest in the country. You can view the arboretum he planted, from the churchyard.

Colesbourne Park as it stood in his day

As well as travelling and planting, he wrote what is still a standard book on lilies, bred Cotswold sheep, founded the Quarterly Journal of Forestry and by 1913 had published all seven volumes of the monumental "Trees of Great Britain and Ireland". His aim had been *hunting up, and personally visiting, every tree which had been recorded in print of exceptional size, interest or rarity.* Research for this work took him to more than 600 locations throughout the British Isles and wore out two cars.

His interest in forestry led him to promote the use of British timbers amongst architects and cabinet-makers and his own home was filled with items made from native woods.

He died in 1922 and is buried in Colesbourne churchyard under a fitting tombstone with a lily on a cross. He deservedly achieved the two finest accolades for a Victorian amateur naturalist - A Fellowship of the Royal Society without the normal academic background and species bearing his name: seven plants as well as the giant snowdrop, fifteen species of butterfly and the horned lark. His collection of 30,000 preserved butterflies and moths was presented to the British Museum.

You may get an opportunity to visit the grounds of Colesbourne Park for an annual open-air Shakespeare production - in 1995 it was "A Winter's Tale".

Double Gloucester Cheese

Milk from the Gloucester cattle was used to make three distinct varieties of cheese and, ironically, while the cattle have been saved from extinction, one of the cheeses has disappeared. Double and Single Gloucester are still made in the County; the third, Blue Vinney[1], was made in Dorset where the cattle grazed on summer pastures around Sherborne, but the little that is made today on a handful of Dorset farms it is only for private sale. Although most Gloucester cheese was made in the Severn vale, the best quality cheese was said to came from the poorer grass of the uplands.

Martell's Single Gloucester

By the 17th century Gloucester cheese making had become an important cottage industry. The annual Ceremony of the Cheeses at the Royal Hospital in Chelsea dates from 1692 when the pensioners living there were first given a Double Gloucester cheese.

Cheese making was women's work. Men's work took them into the fields so they could not have provided the daily attention or careful timing needed to make a successful cheese. Each cheese required 15 days of turning and then a soaking in whey. Another tricky aspect of cheese making was temperature control, no easy thing in the days before refrigeration. Various suitable parts of the farmhouse were taken over by cheese -

[1] See Patrick Rance's account of his dogged search for a true Blue Vinney.

lofts, attics and sometimes a purpose-built cheese room which you may spot from its louvered windows on the third storey of tall farmhouses.

The final touch was scraping the surface smooth to enhance its presentation. If the cheese was to be sold away from the locality, it was painted with the vegetable dye, anatta, mixed with beer to produce a red exterior. The distinctive dark colour of the cheese itself came from the mixture used as the rennet, a combination of the plant Lady's Bedstraw and nettle juice.

In the 1930s Depression, cheese making died out when the price dropped to just six pence per lb. Local farmers could not compete with cheap imported colonial cheeses and turned instead to milk production. Gone were the 19th century days when 1200 tons of Double Gloucester were made in a year, much of it shipped by barge on the Thames and Severn Canal to London.

Why Single and Double? The names may refer to the sizes. While the more open textured Single is two to three inches thick weighing 15 lbs, a Double is four to five inches thick and 24 lbs. Both are circular, about 16 inches across.

Alternatively, the names may distinguish the kind of milk used. Full cream milk is used to make the Double while the Single has a high proportion of skimmed-milk to produce a lower fat cheese. The Single is sold when it is between six and twelve weeks old, the Double when it is three to six months.

In the 1940s Colonel Elwes at Colesbourne Park tried to revive the Double Gloucester tradition but the attempt was not a success and twenty years ago genuine Gloucester cheese was just about extinct. Supermarket "Double Gloucester" is unlikely to have been made in the County and is certainly not made from Gloucester cattle's milk. Happily, today there are a few farms producing the cheeses to the traditional recipe. Diana Smart of Old Ley Court at Churcham produces both varieties. Her Single is delicate, white and mild; the Double is orange in colour, closer textured and has an almost smoked taste. Charles Martell of Dymock is the only other producer of Single Gloucester cheese from Gloucester cattle's milk. Both can be bought along with other local cheeses at Gloucester's Cheese Fayre.

Pub sign at Shurdington

The cheese making tradition is celebrated in the Cheese Rollers pub at Shurdington and in the mayhem of the Spring Bank Holiday (originally Whit Monday) "Cheese Rolling" down the vertiginous 60 degree slope of Coopers Hill. The contest is documented back to 1836 and is almost certainly a great deal older, part of a Wake which included bizarre competitions in grinning, chattering and shin kicking. A cheese protected in a wooden casing is rolled off the top of the hill by a Master of Ceremonies and those sufficiently foolhardy follow its erratic course to the bottom, the winner being the first to run, fall, roll, tumble or dive over the finish line. Minor injuries are frequent for both spectators and competitors but the compensation for the race winners is a whole Double Gloucester made by Diana Smart.

group who pilot these bi-planes in flying displays with young ladies walking (!) on the wings. Built as naval training planes in the 1940s, the craft can never have undertaken duties quite like the current ones. The sport was banned in Britain in 1933 because so many deaths had resulted from reckless stunts and this group is the only one licensed in this country to walk from cockpit to wing whilst in flight. With luck, you may see a free display as they practise.

➤ The present College was built in 1863 for the financier, Sir Francis Goldsmid, as an Italianate country house intended to impress. In doing this he tore down the Tudor manor about which Alexander Pope had written

I look upon the mansion, walk and terraces, the plantation and slopes which Nature has made to command a variety of valleys and rising woods, with a veneration mixed with pleasure.

In fact this manor, since Domesday had passed through the hands of an extraordinary number of great and worthy families; Hutton gives the details.

➤ The stable block is set well away from the main house. It has a spectacularly tall tower with two clock faces and a cupola over an enormous entrance.

➤ The "Scrabble letters" were planted to spell out Goldsmid's name in Hebrew.

➤ The bridge over the road joining parts of the school grounds is cast-iron with ornamental balustrades.

Eight Quarts a Day

It may seem surprising that cider was the traditional man's drink of the Cotswolds when the rich soils and main orchards are down in the valleys. In fact, the light hill soils were said to produce a better taste and every farm had its orchard. They were untidy affairs, never pruned, containing a mixture of varieties to give the cider a balance of sugar, acidity and tartness.

The apple varieties had gloriously evocative names like Fox Whelp, Tremlett's Bitter, Hagloe Crab and Cat's Head. Early in the century Gissing was deploring the dying out of real Gloucestershire orchards in favour of *trees rigidly quincuncial and rigorously pruned whose trunks, if they have any, are greasebanded or white-washed.*

While the fruit was still on the tree, the farmer would reserve enough for his own purposes and auction the rest with the buyer taking the risk of the weather up till harvest time. Harvesting was an unceremonious affair - the trees were shaken or beaten till the fruit was all on the ground. The gathered fruit was put into stone troughs and ground to a pulp by a horse-turned millstone. The pulp was pressed through layers of cloth to produce the juice which went into wooden barrels to ferment. To the horror of modern wine or beer makers, the fermentation was achieved with wild yeasts.

Many farmers had their own equipment. For those who did not, travelling gangs of cider-makers moved from farm to farm pulping and pressing, rather like the travelling Calvados makers who still operate in Normandy.

The resulting drink was very dry, very still and very rough, said to be *sharp enough to cut the throat of a graveyard ghost*, but it formed part of the farm labourer's wages right up till the Agricultural Wages Act of 1925. These men must have had amazing constitutions: a foreman had one gallon a day supplied in a stone jar or a coopered barrel called a firkin; other men were allowed a half gallon. Gissing says that at harvest time the allowance was eight quarts a day. Roy Palmer recounts the story of a carter from Chipping Campden who, having sunk 17 pints of cider in a mere three hours, remarked, *This be doin' I no good. I'll try a pint of beer.*

These quantities must have presented a major annual storage problem on every farm. The most common storage was 110 gallon oak barrels - the ones you probably think of as beer barrels hold 45. Fred Archer's "The Secrets of Bredon Hill" shows a photograph of a cider making gang dwarfed by a ten-hogshead barrel that held about 520.

The ten-hogshead barrel

For three years from 1763 the government imposed a Cider Tax. Locals were so incensed by a tax on their home-brew that many farmers gave their cider away rather than pay up. A group of miners in the Forest of Dean kidnapped an Excise man and kept him imprisoned in their coal mine as a protest against the Cyder Act. It was repealed three years later but the fate of the tax man is not known. At about the same time cider brandy making in England was killed off by over-taxation.

Today we drink more than 60 million gallons of cider a year, almost all of it mass produced, a single factory accounting for two million gallons. Most of this is not like the fiery stuff described here but you can still obtain the real thing. A number of pubs on the route sell real cider and in the north Cotswolds, the Barnfield Cider Mill at Childswickam just outside Broadway, has been producing cider since 1925. All the apples used are local producing dry, medium and sweet ciders. You'll save a little by taking your own container.

If you need a recommendation to try the real thing, this is what Sir J More had to say in 1707:

That a Glass of this Excellent Cyder-Royal, drank half an hour before Meals, procures a good Appetite; and after Meals helps Digestion: That it cheers the Heart, and Revives the Spirits. And as for its Operation upon the Brain, when too much is drunk at a time, the same is less hurtful than excess of strong Beer, Ale, Canary, or High-Country-Wines.

You too can be a pomologist...

In the last 30 years this country has lost some 150,000 acres of orchards. Whilst in 1883 the National Apple Congress at Chiswick displayed 1,500 different apple varieties, just a few years ago there seemed to be nothing available at the supermarket except the ubiquitous and tasteless Golden Delicious. Things have improved and many supermarkets and farm shops now stock a range of apples offering a whole gamut of tastes and textures.

Why not help the revival of interest by planting your own tree of an unusual variety and stake your claim to being a pomologist (yes, honestly)? If you want to make it a local variety, Corse Hill, Dymock Red, Blakeney Red and Ashmeads Kernal are amongst the types developed and grown extensively in Victorian times in the County.

God made the world of Cotsall
And all the world beside,
But every other paltry land
Arose at his divine command;
This only, with a practised hand,
He fashioned as a bride.

JH

8
Rendcomb to Daglingsworth

6 miles

So I'd go walking by Cotswold streams set a-talking
By a short course and steep from hills azure, green
Through the hawthorn hedges, and orchards dimly seen,

IG

Rendcomb to Daglingworth

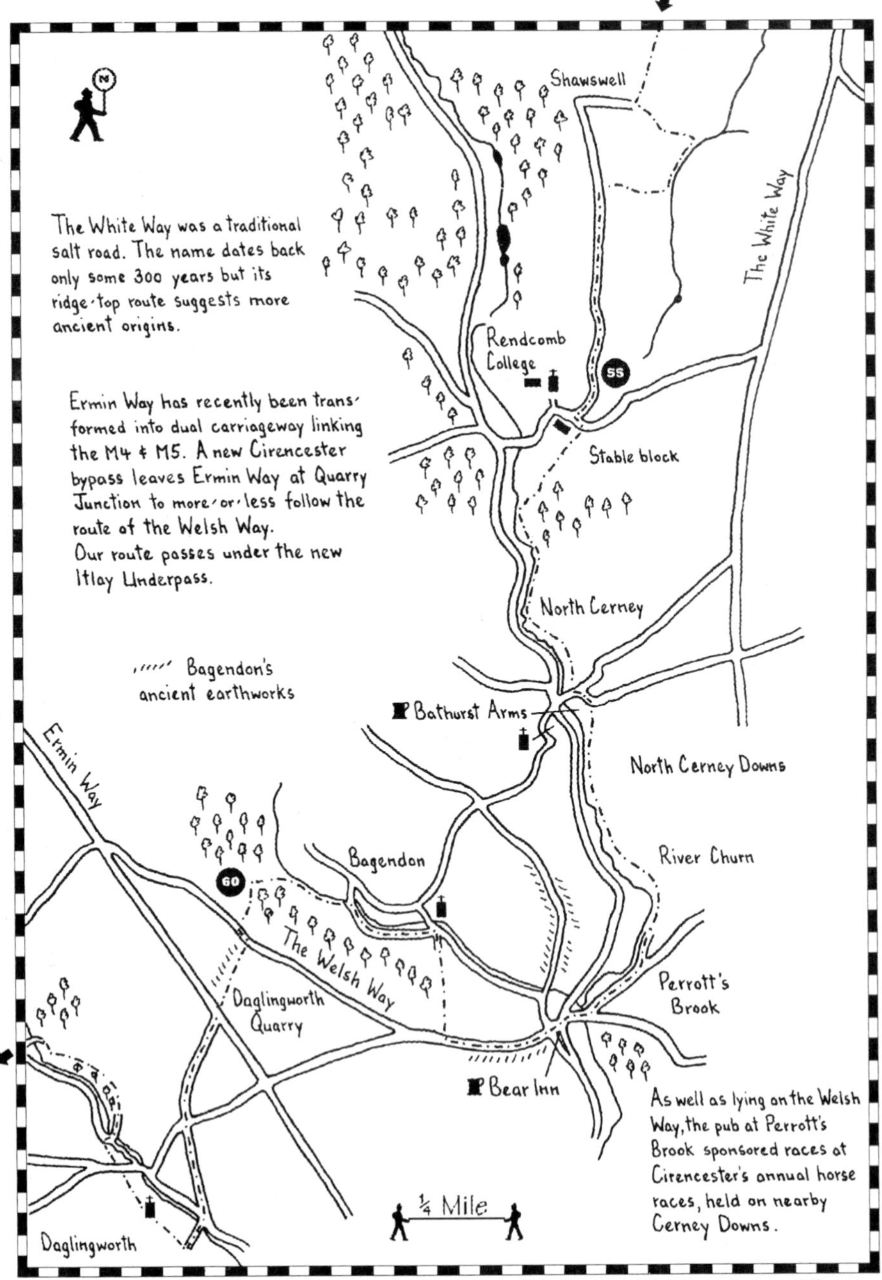

As the road bends left, leave it by the footpath to the right through a gate with Intriguing Gate Fastening Mechanism Number 2. Follow the contour and glance back to the view of the splendid stable block gatehouse looking like a portion of a French chateau but with a rather incongruous satellite dish. Keep to the right of the lake, descending the field, aiming for the middle of the iron railings on the far side.

Pass through a kissing gate and turn left on to the lane. Just before a pair of cottages, strike off right through a gap in the hedge. An indistinct path takes you diagonally down through a scrubby wood to a kissing gate in the iron fence. (If, by mistake, you stayed on the lane and passed to the right of the cottages you would see an old cider press which looks as if it might still work.)

Pass through the kissing gate into a field. Turn left but glance right for a splendid view of the College. Keep to the edge of the wood till you reach a stile with a Y↑ on to a lane.

Your route crosses this lane but a little to the right is a very pleasing, elaborate stone bridge where the Churn forms a small waterfall; it has three arches and a keystone with the mask of a river god[1]. The building you glimpse is the equally elaborate lodge, built where the drive to the new house met the main road.

Return to the unmarked track through the fir trees to a gate. Now follow the left bank of the Churn. Ignore a footbridge and pass through a gate. Keep near the Churn until you see a gate in the stone wall. Go through and turn right. Climb the steep slope until you reach a line of scrubby trees on the brow of the hill. Follow the contour to reach a gate between allotments and a children's playground into **North Cerney.**

➤ The church is unfortunately cut off from the village by the main road but its rich interior is well worth a detour. It is fun to explore. Entry is through the tower and there are several spiral staircases, one leading up on to the modern rood screen. It is easy to imagine a Thomas Hardy style village band playing in the gallery.

> **Bathurst Arms**
> Free house
> 17th century inn with a fascinating open fire. Four or five regular ales and a guest. Try Lady Isabel Angus' prize-winning Cerney goat cheese made just over the road at Cerney House.

➤ The medieval stone altar is unusual. Most were destroyed during the Reformation but this one was hidden under the floor of the Lady Chapel and rediscovered during alterations in 1912.

➤ The attractive organ pipes are from an 18th century barrel organ which played about two dozen tunes when its handle was turned.

➤ Outside are some well-preserved gargoyles and the weird and fanciful Manticores - outlines of mythical beasts carved in the stone wall. The larger one,

[1] It has been argued, even in Parliament, that the Churn which rises at Seven Springs, east of Cheltenham, is the true source of the Thames rather than the conventional Source of the Thames near Kemble. Although the Churn has a good claim on grounds of length, it fails because a river's source is the tributary which rises highest above sea level. Despite this, a plaque at Seven Springs reads HIC TUUS O TAMESINE PATER SEPTEMCEMINUS FONS - Here, O Father Thames, is thy sevenfold source.

on the south wall, has a human head and arms, a lion's body and a scorpion's tail. The other, low on the west wall of the tower, is smaller and more like a leopard with a long tail. It is impossible to date these figures or to understand why they were carved on the wall of a church[1].

➤ The churchyard Maltese cross is 12th century but was recently restored.

➤ An avenue of wych elms leads to the churchyard and separates it from the beautiful plain Queen Anne style rectory which, together with the Old Church House, just above the churchyard, offers a beautiful view.

Return to the point where you entered the village. Turn left uphill and fork right. Notice the variety of shapes and sizes of chimney pots of the 17th and 18th century cottages. Cross a stile to the right into a field, and very shortly cross another stile left to follow the barbed wire fence down to the river, joining it by a group of houses.

When the river swings right, follow the sunken track and embankment for about ½ mile. The track is the remains of channels cut for controlling floodwater on these meadows. Notice on the way:

➤ a channelled spring and a disused brick sheepdip

➤ a tollhouse - the rightmost house in the row across the valley at Churnside.

When you reach a blocked up bridge, go through the gate to cross it and turn right to follow a line of pollarded willows on your right which have been left to their own devices. At the corner of the field take the grassy lane that leads through Perrot's Brook Farm.

Follow the farm drive out to the road, turn right and right again at the junction to cross the River Churn. Follow the road past the inn to ascend the hill by the Welsh Way, noticing the earthworks accompanying you on the left of the road.

Nearing the top of the hill, where a telephone line crosses the road, turn off right through an unmarked gate. Follow the field edge beside a long narrow spinney. The path becomes a track and, as you approach cottages on the right, it becomes a narrow road leading to a T junction at the edge of **Bagendon.**

➤ the church's main feature is its 15th century glass

➤ beside the church is a gabled tithe barn, now a house.

➤ Trinity Mill is mentioned in Domesday Book under the hamlet's lovely 13th century name of Bagingedene.

St Margaret, patron of

- nurses
- peasants
- expectant mothers

---

[1] The manticore appears in classical literature as a man-eating beast and as a bearded symbol in heraldry. In modern Spain the mantequero is commonly believed to be a ferocious monster, with the outward appearance of a man, that lurks in lonely spots awaiting the chance to suck the blood of its victims.

Contd: page 109

Water Meadows

To most people the term "water meadow" will suggest a grassy field. To some it may suggest a field which floods in winter. Its meaning used to be much more specific: a field beside a river which is deliberately flooded. With its beginnings in the 17th century, English farmers perfected an irrigation system at least as sophisticated as the ones used in the Nile delta or in Indonesian paddy fields. It has been called *the supreme technical achievement of English farming*. Since the early years of this century, though, the complex network of ditches and sluices has literally decayed like the one you've been walking across.

Grass does not grow in the winter so it is not until well into spring that the new year's grazing is ready for use. Water meadows developed, before the general availability of fertilizers, to hasten this new growth by several weeks by keeping the meadows flooded from December through to March. The gently flowing water rarely froze so the grass beneath it continued to grow right through the winter helped by a continuous supply of deposited nutrients. As soon as the water was drawn off, lambing ewes got the benefit of the new succulent growth. If a late frost threatened, the meadows would be flooded overnight and drained again next day, replenishing the nutrients and moistening the soil.

Such a system could not rely on haphazard flooding. Water entered the meadows from a river weir by way of channels known as "carriages" which overflowed to spread the water. Set at a slightly lower level, another system of channels called "drawns" returned the water to the river. The whole system was controlled by oak sluice gates and a knowledgeable operator.

After the First World War this labour-intensive way of managing grazing land became impracticable. The channels and sluices fell into disrepair and gradually disappeared under intensive ploughing for wheat growing. Once common to most of the Cotswold rivers which flow to the Thames, the very existence of the systems was forgotten.

Happily, there is an exception. At the Sherborne Park estate on the Windrush near Northleach, the system has been brought back to life on a 140 acre tenant farm. Here, the National Trust working with the National Rivers Authority has responded to the wish of Lord Sherborne to recreate and maintain a fully working traditional country estate.

Recently completed sluice gates at Sherborne

The overgrown channels have been located and cleared using a combination of the 1888 Ordnance Survey map and local memories; new traditionally-designed sluices have been installed built from estate oak and in spring 1994 the meadows were reflooded for the first time in 60 years creating the country's largest fully working water meadow.

The National Trust has clearly marked out footpaths around the water meadows so you can visit them and perhaps see the snipe, herons and moorhens which have returned, and hear the weird, creaky sound of visiting geese overhead.

Eastward Ho!

Roast beef may traditionally have been eaten in Merrie England but, more often than not, it was bred in Wales or Scotland and had to be transported to the English towns. Before the coming of the railways this meant driving the cattle across the country in Wild-West fashion with drovers mounted on ponies assisted, oddly enough, by corgis taking the role of sheep dog. Some of the routes they used can still be traced today, one of them being the Welsh Way arcing for 12 miles around the north of Cirencester, aiming towards the Thames at Lechlade.

A drover coming east out of Wales would gradually add to his herd at a series of collecting points until it numbered several hundred black Welsh cattle, known to the English as "Welsh runts". They travelled at about 12 miles a day, stopping at inns offering a bed for the drover and safe pasturing for the animals. The large house at the uniquely-named Ready Token was originally a drovers' inn on the Welsh Way, the name coming from the practice of not offering credit - only ready (money) taken.

Drovers camped for the night

Two or three weeks on the road necessitated frequent grazing, hence the extra wide verges, as here on the Welsh Way. If the herds were driven any faster they would lose weight and take longer to re-fatten once they reached the Home Counties.

The farmers' livelihood depended on the honesty of the drover; the cattle were taken on credit so the farmers saw no money until the drover returned. To help ensure their reliability drovers had to be licensed, aged over 30, married and householders. The arrangement worked remarkably well and it was drovers who established a sophisticated banking system in 18th century Wales.

Parts of the routes they used are now speculation but to reach Bagendon required crossing the Severn. This must either have been over the bridge at Gloucester or via one of the Severn ferry "passages". We do know that whenever possible the drovers skirted the toll roads to avoid the charges.

So, imagine you are walking along the Welsh Way 150 years ago and you meet a herd coming towards you; they stretch for about half a mile so it's some 15 minutes before they all pass by. This gives you time to notice their feet. The cattle are shod with metal shoes like pairs of half horseshoes, essential protection for the rough roads. But still you can't go on. Your way is now barred by a herd of pigs. Again, look at the feet - little boots like socks with leather soles.

No sooner do you resume your journey than you meet a flock of geese. Surely they're not shod or kitted out with boots? No, but they have been driven through a mixture of tar and sand to give their webbed feet a tough enough coating to manage the journey.

The droves reached their peak in the late 18th century but 50 years later they were superceded by the railways which, of course, did away with the need for all this bizarre animal footwear.

Hugh the Drover or Love in the Stocks

Ralph Vaughan Williams was a son of the Cotswolds, born at Down Ampney near Cirencester and his romantic folk-opera, "Hugh the Drover", written just before the First World War, is set in the Cotswolds of the Napoleonic Wars. The opera opens with a scene of the townsfolk hurling curses at an effigy of the French Emperor and bustles throughout with country town life during a fair with its showmen, jugglers and dancers.

Hugh is not a long-distance drover but he roams the countryside collecting horses for the war against "Bonyparty". At the fair he accepts the challenge of a prize fight with John the Butcher, not for the usual £20 but for the hand of Mary, the town Constable's daughter. Hugh wins the fight but, suspected of spying for the French, he is arrested and put in the stocks. When the sergeant arrives from Gloucester to take him to gaol, he immediately recognises Hugh as the man who once saved his life when he was trapped in a snow drift. He frees the drover who takes Mary to join him in his life as a traveller singing

Now for the road again, the blessed sun and the rain.

The work is magnificent with fine tunes and vibrant orchestral sections and a colourful sense of theatre. Vaughan Williams put his ten years' experience of folk song collecting to good use: some of the music is traditional and the morris tune is one collected by Sharp. Most of the music is original, though, written in the style of folk-song.

It is available in a number of versions on record but is rarely seen in a professional performance. Having begun its composition in 1910, the composer must have felt that he had not quite got it right because he was still tinkering with it 45 years later.

Cold blows the wind on Cotsall in winter, snow and storm,
But the heart of England's in Cotsall, and the heart of England's warm.
O gentle are the men of Cotsall and were since the world began,
But none will fight for England's right like a true bred Cotsall
man, brave boys, like a true bred Cotsall man.

First Century Forgers

Bagendon today is a lovely group of buildings clustered in the narrow valley of Perrot's Brook but the buildings give no clue to this hamlet's importance in the past. You've walked past one clue: the earthworks beside the Welsh Way.

For the first few decades of the first century AD, Bagendon was the capital of the Dobunni tribe which controlled all of the Cotswolds and the Severn Valley. The earthworks enclosed an area of some 500 acres with today's hamlet near its centre. These huge defensive ditches must have taken quite some digging - they were about three yards wide and two yards deep. As well as those you've seen, earthworks still stand to the north of Bagendon at Scrubditch and to the east beside Cutham Lane. They never were continuous around the settlement.

This enclosure gave protection to cattle, sheep and pigs and horses which were about the size of New Forest ponies. The houses were walled with wattle panels on circular stone bases, entered through wooden doors with iron latches.

The main occupation here was sophisticated metal working, making nails, brooches and other domestic items in iron, bronze and lead. They apparently smelted iron ore with coal - a technique which was then lost until its rediscovery in the 17th century.

Bagendon was the tribe's Mint, making gold and silver coins, many with a motif of a three-tailed horse. Some 500 coins minted at Bagendon have been found in Gloucestershire and its neighbouring counties. Curiously, they even made forgeries of silver and gold-plated bronze. The names on the coins are presumably those of the tribal chiefs so the earliest "Gloucestershire" names we know of include Catti and Bodvoc. None of the coins have been found completely intact so these illustrations are based on careful reconstructions made by Derek Allen.

Life must have been pleasant here at least for the tribal chiefs. Evidence of imports includes wine, tableware from Italy and glass vessels from Egypt and Syria and we know that on occasions they ate oysters. In return, we know that the tribe exported woollen cloaks to Rome.

There is no evidence of any resistance to the Roman invasion. Bodvoc seems to have submitted at the first opportunity in AD 43. Bagendon continued to flourish till AD 60, adapting to the Roman way of life, but ten years later the settlement was deserted.

➤ The large house across the valley is Bagendon House, formerly the rectory, dominated by a magnificent Cedar of Lebanon. Mysterious narrow paths lead through shrubberies to a rocky grotto with a pool and a Victorian fern garden.

Pass the former school and continue past houses at the far end of the village. When the road turns sharp right, continue straight ahead to follow the field edge above the little stream. At the far corner of the field go through an open gateway on to a wide woodland track leading through carpets of bluebells up to a house.

Turn left to pass above the tennis court and house - the single seat seems to be for an umpire. Continue on the house's drive to rejoin the Welsh Way. Turn left and after 200 yards turn off right on to a footpath beside Daglingworth Quarry. The embankment you soon notice just right of the path is another part of Bagendon's ancient defences. You'll notice a lot of beehives stationed in the scrubby woodland to the right and, to the left, good views of the stone quarry.

The Itlay Underpass with its beautiful new stone-walling, takes you safely beneath the new A417 dual carriageway, a 20th century "toll" road linking the M4 and M5. Privately financed and constructed, the government will pay the "toll" to the builders for a period of 30 years. The road has dramatically reduced the journey time across this part of the Cotswolds and has provided a bonus of hundreds of yards of drystone wall and some 200,000 newly planted trees. At Latton, just beyond Cirencester, the new road crosses the line of the Thames and Severn canal on a new culvert; without this, the full planned canal restoration would have been impossible.

Cross the main road on to a minor road through the oddly named hamlet of **Itlay**. Cross the road on to a path which, after a few hundred yards, has the feel of a very ancient track. Notice the care taken by the mason in curving the wall at corners and gateways.

The track drops down to the wonderfully secluded valley of the Dunt to emerge by the former village school into **Daglingworth**, a village owned by the Duchy of Cornwall. Turn left then right at the No Through Road sign to pass the gates of Lower End House, the former Daglingworth Manor.

➤ The circular stone dovecote in the Manor grounds is all that remains of a 12th century Priory. Inside is a ladder, called a "potence", which circulates round a central spindle to give access to all 550 nest boxes. The house was recently occupied by a religious cult but now seems to be back in conventional hands.

Tithe Barns

One of the historic treasures of the Cotswolds is its stone barns, some still in use, some derelict and some splendidly preserved with original beams, buttresses and elaborate pinnacles. Many are now converted into homes, sometimes imaginatively and in the best cases with a sensitivity for their original appearance; one has been turned into a mill and exhibition area by the Cotswold Woollen Weavers at Filkins. The oldest barns represent a link with the Medieval world of Lords, clerics and peasants.

Barns were both working areas and places for storage. The word comes from the Old English *bern* meaning barley store. Corn, bound in sheaves, was dried in the sun and then stored at one end of the barn. During the winter months it was threshed on the area between the enormous central doorways. The straw would then be stored at one end of the barn, the corn at the other, while the chaff blew away in the draught between the doors.

The Woollen Weavers' barn at Filkins

These doorways were often enormous to allow a fully loaded cart to pass right through and many had elaborate porches to protect the labourers from the weather. J Arthur Gibbs describes how the vicar's men placed a bough on every tenth stook of corn as it stood in the field and then came with the vicar's horses to cart it away to the tithe barn.

Many of the larger remaining barns were tithe barns. Strictly the term applies only to those used for storing the one tenth of the year's produce paid to the church for clergy's pay, church upkeep and poor relief; those built to store a monastery's or abbey's own produce were called granges. Over the years the meanings have become confused and the beneficiary of the tax has changed. After the Dissolution the rights to the tithes in many parishes passed out of Church hands into those of local landowners.

The finest piece of architecture in England

The oldest barns had sturdy oak frames arranged in "cruck" style, a split tree trunk providing the two sides of an "A". By the time the enormous tithe barn at Great Coxwell was built by Cistercian monks in about 1310, its carpenters had evolved beautifully complex joints and arrangements of beams to support their enormous load of stone slates.

William Morris[1] loved the building and called it *the finest piece of architecture in England, as beautiful as a cathedral.*

The intricacy of Great Coxwell's roof beams

Until the late 19th century this country was self-sufficient in grains so there was a great deal of it to be stored through each year till the next harvest. Every cereal producing farm needed a barn, normally the largest of its farm buildings. Almost invariably the architects of these barns are anonymous but in the Cotswolds we have two 19th century exceptions: Lewis Vulliamy's model farm at Westonbirt and Cockerell's exotic design for Sezincote.

We readily think of tithes applying to cereal crops but the Church took its tenth of all produce - wood, milk, eggs, even new-born livestock. Although in the 19th century many parishes converted the tithe into the payment of a money equivalent, Gibbs quotes examples of how the tithe was paid in some parts of the Cotswolds in the 1890s:

A new milch cow	three pence
A hen	two eggs
A cock	three eggs
Every calf sold	four pence or the left shoulder

Astonishingly, the tithe system of taxation lasted from Anglo-Saxon times through to 1936 when it was taken over by the Inland Revenue. Former tithe payers still paid towards a tithe redemption annuity until its final abolition in 1996. Then the last traces of the tax disappeared but many of the enormous barns still stand dotted around these uplands, as a link with our medieval forebears.

The Green Man

Many of the churches we pass have gargoyles which are nothing more than waterspouts, designed to drain rain water from the roof and throw it well away from the walls. Though they have this simple function, they are often an attractive decoration to the building because the masons were allowed to display their stone-carving skills and their imagination in creating caricatures of human faces or of fantastic beasts. Just occasionally, tucked away in dimly lit recesses, you may find an altogether different character - The Green Man.

[1] William Morris' home at Kelmscott Manor is surrounded by barns: there are three at Home Farm, one medieval, one with a dovecote and a dozen more in Kelmscot village. Morris was a real barns enthusiast and regularly took his friends to see the tithe barn at nearby Great Coxwell. It is now owned by the National Trust who stripped and relaid the roof in the 1960s.

The Green Man is a man's severed head, swathed in leaves. At Guiting Power he is to be found high above your head, carved on to the roof boss; at North Nibley he is hidden amongst carvings on an octagonal stone pillar. There are thousands of examples of the Green Man all over Britain and Europe but who is he?

This Green Man is in North Nibley church

He seems to be a remnant of pre-Christian beliefs, a symbol of the annual cycle of the natural world and the resurrection that occurs unfailingly every spring. He may be a spirit of the woods and the trees or a fertility symbol. It seems that as Christianity usurped the pagan festivals and symbols, the Green Man lived on defiantly, hidden away in sacred buildings by the stone masons.

This Green Man lives in my garden

He seems to have lived on in other ways too. The folk song figure John Barleycorn, the Fool in the Mummers Plays and the character Jack-in-the-Green who appears in many May Day festivities, all seem to be his descendants. Even some of the early Robin Hood stories suggest connections with this powerful symbol of regeneration.

Maybe the unschooled masons knew a thing or two which was a closed book to their learned clerical masters.

Whilst many church gargoyles hold a power to fascinate and even frighten the visitor who seeks them out, more fascinating still is the Green Man and his links to our pagan past.

I've tramped a score of miles today
And now on Cotswold stand,
Wondering if in any way
Their owners understand
How all those little gold fields I see
And the great green woods beyond
Have given themselves to me, to me
Who own not an inch of land.

WH

9
Daglingworth to Miserden
6 miles

Cheerily upon the road
Tramp we all together,
Bearing every one his load
Through the changeful weather
WH

Daglingworth to Miserden

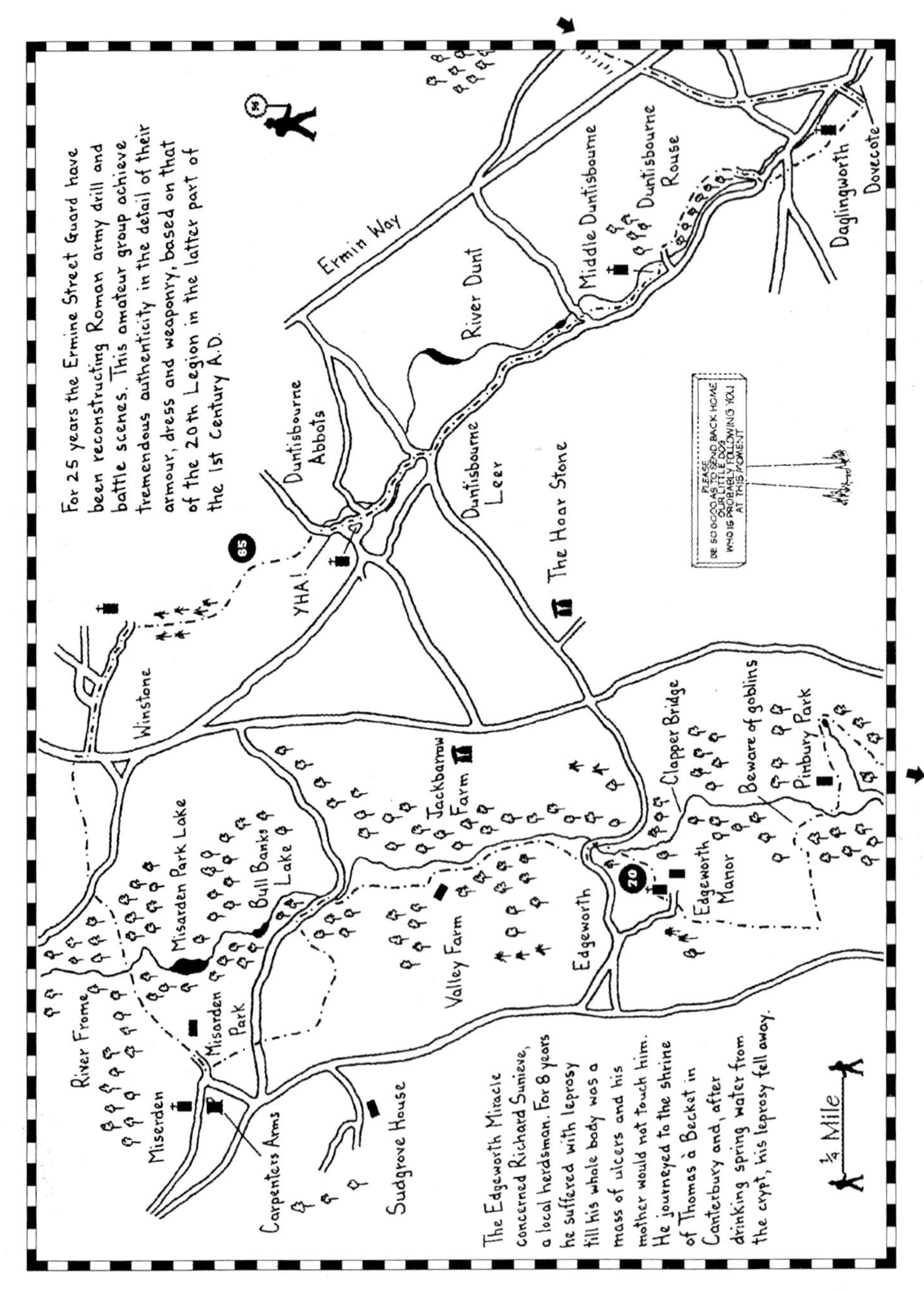

At the brow of the hill turn right through a kissing gate with B↑. Keep to the edge of the field to reach a gate with B↑ which brings you to the church.

➤ Above the Saxon doorway is a fine sundial (remember the porch was added later).

➤ Set into the inside walls are some of the best preserved Saxon carvings in the country. They were found during the Victorian restoration and are now set into the internal walls. The three designs are simple, boldly cut into the stone depicting the Crucifixion with two Roman soldiers, St Peter holding a key and a book, and Christ enthroned. On the outside eastern wall is a second Crucifixion. The straightforward work of the craftsman from so long ago is very moving.

➤ The vestry window is a Roman relic. The two windows are cut into one block of stone which has an inscription on the outside. This once formed part of an altar dedicated by Junia to *the Mother and Genius of this place.*

➤ Set into the floor of the porch are brass memorial plates. One dated 1638 reads: *The dissection and distribution of Giles Handcox who bequeathed his soul to heaven, his love to friends and £5 to the poor.*

➤ Beside the church is the very plain, square and simple Daglingworth House opposite which is a very plain, rectangular and simple fish pond.

➤ A second, 19th century dovecote is to be found in the Rectory garden.

Return to the road and leave it by a stile left before a modern barn conversion. Turn right and over a stone stile with a Y↑. Aim across the field just right of the house with the stone tiled roof. Descend the steps, cross the road and ascend the steps on the other side.

Cross a stile to follow a path at the foot of some attractive cottage gardens, crossing two stone stiles to reach the road.

Turn right then branch left at the No Through Road sign. Branch left on to the bridleway signposted to Duntisbourne Rouse, our route now running up the valley of the Dun or the Dunt or the Duntisbourne Brook, depending on which authority you turn to.

Go through a gate and follow the field edge round to the left above the steep wooded slope, thick with bluebells in spring. Pass through a gate and at the field corner, exit by another. Keep straight ahead to drop down the field to yet another gate to the right of the house. Turn left down the track and cross the stream by the footbridge or the ford.

Pass an attractive house front and turn right up the steps beside the Old Rectory. The first time I walked here I wrote that

> *the Old Rectory garden is currently undergoing a dramatic rethink.*

It had been bought in the early '90s by Mary Keen, a professional garden writer and designer, who has certainly rethought it and now has climbers making their way up just about every vertical surface. She describes the project in her book "Creating a Garden".

Pass through an iron scissor gate, Intriguing Gate Fastening Mechanism Number 3, into the churchyard of **Duntisbourne Rouse** (pronounced Dunsbourne), - or Rous as publications in the church insist on spelling it. This hamlet is idyllic.

➤ The church is built on such a slope that the roofs form three steps, each with a cross. It has a saddle-backed tower, one of several in the Cotswolds.

Contd: page 118

Stone Cottages

A true Cotsaller can do anything with stone except eat it

One of the great treasures of the Cotswold countryside, which makes it so pleasing to the eye, is its stone buildings - farmhouses, barns, manors and, most frequently, cottages. Part of their visual attraction comes from the way they cluster together in the narrow valley bottoms and, as at Chalford or Blockley, clamber up the steep valley sides; part is the way they blend in with the scenery because they are built from the native stone - a creamy grey in the south wolds, pale golden in the centre and a rich orangey brown in the north. John Buchan, who lived just outside the Cotswolds in Oxfordshire, wrote in a story, "Fullcircle", of Cotswold stone's chameleon quality:

The stone of Cotswold takes curiously the colour of the weather. Under the thunder clouds it will be dark as basalt; on a grey day it is grey like lava, but in sunshine it absorbs the sun.

The cottages have a style developed from Elizabethan houses which has given them a pleasing consistency throughout the area but despite their common features, no two are identical. It's as if each mason or architect was working from a slightly faulty memory, each time creating a unique arrangement with the familiar components, the characteristic features appearing again and again in an endless sequence of variations.

You'll see many 17th century cottages and a few from the century before but none of an earlier date. That is because until the late 16th century the homes of ordinary folk generally had thatched roofs and wooden walls. Those which were built with stone were made from reused rubble by unskilled hands and had to be rebuilt every ten years or so. The wood, of course, has perished so the only buildings we see from an earlier date are castles, churches and manor houses, built by craftsmen using dressed stone. The period 1560 - 1620 is known as the "Great Rebuilding", stone replacing half-timber dwellings, financed by the region's increasingly prosperous wool trade.

Architectural styles later than the Elizabethan have almost passed the Cotswolds by. In a few cases, such as the Old Manor House at Upper Slaughter, Classical revival pillars were incorporated in the design. In most cases, though, the only nod to changing fashion was the elaborate shell hoods over doorways such as the one at St Mary's Mill House at Chalford.

So 300 years of building have produced a continuity of design perhaps unique to this part of the country. Architects connected with the Arts and Crafts Movement prolonged the tradition and the Cotswolds' most well-known show-piece cottages, Arlington Row in Bibury, were saved from decay by William Morris. He called Bibury *surely the most beautiful village in England.* In recent years building controls have ensured that the rural Cotswold scene, so pleasing to the eye, is preserved for future generations.

Of course, the attractiveness of stone cottages today tends to romanticise the rural life of the past. Beatrix Potter, staying at Harescombe Grange in 1894, balances this view by talking of

....labourers, their miserable wages of eleven shillings a week, their unsanitary cottages, their appalling families and improvidence.

And, just in case the life of a stonemason appeals, Richard Garne describes the working conditions of a man from Filkins who started as a mason in 1899. He left home at 6am to walk about four miles to work. He worked through to 8pm with a half hour break for breakfast, an hour for lunch and another half hour for tea. Work finished early though on a Saturday - 5pm in summer, 4pm in winter.

Arlington Row, Bibury, began life as a wool store in the 1380s and was converted to weavers' cottages in the 17th century

Under the chancel is a barrel-vaulted Norman crypt, originally a chapel, with a spiral staircase, now blocked off. You can, though, enter through an external door. The crypt was restored in the '30s - up till then it was being used as a coal shed. High on the outside of the tower is a stone clearly bearing an inscription; it records the rebuilding of the top portion in 1587.

➤ The wall paintings of long-stemmed daisies are 13th century while the churchyard cross which has its original head is 14th century.

➤ The harmonium has miniature gaily-coloured pipes reminiscent of pan pipes. It was given in memory of Katherine Mansfield, the short-story writer who died in 1923, by her sisters, one of whom came to live here at the Rectory.

➤ West of the church another scissor gate leads to a fine stone-roofed lych-gate.

➤ Manor Farm has an old stone dovecote in its garden.

Don't leave the churchyard by the lych-gate. After admiring the view over this charming hamlet in its hollow, backed by the wooded slope, leave the churchyard northwards via a stone stile by a Y↑ on a tree. Go through the woods, dropping down to the stream and a stile with a Y↑. Aim across the middle of the field to reach a gate on to a road at **Middle Duntisbourne**. Turn right and at a U-turn in the road take the unmarked lane left. The hamlet is a small group of farm buildings and cottages with another ford over the Dunt.

Follow the shady track, an older road than the metalled one above. Emerge right on to the road and follow it uphill. Go left at the T junction and then right into the hamlet of **Duntisbourne Leer**. Go down the hill to the ford which you might recognise from a television advert for telephones.

➤ The 16th century Leer Farm has fleur-de-lys carved on a chimney and above a door, a reminder perhaps of the manor's early ownership by the Abbey of Lire in Normandy. The farm buildings include a brewhouse and a barn with a pigeon loft.

Return up the hill and take the Unsuitable for Motor Vehicles road now on your right. You will find the reason beside the house called Long Ford. The stream here was diverted to make a convenient place to wash carts and horses. Approaching **Duntisbourne Abbots,** notice the spring made into a garden feature with a pond and a little further on, by the phone box, another attractive spring, once the village water supply, fenced now by the WI.

➤ The church has a curious centre-pivoted lych-gate.

Take the path uphill aiming to the right of the church. Follow the road up and branch to the right of the Youth Hostel. The road drops to a gate and stile on the left signposted to Winstone. It's an excellent gate to sit on and look back at the V shape of the little valley.

The next section is charming and strange. Follow the dry valley bottom as it winds gently uphill. It is eerie to think that you are walking where the stream once ran, cutting the valley. The steep valley sides have thousands of cowslips interspersed with orchids. Cross two stiles, the private road to Rectory Farm and through two gates with Y↑. The valley is less distinct now but follow the right side of the wall entering a narrow field by a gate below the conifer plantation of The Grove.

Swinging right you will soon have trees on both sides. In winter you'll find this field has an identity crisis - is it a pasture or is it a stream?

As the field opens out, aim for its far left corner. A stone stile brings you on to the road and turning left brings you into the village of **Winstone** beside a couple of barns, one with a neatly arched stone entrance. Notice how the village grew up well away from the parish church which stands in windswept fields behind you.

St Bartholemew, patron of

- bookbinders
- glovers
- shoemakers
- vine growers
- plasterers
- tanners
- dyers
- cheesemongers

➤ The church is tiny, a mixture of Saxon and Norman but the interior was thoroughly "scraped" by the Victorians.

➤ You may be disappointed to find that the public house marked on the Ordnance Survey map called its last orders many years ago.

When the road forks, go left through the rather nondescript village. Notice the water pump in the yard of Townsend Farm on the left. When the road turns sharp left, go right into a road that soon becomes a lane. Pass Pound Cottage and take the footpath left over a stile. The footpath has been re-routed here to avoid arable crops. Keep to the field edge to the right of the hedge. At the end of the field a post with Y↑ points through a gap in the hedge left. The route is clearly marked now with a series of Y↑s on posts which will guide you across two fields and through the edge of two small copses.

Turn right on to the road for 100 yards or so, leaving it at the Miserden sign. Walk beside the hedge to the edge of the woods of Winstone Hill. Notice the pollarded ash just the other side of the hedge.

Enter the woods over a stone stile with a steep drop on the far side. Follow the Y↑s on trees obliquely down through the wood of young beeches in a sea of bluebells early in the year. This will bring you to a paved estate road. Turn right and follow it down to the bridge noticing the pleasing trees, mainly conifers. Just before the bridge is a striking group of pollarded scarlet willows, their new

The Hoar Stone

This is a large lozenge-shaped stone, between five and six tons in weight, with just half its full length standing 12 feet above the ground. It is the eastern end of a ruined long barrow. Eight or nine skeletons were found when it was excavated in 1806.

Jackbarrow Farm Barrow

Late in the last century this barrow was found to contain skeletons, a stone chest and an enormous sword. They are reburied in the churchyard, the position marked by a cross carved from a stone slab taken from the barrow. This is an unusual mark of respect at a time when the Cotteswold Naturalists' Field Club treated the opening of barrows as something of a sport.

Contd: page 123

Misarden Park Gardens

The mansion dates from the early 17th century but has been considerably altered, most recently by the rebuilding of the east wing by Lutyens in the 1920s following a fire. The house strikes me as dark and gloomy even on a bright summer day which is a pity because its location at the head of the most varied of Cotswold valleys, the Golden Valley, is spectacular. Fortunately, the garden does make the most of the site.

The original walled garden dates back about 300 years and contains vast herbaceous borders, a formal garden of beautifully scented roses, a splendid wrought-iron gate through a stone archway and a magnificent yew walk - magnificent that is so, long as it's not you who has to clip the dozens of uniformly-domed yews. At the corner nearest the house an extraordinary ancient sycamore seems to float six feet in the air, its exposed roots entangled with a wall to such an extent that it is hard to say which is supporting which. Between here and the house is the striking collection of plants which make up the Silver and Grey borders.

Peering from the Yew Walk into the Rose Garden

The loggia and the series of terraces were designed as an extension of the new east wing. Here you will find a quince amongst a variety of planting mainly by Mrs Huntly Sinclair between the wars. The view is over the arboretum which includes an Indian Bean Tree and a range of Cedars - Atlas, Incense, Deodar and Blue Atlantic. Descend the steps to the north of the house and from the Butler's Walk you will spot a cunningly disguised squash court.

The most unusual feature is the two flights of steps which join the different levels of the lawns: the treads are of turf and the risers are miniature stone walls.

The gardens lie at the heart of the 3,000 acre Misarden estate, which embraces the whole village apart from the pub and the church and includes 700 acres of forest. Bought by the Wills tobacco family in 1912 it is now run by Major Tom Wills who operates the estate on traditional lines, aiming to preserve the integrity of the landscape. The seriousness of this aim is illustrated by the clearing of scrubby patches within the woodlands as a habitat for the Duke of Burgundy Fritillary, an orange-brown butterfly which feeds on primroses and cowslips and can be spotted from May to August.

Jumping for Joy

Show jumping today is dominated by commercial sponsorship and has always had the image of a pursuit for the wealthy, but in the years just after the war, Pat Smythe became the world's most successful woman in the sport without either of these advantages, in one of the few sports where men and women compete directly.

She learnt to handle horses at Miserden where she lived with her mother in the Dower House of Misarden Park. Money was short: her mother took in paying guests and students from Cirencester Agricultural College and grew vegetables to sell in Cheltenham. Pat worked her school holidays on a local farm, milking and harrowing for 5d per hour, and the horse that first brought her to public notice, *Finality*, was borrowed. Her training facilities at Miserden were the same as for any gymkhana enthusiast: poles resting on oil drums.

At her first international competition in Belgium in 1947, dressed in her mother's stock and hunting breeches, she entered the ring on *Finality* and exited, unconscious, on a stretcher. The horse had done a somersault over the final fence. Ironically, being in the British team had its drawbacks for her because, while she travelled and competed abroad, she was forfeiting the prize money from the summer round of Horse Shows.

Pat Smythe on her favourite, "Prince Hal"

She did not compete in the 1948 London Olympics although *Finality* was borrowed to be trained for the team. After six weeks the horse was returned, not used by the team and without compensation. The same thing happened with *Prince Hal* in the 1952 Helsinki Olympics.

1956, though, was a very good year. In the Grand Prix Militaire in Lucerne she rode 23 rounds on three different horses, clearing 273 obstacles and hitting only two. Although she won the competition on points, a woman was not allowed to receive the cup. She had to settle for the title of Leading Lady Rider and the award of an OBE. Shortly afterwards in Stockholm, with Peter Robeson on *Scorchin* and Wilf White on *Nizefela*, Pat on *Flanagan* won the Olympic bronze, the first ever Olympic show jumping medal to be won by a woman. They made up for the disappointment of third place by winning the Nations Cup on the final day. As a woman, she never was allowed to compete in the World Championships.

Pre-war, the sport was dominated by cavalry officers but this changed dramatically during the 1950s. These British riders, together with David Broome, David Barker and a handful of others raised the standard of British show jumping to equal that of any country in the world. In the company of these men, Pat's success was based not on strength or technique so much as a tremendous rapport even with a horse she had known only a few days.

And it is the horses that have lived on in the public memory. Among her best-known were *Kilgeddin* with whom she set the European height record at six feet ten and seven eighths, *Tosca* who once cleared 200 consecutive fences without knocking a single one down and *Prince Hal* who had a reputation for biting and a nameplate on his stable reading *The Vampire, feed this horse on fresh blood.*

In the stable yard at Miserden with Prince Hal (and Windy and Bliss)

She was Sports Woman of the Year in umpteen different polls. A measure of the popularity of the sport in those years is the result of the 1954 junior Mirror "Sports Hero" award: in descending order:

Roger Bannister
Pat Smythe
Stanley Matthews
Len Hutton
Denis Compton
Stirling Moss
Don Cockell.

During her 17 years at the peak of her sport she followed a parallel career writing 13 hugely popular pony books for children, "The Three Jays" series, which went some way to ease her financial situation. In 1963 she married Sam Koechlin, a Swiss Olympic rider and lawyer who later became Chairman of Ciba-Geigy. She divided her time between living in the Swiss Jura and at Sudgrove House, a dilapidated manor just a mile away from Miserden.

After her husband's death she returned to Sudgrove and poured her energies into the World Wildlife Fund, as a Trustee of its international committee, conducting a dizzying series of visits to hundreds of conservation projects around the globe.

The prize money for the Hickstead Show Jumping Derby in 1994, a competition which Pat was the first woman to win, may well have caused her a wry smile: £35,000 to the winner and another £5,000 for achieving two clear rounds. Her prize money in 1962 was £200.

Pat Smythe died in 1996.

shoots an unusual brilliant red in the autumn.

Keep to the road to climb to the far side of the valley. When three roads meet, go straight ahead up the steep muddy forest track - a Y↑ on a tree confirms the route through a beech wood, heavy with the scent of wild garlic. When this track bends left, go straight ahead on an indistinct footpath. Cross a stone stile to emerge in parkland. Continue straight up the hill and you will again meet the estate road.

Follow it uphill to a white gate and kissing gate beside the entrance to Misarden (sic) Park. Swing right for the centre of **Miserden** village.

➤ On the village green is a hexagonal shelter built around a sycamore.

➤ Some of the pairs of cottages at the top end of the village were designed by Sidney Barnsley and dated 1920. One has the name Norman which seems overly human for a house until you notice the one next door is called Saxon.

➤ In the church are three magnificent 17th century effigies. Sir William Sandys, dressed as an Elizabethan knight, and his wife Margaret are beautifully carved in Italian alabaster. At her feet is a vicious-looking falcon; at his, another falcon being attacked by a griffon.

On the sides of the tomb their ten children are depicted, three in clothes showing they died before baptism and three carrying skulls meaning that they predeceased their parents. The effigy of William Kingston lies bizarrely with his feet resting on a goat which is munching a cabbage.

P **Carpenters Arms**
Free house.
Boddingtons, Brakspear, Wadworth 6X and Stowford Press cider. The splendid inn sign marks a village pub, closed for a couple of years but now "back on the map" of village pubs.

Whiteway Colony

Whiteway presents a quite untypical Cotswold sight: a settlement of mainly wooden bungalows clustered around private roads on an exposed part of the wolds. Yet, at the turn of the century, Whiteway was no more than a single stone shepherd's cottage. It was created by a small group of idealists attempting to live life in their own way.

Nellie Shaw

In 1899 eight settlers arrived from London by bicycle, bought 42 acres of bleak farmland and set about trying to live by the teachings of Count Leo Tolstoy[1], the author of "War and Peace". Their first action was to burn the title deeds to the property, believing that land should be held in common for the use of anyone who could make it productive.

Their aim was to live off the land without the use of money, without recognising the authority of the government or the police, and without using any violent force. They wanted to live according to their own dress code and morality and without a leader. Nellie Shaw, who joined the settlement in 1900, recounts in her book, "Whiteway", the ecstacies and agonies of adopting a communist lifestyle 17 years before the communist revolution in Russia.

Francis Sedlak

The first winter was the hardest of all, living off potatoes and parsnips, with £6 left in the communal moneybox and no source of income. Some settlers persisted for a few years in refusing to use money but repeated jail sentences for non-payment of rates led them all to seek a modest income; some worked for local farmers, others turned to handicrafts.

The avoidance of force and their reluctance to call in the police, led to problems: neighbours' cows trampled the first year's crops and local people took much of what was left and helped themselves to tools. Their principle of giving what they had to anyone who needed it, meant even more of their precious food was given to scroungers who stayed for days or weeks, abusing their welcome. Reluctantly, the farmed land was hedged for protection.

---

[1] Tolstoy's unhappy marriage and the deaths of several of his infant children led him to a mid-life crisis and a conversion to an anarchic form of Christianity. He renounced private property, including the rights to his books, he opposed organised government and preached non-resistance to evil. He resolved to forego any sexual relationship and live out his life as a peasant. Although he wrote a good deal about his new-found communist-like philosophy and spawned hundreds of disciples who came to visit him at his Yasnaya Polyana estate he, illogically, continued to live the luxurious life of a Russian aristocrat apart from giving up meat, making his own boots and dressing in a peasant's smock.

The settlement soon became a tourist attraction. Coaches would drive out from Gloucester to catch glimpses of nude bathers and strange dressers: while some of the men wore shorts and coloured shirts and walked barefoot, the women were to be seen in sleeveless dresses that failed to cover their knees. There were also couples living together without the benefit of a marriage certificate - all very unconventional in the 1900s.

Sinclair's house has not stood the test of time

Gradually the communist experiment failed and was replaced by "individualism" of a pretty remarkable order. One man quarried the stone to build his own shanty. William Sinclair dug the clay, made the bricks and thatched the roof of his, at a cost of absolutely nothing. Some of these original houses remain: Sunnymedes, built by Shaw and Francis Sedlak, and Sud Protheroe's Meadow Cottage, both date back to 1902.

Some made a living selling milk, peas, strawberries; Sud built the bakery which baked bread right up till 1988, its famous double ovens each baking 110 "Old English" loaves with stone-ground flour from Ebworth Mill. For eight years a number of settlers operated as the Cotswold Cooperative Handicraft Guild, making and selling cloth, sandals, baskets and wood products but personal frictions led to their disbanding.

Shaw's book glows with the satisfaction gained from communal musical evenings, dances, the writing and performing of plays (once in a cow-shed) and listening to visiting lecturers. By the 1930s the settlement had reached a certain maturity with the building of a village hall and a school room. Many colonists stayed only a matter of months but a number lived at Whiteway for 20 and even 30 years. Shaw died here aged 82 in 1946; Jeannie Straughan, another original colonist, died here in 1950.

Protheroe's Bakery still stands but no longer trades as a store

From the start there was never any consistent set of beliefs apart from the assertion that here was a haven to live in as one pleased. The community never did have a leader. Even today, land at Whiteway must be applied for and decisions made by the monthly meeting of the colony are legally binding.

The craft tradition continues with a number of artists such as Peter Evans who carves in wood and Mike Hawkes who is a freelance inn-sign painter.

For two days at Easter 1994 Whiteway was opened to the public to raise money to improve their private roads. A visit confirmed that Whiteway is still a special place peopled with folk who want to live their life outside the mainstream. The colony has also inspired a play with music, "Walking to Whiteway", by Frank Hatt which toured Gloucestershire in 1995, portraying the dilemmas faced in the first couple of years by Whiteway's original pioneers.

After that early period the colony built up a network of friends who supported them, staying for short periods without ever moving in. Some of these were very curious characters like Frances Jennings, a 28 year-old woman, paralysed from the waist down, who travelled on her own by donkey cart, refusing even on Christmas Day to eat inside anyone's house. The last word goes to another of these friends of the colony, a Captain Jack White:

> *I have always considered that no man understands how to live who cannot be happy leaning over a gate and spitting. Whiteway provides so much food for reflection that the latter activity can be dispensed with.*

There's a magic in living on Cotswold
That only the hills can impart,
And those who were bred on the uplands
Have Cotswold pressed deep in their heart.
FM

10 Miserden to Daneway

6½ miles

Walking all morning, afternoon too, the lanes
Or high roads - To return dusty, tea thirsty
To friends, the piano, sketching ambitiously
Such works as broad country might bring to attempt

IG

Miserden to Daneway

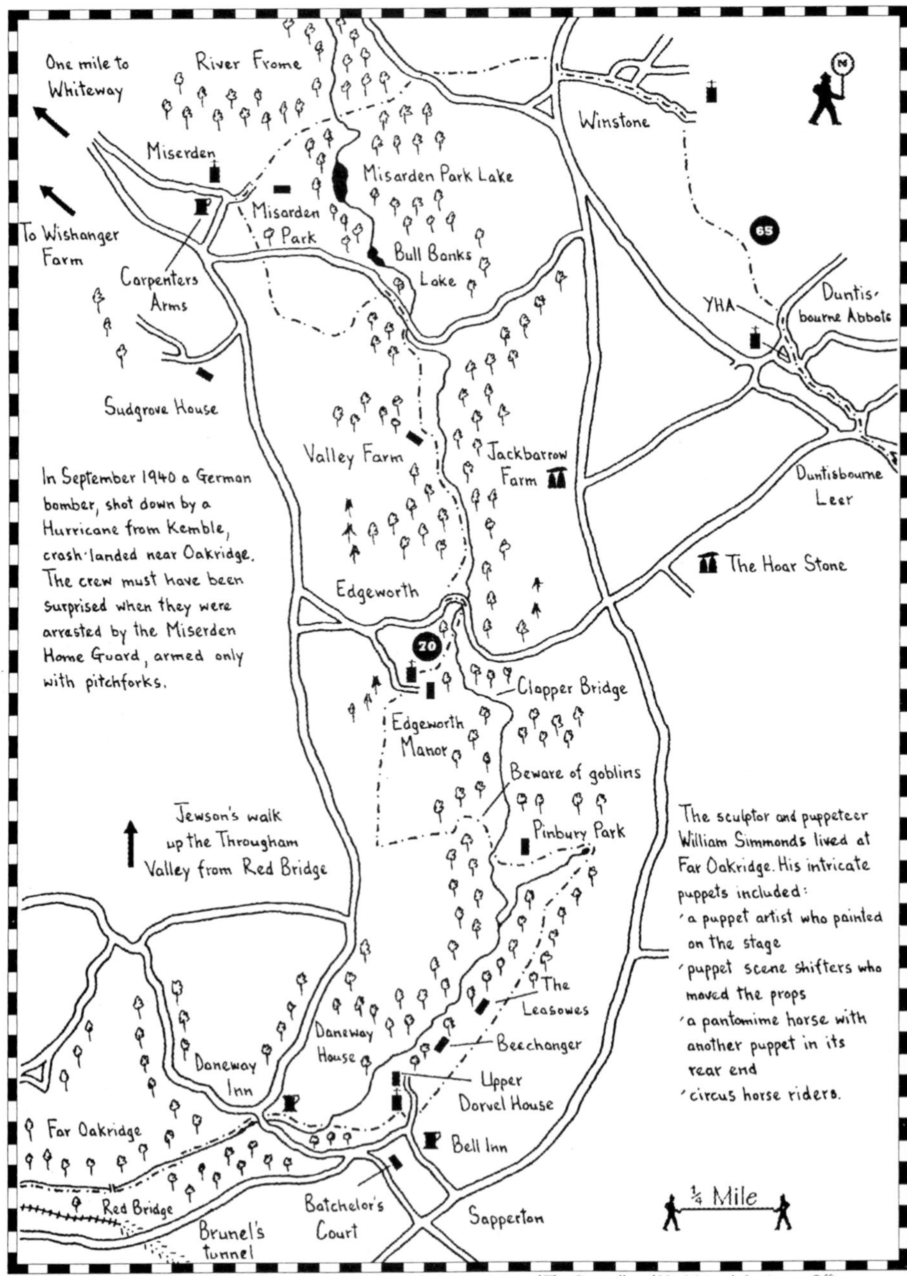

Retrace your steps back towards Misarden Park and take the footpath right, beside Yew Tree Cottage which soon becomes a bridleway. Cross a stone stile to be channelled between a fence and a wall at the back of Miserden Nursery. At one point the wall turns some fancy corners but it is hard to fathom why.

Leave the path by a stone stile and cross the road with a splendid view behind of the Park presiding over its valley. Follow the field boundary across two fields then take an unsignposted left turn on to a track between stone walls. The track curves right above Sandy Flats Plantation, growing in a small old quarry. At the fork, take the left track, down through trees, to a gate with Y↑ into a field. Aiming to the right of three large beech trees, leave the field by a gate on to the road. Turn right.

Go down the road 300 yards, the bank on the right white with wild garlic flowers and turn right just before the bridge. Then take the indistinct left-hand path. Cross a stile after 150 yards. Initially the path leads to the right, then it turns sharp left to climb diagonally through the trees of Parson's Hill. The path levels out to run along the contour on this very steep slope,offering attractive views of Bull Banks. A rise to a stile takes you out into a field. Aim straight across it and veer right into a grassy lane.

After 250 yards, where the path levels out, turn sharp back to the left beside a fence and beneath a young plantation of beeches to reach a stile. Head for the cattle shed where a Y↑ on a gate points you out across the field. Join a farm track that leads to an open gateway with Y↑ into a lane that brings you to the buildings of Valley Farm. Notice the small building with the wonderful hipped stone slate roof.

A little before the farm house a notice announces a right of way diversion. At this point go left through a gate with B↑ and Y↑s into a field. Turn right and aim along the contour for a small stone building. To the right is the attractively extending garden of the farm and to your left a tiny waterfall on the infant River Frome. Pass left of the small building to a gate with B↑.

Keep to the contour, below the tree line, until you emerge by a cattle grid on to the farm's access road. Follow it as it passes above the splendidly restored buildings of Edgeworth Mill Farm and a former mill pond. When you reach the public road turn left on to it. After it takes a sharp right turn, take the second footpath sign to the right. Cross the field using the stout wooden footbridge over the meandering stream. The view of Edgeworth Manor standing high on its dramatic site is spectacular. Veer right to the corner of an ancient mossy wall with Y↑.

Keep a straight line steeply up through the scrubby trees to reach a stile

---

De tour — Misarden Park Lake

Turn left on to the road and take the first footpath left. You find a sizeable lake with an island. On a cold autumn afternoon, with mist blurring the line between water and trees, this is a place of mystery.

In wet weather the sheer quantity of water escaping over the weir powerfully demonstrates the potential of water powered mills in the past and explains why we find mill sites on the smallest of brooks. Retrace your steps to the road.

---

with Y↑, designed by someone who has evidently never tried to use one, leading into a field. Cross it, aiming for the charming lych-gate to the right of the church. If the field contains large, long-horned bulls, you might prefer to climb quickly up to the Manor outbuildings and over the fence into **Edgeworth** churchyard. Pass through the lych-gate and take the churchyard path between neat box hedges branching right out to the road.

➤ The church has a Norman doorway with a zig-zag arch, part of a Saxon cross and 11 gargoyles, some in excellent condition. Most interesting, though, is a finely crafted window of 14th century glass showing a mitred Archbishop, thought to be Thomas à Becket.

➤ On the backs of bookmarks on sale in the Church the story is told of the Edgeworth Miracle. Richard Sunieve, a local herdsman and leper, was cured of his appalling disease at the shrine of Becket in Canterbury Cathedral.

➤ On no account miss the brass plates on the ends of each pew, an astonishing throwback to a vanished society.

➤ There is a ½ mile sycamore avenue leading from the church and manor to the village itself, following a line a little above the modern road.

➤ The Manor house that loomed over your route up the hill dates from about 1700 but is not open to the public. In its gardens is Scriven's Conduit, an octagonal stone building with lions' heads and a statue of Jupiter, brought here in the 19th century from Gloucester.

➤ This western front of the house looks Elizabethan, similar to that at Misarden, but it was in fact re-fronted in 1889.

De tour

The Stone Clapper Bridge

Appoach Edgeworth House on the gravel drive. Wave a greeting to the figure who waves at you from near the house. Take a narrower gravel path right marked with a B↑ which leads you down beside the gardens of the Manor. Pass through a venerable iron gate and squeeze style until you approach the estate bridge over the stream.

From beside the gate marked No Footpath you can see the clapper bridge made from three large stone slabs in a beautifully secluded spot. Although the stream is of no great width it was important in the days of the Cotswolds' wool trade to have a dry route suitable for pack mules laden with wool sacks[1].

The bridge had no parapets because they would be an obstacle to the mules' load. Take a look at the gate on the estate bridge to find Intriguing Gate Fastening Mechanism Number 4.

[1]On Whit Bank Holiday you can see the World Championship Woolsack Races at Tetbury. Competitors from around the County race over a 280 yard course up the 1-in-4 Gumstool Hill, between the Royal Oak and The Crown, carrying a 60 lb woolsack (35 lb for the women) across their shoulders. The world record for the four-man team stands at 3 minutes 29.81 seconds.
The races hardly count as a traditional pastime as yet - they began in the 1970s and have raised thousands of pounds for local charities!

Contd: page 133

Winson Invincibles
v
Edgeworth Daisy Cutters

J Arthur Gibbs lived in the 1890s at Ablington Manor on the River Coln. There he wrote "A Cotswold Village", perhaps the classic description of rural life in the Cotswolds. Much of the book concerns gentlemen's sporting pursuits - riding to hounds, shooting, fly-fishing for trout and, his greatest accomplishment, cricket. He learned the game at Eton, played for the MCC and five times represented Somerset. In 1892-3 he toured India with Lord Hawke's XI.

In the book he describes in Dickensian fashion an away game for a Winson XI at Edgeworth. His team comprised the village miller and carrier, the carpenter's two sons, the curate (capt.), Gibbs, his footman and butler and three farmers. When the carrier deposited them at Edgeworth:

... they proceeded to look for the pitch. They knew it was somewhere in the field they stood in because a large red flag floated at one end proclaiming the field of

Gibbs faced his first ball and caught it, just as it pitched in a rabbit hole, and sent it straight up into the air. He describes the second ball:

I was quite certain that the man who bowled me out was a direct descendant of Julius Caesar. He delivered the ball underhand at a rapid rate. It came twisting along, now to the right, now to the left; seemed to disappear beneath the surface of the soil, then suddenly came in sight again, shooting past the block...It was generally agreed that such a ball had never been bowled before.

Gloucestershire's most famous cricketer, WG Grace, in a spoof "portrait by Vincent Van Gogh"

In the confusion of missed catches, colliding fielders, overthrown stumpings and lost balls, he ran seven runs while his partner ran five. How to score this? The compromise of six seems reasonable but a team mate's suggestion that the five and the seven should be added strikes me as unlikely to be upheld by the Laws of Cricket. Gibbs' international experience did him little good on this Edgeworth pitch.

He lived a rich but short life, dying at the age of 31 from complications following a hernia operation.

Pinbury Park

Pinbury Park enjoys a beautiful setting overlooking the beech-clad valley of the Frome, on the alleged site of the royal residence of 7th century King Penda. At the time of the Conquest the manor belonged to the Abbess of Caen who was William's daughter. In 1415, when foreign religious houses were being suppressed, Pinbury was given to the Nuns of Syon Abbey.

The house has some 15th century features but it has mainly grown piecemeal from the 17th century. By the 1890s it was a mere farmhouse falling into disrepair, part of Lord Bathurst's Cirencester Park estate. At the turn of the century, Gimson and the Barnsleys added a drawing room, a bay window and a fine carved stone chimneypiece. The grounds include a large sunken garden, a circle of wych elm and the neat topiary includes an eagle who overlooks the croquet lawn.

Despite the early ownership by nuns it is by no means clear that any ever lived here. However, stories involving them cling firmly to the house.

The most persistent concerns an elderly nun and a housekeeper who lived here looking after a group of ladies from noble families. When the religious houses were closed, the housekeeper was allowed to remain. She seems to remain here still, the source of modern supernatural happenings.

A fanciful view of The Nun's Walk

Some say that a ghostly nun rolls a Double Gloucester cheese along the avenue known as the Nun's Walk. A party of locals bound for a cricket match, recently claim to have encountered the housekeeper.

John Mullings, the present occupant, has many times heard his wife return from evenings out long before her actual return. He tells of the family living here just after the last war with three small children. They had taken care never to frighten the children by talking of the nun. One day, walking in the garden by the yews, the smallest child asked, who was the lady following them in a black dress with a strange belt. Of course, no one was there.

You may be followed yourself as you walk up the lane and pass in front of the topiary garden. It's probably just the Mullings' dog but you'd better look back, just to be sure...

Take the road leading away from the front of the manor. Branch down the road to the left, passing between cottages to a step stone stile and gate. In the field turn a little to the left and aim for the fencing silhouetted on the skyline. Go through the gate with B↑. The views back to Edgeworth are magnificent.

Keep right of the iron fencing and stone wall, passing through three gates. At Gloucester Beeches cross the stile and turn left through a gate. Follow the track to the right of the hedge. It swings right to reach a gate into a wood. Take the path forking left.

This muddy bridleway swings first to the left and then gently right, down through the woods till you emerge with surprise into a neat flat field surrounded by trees; a magical place where a glimpse of pixies or goblins wouldn't surprise you. Cross the field, pass through a gate and cross the Frome either by the footbridge or, if you're feeling playful, the ford.

A sunken lane swings steeply up to the left. Pass the front of Pinbury Park and its cottages and outbuildings, turning right off the access road between the fishpond to the right and a powerful spring to the left. Go through a double gate and then keep to the contour passing to the right of the trees. The path swings left just below a wall and the edge of the trees as you regain the Frome valley. Pass through a gate (with five assorted ↑s!) and take the track uphill. Go the length of this long field to join a track used by farm vehicles.

When the field narrows, the trees closing in on both sides, go through the gate (with only two ↑s). The short lane soon becomes a path beside a fence leading left up to a gate.

The house to the right is The Leasowes, designed and built by Ernest Gimson. Its original thatched roof, destroyed in a fire, was replaced by tiles. Through the gate, continue on the path beside the fence. Masked by the trees down to the right is Beechanger, designed and built by Sidney Barnsley. The path eventually reaches a gate with B↑. Cross the field to the kissing gate beside the telephone box in **Sapperton**, which Hutton calls *lovely Sapperton - no, enchanting Sapperton.*

➤ Just to the right is the entrance to Upper Dorvel House, built by Ernest Barnsley by adding two wings to an existing cottage.

➤ The cottages date from the 17th to the 20th centuries but you would be hard pressed to distinguish when many of them were built; those designed by the Sapperton Craftsmen are firmly in the Cotswold tradition.

➤ Batchelor's Court, the former home of Norman Jewson, has topiary yews shaped as an archway, cheeses and peacocks; School House has a yew clipped to form a room; there are marvellous topiary mushrooms at the rear of the church and a house near the Bell Inn has a topiary cottage.

Bell Inn
Free House
Spacious village pub offering Wadworth & Whitbread, guest ales and a couple of draught ciders.
A log fire in the lounge but oddly bare stone walls.

Contd: page 137

The Sapperton Craftsmen

At the turn of the century the Arts and Crafts Movement was a significant force in the Cotswolds with Ashbee's Guild of Handicraft at Chipping Campden and the memory of William Morris still warm on the Oxfordshire border at Kelmscot. Here in the Frome valley, an equally remarkable group of craftsmen lived and worked for 25 years.

Three young architects, Ernest and Sidney Barnsley and Ernest Gimson, rented Pinbury Park as both a home and a workshop. Disenchanted with Victorian manufacturing, its poor design and lack of craftsmanship, they sought to produce work that was *useful and right, pleasantly shaped and finished, good enough, but not too good for ordinary use.* Their inspiration was not the delicate cabinet making skill of the 18th century but the plain solid furniture of the 17th century and the rural craft traditions of blacksmith and wheelwright, a remnant of which lived on in this part of the Cotswolds. Their furniture designs are reminiscent of Shaker furniture, popular again today. Rather than conceal the constructional joints, they were often boldly displayed and even accentuated.

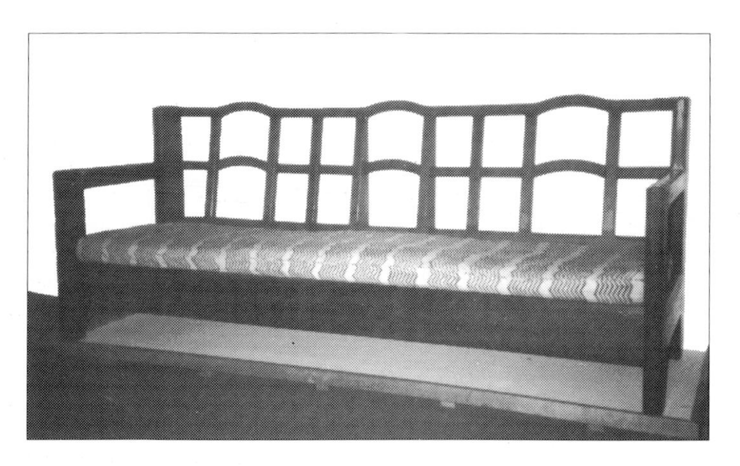

Oak settee designed and made by Sidney Barnsley

These craftsmen developed an astonishing range of expertise. They designed and supervised the building of scores of traditional style cottages in the Cotswolds, Rodmarton Manor being their greatest architectural achievement. They produced plasterwork ceilings, friezes and decorations with rural motifs, candlesticks and lecturns for churches, book bindings in tooled leather and book plates like designs from illuminated manuscripts, embroidery designs, carved stone fire-places, ornate leadwork for drainpipes...an amazing array of skills worthy of a whole village of master craftsmen. Sapperton became a thriving craft community with local men trained to work to their demanding standards.

At the time it must have seemed that a new age of quality design and rural self sufficiency could triumph over mass production. At Pinbury Park they fermented their own cider and built up a stock of 1000 gallons; at Christmas they revived the local mummers play; in the village hall, on a Saturday night, Mrs Gimson accompanied folk songs on the piano while Cecil Sharp listened out for songs to collect and sang George Riddler's Oven[1].

A writing cabinet by Ernest Gimson, 1919

Exciting as the experiment was for many years, it was doomed to failure. It is not possible to produce hand-crafted work which sells at man-in-the-street prices. Inevitably, their customers were the wealthy who could afford to commission their work. While some will dismiss their designs as whimsically rustic, many view it as a noble attempt to revive fast-disappearing skills, driven by a belief that valued the relationship between man, tools and materials in the act of creation.

Norman Jewson continued the work after their deaths in the '20s, but he retired at the end of the Second World War, unable to find men willing to work to his exacting standards.

My favourite story about the group concerns the houses they built for themselves. After nine years of renting Pinbury, Lord Bathurst decided he wanted the house for his own family. The three craftsmen had to find new homes. His Lordship, though, was so impressed with their restoration of his house, that he offered each of them their choice of a plot of land on the estate together with the materials to build a house to their own design entirely at his expense. So in 1903 each was able to create his own new home. At the same time Lord Bathurst made Daneway House available as a workshop and showroom. What a vote of confidence in the talents of three budding craftsmen and what a mark of respect for those who create things with their hands.

Ernest Gimson armchair

The country's premier collections of Sapperton Craftsmen furniture, along with the artefacts of other Arts and Crafts Movement artists, are to be found in Cheltenham Museum and at Rodmarton Manor.

---

[1] J Arthur Gibbs records the words to this very old drinking song, adopted by the Gloucestershire Society, founded in 1657 to promote the restoration of Charles II. Its meaning is deliberately impenetrable, involving Dick the treble, John the mean, a wench called Nell and endless references to stwuns (stones). Try to hear it performed by Ken Langsbury, who declaims it with amazing energy in an extreme version of a Gloucestershire accent. He even manages to give the impression of knowing what it is all about!

I Must Go Down To The Sea Again

Since Ted Hughes became Poet Laureate in 1985 the public has rather lost interest in odes written to order by a public versifier but, for more than three centuries, "laureate" has been the greatest honour that can be bestowed on an English poet. In 1930 John Masefield became Laureate and in 1933 he came to live for seven years at Pinbury Park.

Such an honour looked most unlikely 20 years earlier. He started his working life as an apprentice on a windjammer that sailed round Cape Horn. Deciding that a life at sea was not for him, he jumped ship in New York and did spells as a barman, a farm hand and worked in a carpet factory.

His sailing experience influenced the 1902 Salt-Water Ballads which included the well-known "Sea Fever" and "Cargoes". In 1911, though, the long narrative poem, "The Everlasting Mercy", shocked the establishment with its oaths and curses but it certainly pleased the general public: the publishers sold edition after edition. The language seems tame to us today but at the time poems were not expected to contain everyday spoken English. He immediately became the most widely read poet since Kipling and went on writing profusely, poems, plays and novels.

On an American lecture tour in 1916 he had met Florence Lamont, the wife of a New York banker. Over the next 35 years he wrote her more than 2000 letters. Portions of these illustrate his life at Pinbury:

This is certainly a heavenly place, and time slips away fast...

The ghost has not been seen, but a friendly seer says that her influence is good...

The place is as lovely as ever, now that the leaves are off. The jasmine and the violets are out: the berries are scarlet on shrubs and trees, and the storm-cock loudly sings...

...very soon, now, the snowdrops will be in a great mass all over the garden and spring visibly here. Who would not be a Briton? Think what your ancestors so rashly flung away at Boston Harbour.

...we have been busy, clearing moss off walls here. Lately, have taken to clearing ivy also; it is a ruin to walls and to trees, too. So I go around with an axe, a very sharp and nice one, newly bought.

A depression in the garden revealed underground brick and stone work. Masefield speculates on what it could be:

The country folk are of the opinion that it is the secret passage, so often talked of in English country places, by means of which they old nuns went to visit they old monks (never the other way about, which seems odd to me) but perhaps they old monks were a lot less coy, and went on the surface.

Florence died in 1952. Masefield left Pinbury Park because of the noise from the planes at Aston Down. He died in 1967, aged 88.

➤ The church is much larger inside than appears possible from outside. It is dedicated to St Kenelm who allegedly became king of Mercia at the age of seven in 822. A series of bizarre miracles attached to him after his sister arranged his murder. The church was rebuilt by the Atkyns family in Queen Anne style, rather eccentric and very unusual for the Cotswolds. The box pews have elaborately carved ends, rescued from Sapperton Manor, showing naked eastern figures who sit rather uneasily in a church.

➤ The Atkyns chapel contains the effigy of Sir Robert who, as the County's first historian, wrote the "Ancient and Present State of Gloucestershire". He looks a wonderful man, reclining, life size in white marble, holding his book. Two earlier effigies, too gharish for my taste, are of earlier owners of Sapperton Manor, Sir Henry Poole in an ermine cloak and armour, and his wife, Anne, in a full gown and a bodice studded with jewels.

➤ Gimson and the Barnsleys are buried in the churchyard in graves marked with brass inscription plates. These are a common feature of the Cotswolds because the local limestone is too soft for carved lettering. Here are some of the best examples in the Cotswolds, those nearest the church ranging back 300 years.

Take the path to the left of the churchyard, bearing right when it forks. A kissing gate leads into a field. Turn left to follow the hedge. This terraced ground gives no clues that it is the site of the former Sapperton Manor. At the muddy patch by a spring take the well-worn path diagonally downhill to reach a stile leading on to a path across the western portal of the Sapperton canal tunnel. Although the entrance is blocked, the tunnel offers a very satisfying echo.

The towpath takes you past the extremely dilapidated lengthsman's cottage and on beside the former canal through woods to The Daneway Inn. You are passing beside the Daneway Banks nature reserve with buzzards to be seen in February and March and nightingales to listen for in April and May.

Daneway Inn

Canal-side pub.
Built originally to refresh the diggers of the canal tunnel.
At least half a dozen real ales, real cider & its own "Daneway" Bitter.
Scary warning notice about *Unattended Children.*
The Bisley mummers play is performed outside the pub a week before Christmas.

A squeeze stile brings you up to the road. Turn right, cross the bridge and turn immediatey left, signposted Chalford to enter the Golden Valley, a unique Cotswold valley with its own history and identity, quite unlike anything we have seen so far.

Sapperton Manor

Just as fascinating as the sights you'll see on the Cotswolds are some of those you can't see because you're too late and they're long gone. One of these is right here, or it was till 250 years ago, and you're standing in its front garden.

Sapperton Manor stood here for about 100 years, one of the most substantial houses in the County. According to the 1672 Hearth Tax return it had 30 rooms with fireplaces. The house boasted a huge stone front with its three storeys and six bays. In front was a formal layout of lawns and trees with a stone summer-house perched on a high terrace. To the rear, rows of trees marched into the distance. You have to imagine several generations of Pooles and Atkyns, long-established Gloucestershire families, unfolding the drama of their lives in and around the house. Kip's engraving from the 1700s, which you can see in the church, views it from somewhere above the trees[1].

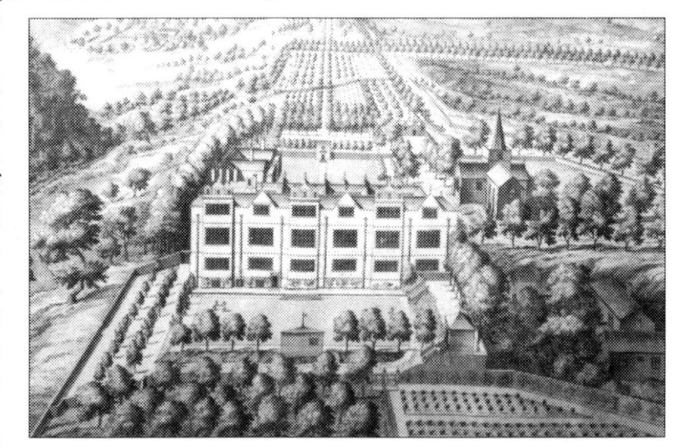

Kip's 18th century aerial view

In 1730, the first Lord Bathurst acquired the house and immediately had it demolished. Some of the woodwork found its way into the Parish Church to provide the fascinating Jacobean carved figures adorning the end of each pew. Much of the stone, though, was carted away to be incorporated into Alfred's Hall, a folly in Lord Bathurst's newly-created Cirencester Park.

Strange to think of the wealth that can cause a 30 room house to be knocked down to provide building materials for a whimsical adornment to a garden.

Daneway House

This is a lovely building that has been altered and extended over 700 years. The oldest parts are the 13th century hall and oratory. In the 16th century a chapel was added together with the "high building", five storeys with a room on each floor connected by a spiral staircase. At one time it was a dower house let for a rent of just one red rose at midsummer.

Between 1901 and 1908 the building was enhanced by Gimson and used as showrooms and workshops by the Sapperton Group.

Since Gimson died in 1919 and the group broke up, the house has been the creative haven for a string of artists - Sir Emery Walker whose Doves Press produced the magnificent five-volume Doves Bible, Oliver Hill, the Queen

[1] Look at the engraving in the church and you will see a house in the background. Presumably it is Pinbury Park but it is hard to reconcile either the buildings or garden layout with what we see today.

Mother's architect and Simon Verity who has sculpture in Canterbury Cathedral. Other occupants have included a painter, a designer, a basket maker, a wool spinner and knitter, all continuing the craft tradition at Sapperton.

From the road or the footpath you can see little more than the roofs of this historic place nestling in a fold of the hillside, just out of sight of the 20th century.

The house can be viewed by appointment at reasonable times between March and October.

Serendipity

Norman Jewson walked into this book Robert Louis Stevenson-fashion, leading a donkey. He was a young architect taking his 1907 summer holiday sketching Cotswold buildings and in these hills he found his vocation.

Near North Cerney he saw a man ploughing with two yoke of oxen and he became entranced with the County. Meeting Gimson and the Barnsleys at Sapperton, he discovered a craft community who wanted, like him, to make and to build, combining their own ideas and skills with those of local craftsmen.

He joined the Sapperton Group as their assistant and disciple, working with them till their deaths in the '20s and continuing in their tradition till the Second World War. Immersing himself in the community, he married Mary Barnsley and lived in the inappropriately-named Batchelor's Court. He is best known for completing the building of Rodmarton Manor, restoring Owlpen Manor and altering Iles's Green, at Far Oakridge, for Sir William Rothenstein. Louise Wright describes a visit to him at Batchelor's Court when she saw a beautiful round-backed child's chair, its back rail supported by carved and painted village characters - shepherd, baker, blacksmith, wheelwright and parson.

Whenever he could, he walked his beloved Cotswolds, describing many of the very long walks in his biographical "By chance I did rove". In the first quarter of the century he enjoyed the luxury of wandering at will, not restricted to rights of way.

This is one of his favourite walks, up the Througham Valley, which you can follow pretty closely on today's footpaths if you use these rough instructions as your guide:

➤ *Start from the Thames and Severn Canal at Red Bridge, the first bridge below Daneway*

➤ *Pass Tunley to a fine old house called Rookwoods*

A long case clock from 1931, designed by Peter Waals, the panels made by Jewson

➤ *Go through meadows to pass a farm called Battledown*[1] *with Juniper Hill on the opposite side*
➤ *Pass the site of The Greys, now only bases of stone gate piers, once a Jacobean house*
➤ *Pass a house called Throughham Slad*
➤ *Pass two more fine houses at Througham*
➤ *From Honeycombe Farm, finish at Wishanger with its three storey porch.*

His walks clearly did him good - he lived to be 92, dying in 1976.

The Sapperton Tunnel

In 1789 when France was erupting in revolution and George III began to go mad, Sapperton became a world record holder: the world's longest canal tunnel was completed to link London with what was then the great sea-port of Bristol. Although conceived 140 years earlier, the Cotswolds had always been too formidable a barrier to cross until the years of "canal mania".

By 1776 the Stroudwater Canal had reached from the Severn up the Frome valley to Stroud. By 1786 the Thames and Severn Canal extended the navigation to the basin at Daneway, the steepness of the valley requiring 28 locks in 36 miles. But, to link Daneway with Coates, the route had to pass through the hill.

The eastern portal at Coates

The 2¼ mile Sapperton tunnel took six years to dig, working simultaneously from both ends. A cord was laid across the hill to mark the route and 25 shafts were dug to allow men and materials to be let down and the waste rock to be got out. The project was accomplished with the simplest of hand tools, gunpowder, muscle-power and candlelight and was dug accurately enough for daylight to be seen from the far end. This ambitious engineering project was very successful despite the original contractor, Charles Jones, being imprisoned for debt after failing to pay his 2-300 navvies. He was described in the court case as *Vain, Shifty & Artful in all his dealings.*

The first coal barges to reach Cirencester were met by thousands of spectators. In Victorian times, civil engineering feats of this kind were greeted with patriotic excitement, firing the popular imagination even if the crowd's interest contained an element of voyeurism, speculating that perhaps the thing wouldn't work, would break down, or would sink. Today, the completion of the Channel Tunnel is greeted with a general indifference. The cheering crowds at Cirencester,

[1] If Jewson means Battledown Farm then you reach it before Rookwoods. I think he means Battlescombe because it makes sense of *with Juniper Hill on the opposite side.*

though, lined the canal banks to applaud the achievement and the novelty of the sight.

The canal never did become the great east-west route that the speculators had envisaged. Its coal traffic amounted to little more than distributing Forest of Dean coal to the upper Thames valley. The cargoes that were carried were varied but hard for us to visualise as we have become unfamiliar with the language of their packaging:

➤ sugar	in lumps, bags and loaves
➤ hops	in bags and pockets
➤ butter	in firkins
➤ oil	in runlets, hogsheads, puncheons and pipes

The tunnel itself was a constant problem with frequent leaks and roof collapses. The boatmen also had to contend with its lack of a towpath. While donkeys could bring the barges as far as Daneway, the boatmen had to "leg" for five hours, lying on the deck on their backs "walking" along the tunnel roof[1]. Not surprisingly, this produced a lumbar complaint known as "lighterman's bottom".

When the Great Western Railway was completed between Swindon and Cheltenham in 1845, the canal's short life was doomed. It limped on till 1933 and the Stroudwater Canal was not finally abandoned till 1952.

The restored Blunder Lock on the Stroudwater Canal, at Eastington

Both canals have deteriorated since then but a three mile stretch is once again navigable; two locks at Eastington are fully operational after a gap of 40 years and work has begun on 20 more. Both tunnel portals have been restored and the western portal is once again complete with stone castellations. At Bondsmill a new lifting bridge has been installed and at Wallbridge in Stroud, a section is being renovated to make it suitable for disabled anglers. An engineering survey of the tunnel itself has been commissioned to establish just what problems need to be overcome in addition to the known collapse of part of the roof.

[1] Bob Simpson, who has studied and explored the derelict Oxenhall Tunnel on the Hereford and Gloucester Canal, thinks this is apocryphal. He believes the canal men "walked" along the tunnel side - which sounds equally uncomfortable.

This restoration work has been achieved over the last 25 years by the Cotswold Canals Trust which has gained several hundred thousand pounds of Government grant to supplement its voluntary efforts. This demonstrates great faith in the Trust's ambition to raise the estimated £35 million needed to restore the whole 36 miles for recreational use by the year 2010.

The western portal, now restored

The task is made more difficult because parts of the canal have been filled and some stretches have been built on. The biggest problems will be forging a way across the A38, the M5 motorway and the Gloucester-Bristol railway line, which were built with no thought for any future life for the canal.

If the volunteer restorers, who refer to themselves as "navvies", can succeed, we might once again see narrow boats plying across England between the Thames and the Severn. I doubt, though, that any of these modern navigators will want to "leg" through the Sapperton tunnel.

The little roads are quaint roads
That wander where they will,
They wind their arms round all the farms
And flirt with every hill.
But the high road is my road
And goes where I would go,
Its way it wends as man intends,
For it was fashioned so.

JH

11 Daneway to Avening

7½ miles

Only the wanderer
Knows England's graces
Or can anew see clear
Familiar faces

IG

Daneway to Avening

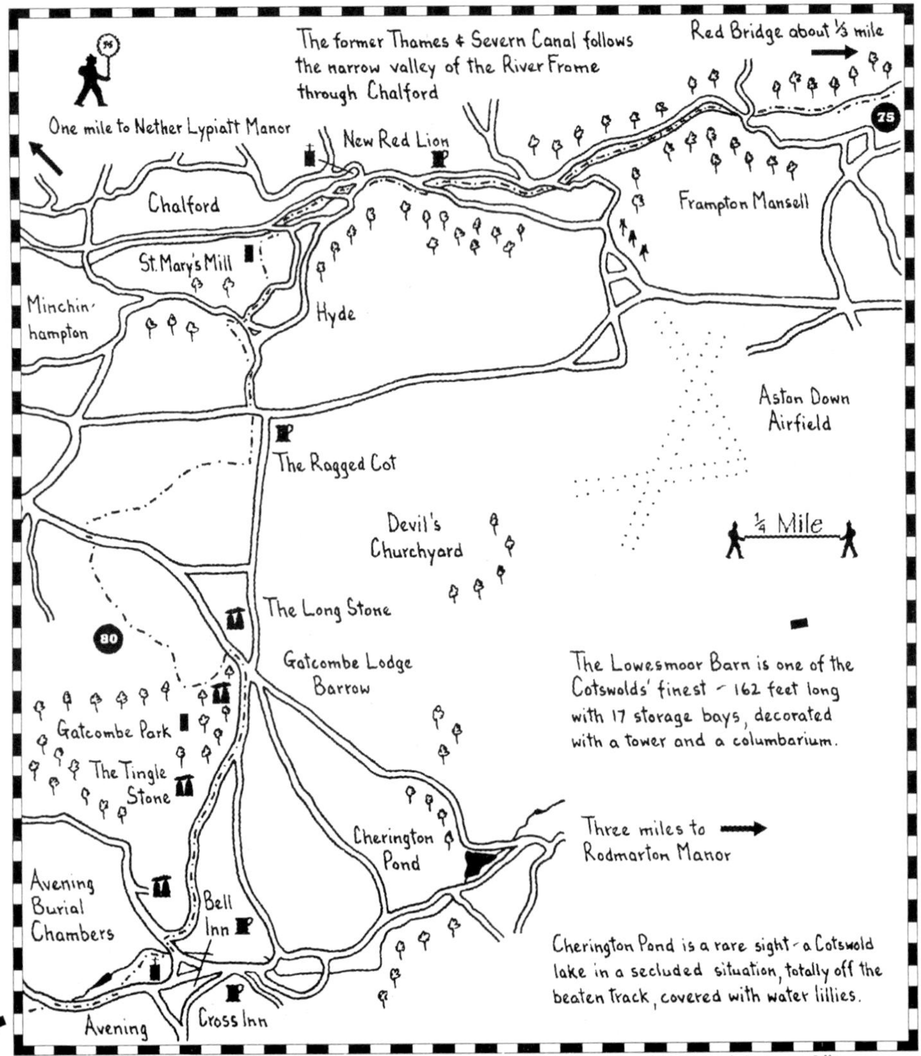

The route from the Daneway Inn along the canal to St Mary's Lock at Chalford does not need detailed route instructions because it follows the line of the Thames and Severn Canal. There are, though, many points of interest along the way so the text for this section is in the form of an itinerary. The central column shows the locks and bridges that lie along the canal route. Features are shown either to the left or right. Be sure to read **up** the pages, from A to B, B to C and then C to D.

B

The house with the sculptures was formerly the Oak Inn though it is hard to "match" with contemporary photos.	**Puck Mill Upper Lock -** cross here.	
The former lengthsman's cottage has a private footbridge. A lengthsman was responsible for about 5 miles of canal.	**Whitehall Lower Lock**	The farm track passing over the bridge is the start of Jewson's walk up the Upper Througham valley. He calls it Red Bridge.
The canal was abandoned eastwards from here in 1927.	**Whitehall Bridge -** datestone 1784.	
	Whitehall Upper Lock	
	Bathurst's Meadow Lock	
The side ponds were added in the 1820s to try to improve the canal's water supply.	**Lower Sickeridge Wood Lock -** footbridge over canal.	The reserves now have about 150 dormouse nest boxes, information going to a national dormouse survey.
The water meadows and silted canal form the Sapperton Valley Nature Reserve. Moorhen, mallard and grey wagtail breed here; herons, kingfishers and fallow deer visit.	**Middle Sickeridge Wood Lock**	Siccaridge Wood Nature Reserve runs alongside the canal as far as Whitehall Bridge. It is noted for lily-of-the-valley, bird's nest orchids and "Roman" snails!
	Upper Sickeridge Wood Lock	
Daneway Basin was used for turning and for waiting to pass through the tunnel.	**Daneway Basin Lock**	

A

C

Bell Lock -
cross the road & take the path beneath the Elbesee Products sign.

Bliss' Mills, now the Chalford Trading Estate, was converted in 1856 to making walking sticks. By the 1870s 2000 people in the area worked in this industry using local beech, birch, maple, olive, cherry and even orange and gorse woods.
Above, in the trees, was the site of Chalford station.

The Arnolds Designs building was used as a workshop by Peter Waals who had been foreman to Gimson & the Barnsleys. From 1920 to his death in 1937 he continued working in their tradition. His furniture for Queen Mary's dolls' house can be seen at Windsor.

Red Lion Lock & Clowes Bridge

At last a pub that still exists! A free house with four regular ales, a guest beer and a range of real ciders.

Valley Lock

The house on the bridge was known as the Clothiers Inn & then the Valley Inn - look for the feint lettering on the wall.

Approaching Chalford with its strikingly alpine appearance with houses built on the steep hillside. Some houses' back doors are three storeys higher than their front doors! Some old folk recall bread being delivered by donkeys with panniers.

Baker's Mill Lower or Boulting's Lock

The brick building was the Chalford Water Works, built in the 1880s. The coal for the steam pumps was brought by canal.

Approaching the site of Ashmead's silk mill, demolished in 1903. Look out for a milepost.

Baker's Mill Upper Lock

Baker's or Twissell's Mill was originally for cloth and later for corn.

This reservoir holding 3¼ million gallons of water obliterated the former mill pond in a late attempt to improve the water supply.

Puck Mill Lower Lock

The pound between the Puck Mill locks was a constant problem. It was "re-puddled" with clay in 1907 to try to prevent leaking water.
Frampton Mansell rail viaduct comes in view.

Notice the stone wall being rebuilt by the Cotswold Canal Trust. Formed in 1972, it aims to restore the entire length of this and the Stroudwater Canal.

B

D

St Mary's Mill produced cloth, then paper from 1846-51; for 30 years it was a flock mill then produced walking sticks and umbrella stems, employing 100. The Phoenix Stick Co still uses two floors.

After passing through
a subway,
St Mary's Lock

Iles's Mill, gutted by fire in 1913, is now a private house.

Iles's Mill Lock
with remnants of lock gates.

The cottages were formerly Clayfield's Mill.

Ballinger's Lock
beneath three garages!

Chalford Wharf has one of five round lengthsman's houses with three floors; the ground floor doubled as stable & kitchen.
Belvedere Mill made Napoleonic War uniforms.
15th century Chalford Place was the Company's Arms Inn (yes, another), the company in question being the East India Company.

Site of
Chalford Chapel Lock
by Noah's Ark.
Milestone plate built into
culvert arch.

Approaching Christ Church, 1724, with a font cover by Jewson & lectum by Peter Waals.

A foundry here makes life-size bronze statues of horses & elephants. One replica of a Namibian bull elephant recently completed weighed 4½ tons and stood 12 feet high.

C

The Flower of Gloster

It's very unlikely you've heard of E Temple Thurston. It's not the address of some religious cult but the name of a writer. Between 1895 and 1933 he published some 30 novels, two books of poems and 11 plays, with bizarre titles such as "The Wonderful World Of Reality", "A Hank Of Hair" and, my favourite title, "Mr Bottleby Does Something".

If he is remembered at all today it is for "The Flower Of Gloster" which purports to be the account of a canal boat journey he undertook, accompanied by one, Eynsham Harry, in 1911.

Thurston describes setting off from Oxford, northwards on the Oxford Canal towards Stratford. He then abandons the boat and walks to Tewkesbury, forgetting, incidentally, to describe anything of the 30 or so miles down the Severn and up the Stroudwater Canal to Stroud. He does, though, describe the journey up the Golden Valley and four hours of legging through the Sapperton Tunnel, although, somehow, he manages to both enter and exit at the western end!

Thurston seems to have pieced together first-hand details from visiting the Oxford Canal, with bits and bobs gathered from other canal walks he took from various railway stations, to concoct a sugary adventure story. Historians and canal enthusiasts such as Tom Rolt and David Viner have found many inconsistencies in the alleged account but it does contain this wonderful exchange between the writer and the probably fictitious Harry who has just cooked their meal while moored a little above Chalford:

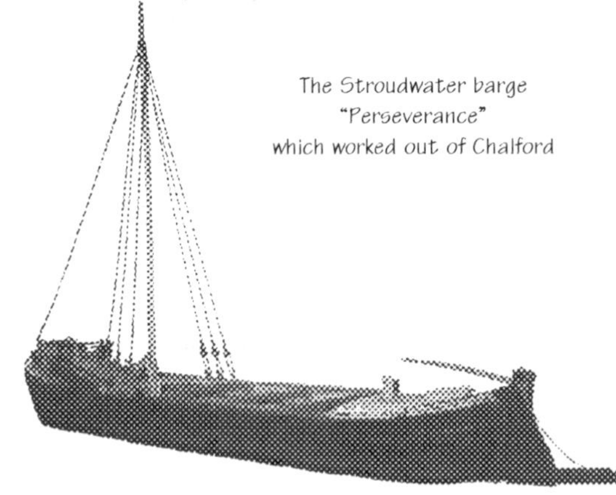

The Stroudwater barge "Perseverance" which worked out of Chalford

I returned silently to the barge; as silently sat down to my mid-day meal. Presently I became conscious of the fact that Eynsham Harry was watching me while I eat.

"What is it?" I asked.

"I be waiting for you to taste that dish, sur," said he.

It was a dish of green vegetable, looking as much like spinach as anything else. I thought it was spinach.

'Where did you get it" I inquired.

"Would you be so good as to just taste it, sur" he repeated.

I obeyed, looking up at him as I did so with that pensive expression which I am sure all professional tasters must adopt. You must put on an expression when you specialise. It is part of your uniform, whether it be in the tea factory, the pulpit, or the house of parliament. All specialists are actors.

"Tastes like asparagus," said I. "Where did you get it from?"

Still he would not tell me.

"You like it, sur?" he persisted.

I tried another mouthful.

"It's better than asparagus," said I.

"Put a little pepper wi' it, sur."

I put a little pepper and tasted again.

"By Jove," said I, "it's damned good! Where did you get it?"

He pointed to a line of hedge half-way up the hill.

"There be hops growing up on that hedge, sur," said he; "these that you're eating be the young shoots, cut off about six inches from the top and boiled the same as other greens. In the month of May we takes 'en whenever we can. The wilder the better."

"I'll remember that,"

said I; and I have, but can find no hedges in London where the wild hop-vine grows. I shall think of it, however, when next May-time comes. I shall surely taste that dish again.

Stroudwater Reds and Uley Blues

The Cotswolds' wealth, for several hundred years up to the close of the 18th century, was based not so much on breeding sheep for their wool, but on turning that wool into a superfine, high quality broadcloth. It was the export of broadcloth that financed the building of many of the County's mansions and churches, and it was weavers' cottages built with a room large enough to accommodate the loom, that crammed the steep hillsides of Chalford or Painswick.

A broadcloth was five feet wide and about 27 yards long, taking a handloom weaver between two and three weeks working 14 hours a day to weave. When complete he took it to the mill and collected the wool for the next.

In Elizabethan times the cloth was sold "white", that is undyed, but by the 17th century the purity of the spring water of the south Cotswold valleys was recognised as ideal for the dyeing process.

The scarlet uniforms of the Guards and the East India Company were made in the Stroud valleys as early as the 15th century; Uley became famous for blue cloth - quite the thing for the Squire to wear to church on a Sunday; olive or dun coloured broadcloths were favoured by coachmen while the "Red Coat" and "Blue Coat" Charity Schools took their names from the children's coloured cloaks.

Uniform of the 28th Regiment of Foot - the North Gloucestershire, about 1815

Today we think nothing of this as synthetic dyes are so prevalent, but at that time all dyes had to come from the natural world. So what were the sources of the colours? The dyers' ingenuity made use of bark, fungi, insects, seaweeds, lichens and even shellfish but in the Cotswolds the main sources were local plants:

➤ **Woad,** beloved of Ancient Britons, was grown as an important base for blues and blacks. Dozens of acres in the Cotswolds were planted with this member of the cabbage family which grows up to three feet high, producing yellow flowers and purple fruits. The useful part is the slender leaf, harvested three times each year, which was sun-dried, ground to a paste and formed into balls to dry. Two months later the balls were broken up, mixed with limewater, urine and wood ash before undergoing a complex, two-week, foul-smelling fermentation to bring out the inky colour.

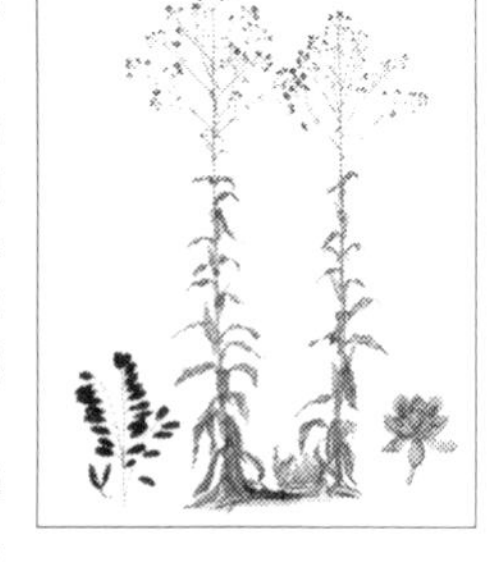
The woad plant

Woad was particularly versatile because, mixed with other dyes, it could produce a range across all the blues, purple, green, brown and black.

A field called Woad Range near Saltford had a building where the pulp from the vats was formed into balls and a woad mill stood on the Eye Brook near Moreton-in-Marsh. Once indigo was introduced from the East, woad fell out of use and has not been grown on the Cotswolds for 100 years[1]. Ironically, natural indigo, which was the original dye for Levi jeans, has now all but disappeared from use.

Rolling woad leaves on a "balling horse"

In the 19th century, woad turned the marl of Tewkesbury's Mythe Cliff on the River Severn from red to golden in late May. This was Britain's last natural stand of woad but in the last couple of years the flowers there have failed for the first time in living memory.

➤ **Weld,** also known as **Dyer's Rocket** or **Wild Mignonette**, was said to produce the best natural yellow. It grows on poor soils as a weed and was used for various yellows, the exact shade varied by adding alum. The flower spikes mixed with either woad or indigo produced Saxon and Lincoln Greens.

➤ **Woodwaxen,** also known as **Dyer's Broom** and **Dyer's Greenwood,** grew wild on the clay areas of the Cotswolds and was cultivated in Herefordshire. It was used to prepare woollen cloths for receiving other dyes, as a base for a range of greens, or on its own for a dull yellow.

[1] One small factory in Lincolnshire continued producing woad dye for making Metropolitan Police uniforms up until 1932.

> **Madder** roots, grown in clamps like potatoes, yielded a red dye when crushed and ground, which could be treated in a variety of ways to produce a colour range from brown to purple. This was the base of traditional "hunting pink". From the same family, **Lady's Bedstraw** roots provided the red used for colouring Gloucester cheeses.

Royal Gloucestershire Hussar of about 1890

> **Alder** bark, rich in tannin, produced a good black when mixed with iron.

A hint of the richness of colours available is provided by the evocative list in a dyeing book found at King's Stanley: it includes Rich French Grey, Pompodore Mixed, Plumb Crimson and Eye White.

The sheer amount of work needed to extract these dyes meant that when cheaper imported substitutes, and later, synthetics became available, they quickly replaced the local sources. Local plant dyes, though, are still preferred today by some handloom weavers who have developed the craft from its rather sturdy but uninspiring traditions to new levels of quality and design. The Cotswold Natural Dyers at Filkins sell hand-dyed wools, producing a range of some 40 colours from the plants mentioned and from other natural sources such as onions, nettles and walnut, which gives a range from coffee to deepest black.

Curiously, these natural dye plants may once again have their day on the Cotswold scene: the Long Ashton Research Institute in the South Wolds near Bath is experimenting with woad, weld and madder, updating and simplifying the processing, to see if they could become viable British farm crops for set-aside land, stemming the enormous world-wide demands for petroleum-based synthetic colourings.

Friar Bacon's Study

It seems likely that Roger Bacon was born at St Mary's Mills in 1214[1] and until the middle of the last century a room in a house there was known as Friar Bacon's study. Not exactly a household name nowadays, he was better known to the Elizabethans, familiar with Robert Greene's play, "Friar Bacon and Friar Bungay". He deserves to be better known to us today as the forefather of modern scientific thinking, in fact the originator of our "scientific method" based on experimental research.

At Oxford, Bacon studied Latin and Greek and translations of Arabic mathematical writings which were just becoming available in the West. He lectured at the University in Paris where he studied optics and astronomy, experimented with magnifying lenses and invented the magic lantern. Working from the reports of travellers to China, he was the first western writer to discover the correct proportions of charcoal, saltpetre and sulphur for making gunpowder.

[1] The rival claimant as Bacon's birthplace is Ilchester in Somerset.

Realising the terrible consequences if his recipe got into the wrong hands, he coded it in his writings by recording it as a Latin anagram.

In 1251 a career change led him to become a Friar of the Franciscan Order, an unhappy arrangement because the head of the Order banned him from publishing and experimenting for many years and had him virtually imprisoned in Paris. He was freed after ten years at the request of Pope Clement IV who was anxious to learn the "true knowledge" Bacon seemed to have acquired. How had he displeased the authorities to such an extent?

To be honest, this monk is the Venerable Bede, taken from Chalford Parish church

He believed that studying many of the writers revered by the Church at the time, such as Aristotle and St Thomas Aquinas, was a waste of time. He pointed out the foolishness of pinning contemporary beliefs on the mere speculations of the ancient writers. Instead, he insisted that the secrets of nature could only be based on observation and he defined the three-stage scientific method - suggesting a hypothesis, testing it and only then reaching conclusions. This was, of course, anathema to the Church so he was treated as a heretic. As the most learned man of his age, Church suspicions were easily aroused and fuelled by his reputation as an alchemist.

It was to be another 300 years before his scientific method was generally accepted, promoted by his namesake Francis Bacon. As a thinker he was well ahead of his time; as a visionary he was quite remarkable, predicting in the middle of the 13th century two methods of manned flight:

Pub sign in Oxford

...an engine for flying and of moving in chariots without animals at an incomparable velocity...flying machines can be made, and a man sitting in the middle revolving an engine by which skilfully made wings beat the air much after the fashion of a bird's flight.

A large hollow globe...filled with ethereal air...would float on the atmosphere as a ship on water.

Astonishingly, he made these predictions 300 years before even Leonardo da Vinci began to imagine and sketch his visionary flying machines.

Leave the canal at St Mary's Lock by climbing the steps. A small signal box on the railway confirms the correct lock. Turn left through a gate with Y↑. Cross the yard of St Mary's Mill to a flight of stone steps with a Y↑ on a tree. A short path leads to a stile into a field. Keep beside the hedge to climb the steep grassy field to reach another stile at a very muddy spot beside a spring. A path through trees leads to a gap into a lane. Turn right to follow the steeply winding lane which becomes a road leading into the hamlet of **Hyde**.

At the house with the postbox in its wall, turn right passing under the magnificent copper beech in front of the gates of Hyde Grange. Cross the road, pass the National Trust sign and follow the track up to a stone stile where three footpaths meet. Cross the stile but do not follow any of the directions indicated. Instead, turn sharp left to follow the wall to the next stile. Don't miss the last magnificent views back across the Golden Valley.

From the stile, cross the field aiming about 50 yards to the right of the red-tiled roof. Crossing two wooden stiles, continue between the fences to reach a gated stile on to the road. Turn right, passing Hyde Riding Centre and continue 250 yards to the main road. Notice in the wall of the house on the right, the blocked-up ticket window of a toll house.

Cross the main road and the stone step stile beside Burnt Ash Farm. Follow the lane and, where it opens out, take the stone stile left opposite the caravan. The right of way takes you to the diagonal corner of the field but it is simpler to turn right, keeping to the wall till the end of the field. Turn right over the stone stile, following the wall to the next stile.

Ragged Cot

16th century Free House.
At least five real ales including Uley's Old Spot.
The pub has the ghost of a former landlord's wife, killed in 1760. The "chambermaid" who recently disturbed guests at five in the morning was not one of the staff!
Log fires and an excellent menu.

Devil's Churchyard

Though marked on the Ordnance Survey map, what once stood here is mostly speculation as the large stones were moved away at the insistence of a vicar of Minchinhampton early in the 19th century. They may have formed a stone circle. Two of them have found their way to the garden of Lammas House. Here they have been used to form a footbridge over a hollow way that leads to the Minchinhampton spring. The gardens open a few days each year.

The story is told of a man who went nutting here in the lane leading to the "churchyard". He reached out for a bunch of nuts saying *Here goes one!* He walked on, saw another and as he picked it said *Here goes two!* Before he could pick any more, a huge black hand shot out of the hedge and grabbed him, saying *Here goes three!* He died from shock and is said to be buried in the Devil's Churchyard.

Contd: page 157

The Dangers of Travel

Chalford Bottom,
25th July 1763:

The Gloucester Journal had published a description of a highwayman, with his horse, who had shot a man on the Bath Road three weeks before. A group of local citizens, believing they recognised the man, seized him and took him to the local Justice who found him to be carrying two pistols.
He was locked up in the George at Bisley while a man robbed that morning on the road near Cirencester was summoned to identify him.
The identification took place while the man ate his prison supper. When asked if he would swear to the identification, the arrested man intervened saying *Why then, I might as well die first as last* and cut his own throat *in a shocking manner.* He lived on for some days.

Near the Ragged Cot Inn, Hyde
8th July 1777:

...two lusty footpads armed with horse pistols attacked Mr William Capel in a chaise and robbed him of about 8 guineas, a silver watch, a steel-mounted gun. One of the fellows had on a light coloured frock (coat), believed to be Russia drab, very dirty; the dress of the other...thought to be a darker colour. 20 guineas reward.

& on 30th March 1778:

On Friday last Thomas Smart and Samuel Warren, for robbing Mr Capell (sic) on the highway, were executed.

Extracts from the **Gloucester Journal**

Aston Down Airfield

During the Second World War the Cotswold skies bristled with warplanes - bombers, fighters and trainers based at 18 operational airfields in Gloucestershire or on its borders. The County was far enough away from the Channel to give a margin of safety yet within effective striking distance of occupied Europe.

Many of the airfields have vanished but one that remains and retains its massive hangars is Aston Down, known during the First World War as Minchinhampton airfield.

Aston Down played an important role throughout the war years but that role kept changing as different operating units were based here. In the first year of the war the most frequent planes to be seen were Harvards, Gladiators and Blenheims of Fighter Command. By 1940, Spitfire and Hurricane pilots were trained here, each for a few brief weeks before being sent to the front. Spitfires might now seem the epitome of wartime glamour but at the time, flying one was a pretty hazardous way to serve your country.

Another role was in helping our allies. In 1940, pilots of the Royal Yugoslav Airforce were being trained to fly Bristol-built Blenheims. Later in the war you could have seen Chinese airmen learning to handle Spitfires and Americans flying Mustangs and Typhoons and the less-well-remembered Martinets and Masters. At times it was the base for Anson flying ambulances and rocket-firing Hurricanes.

In 1941, though, Aston Down became a base for the ATA, the Air Transport Auxiliary, otherwise fondly known as the "Ancient and Tattered Airmen". Formed in 1939, this was a pool of civilian pilots who originally flew light aircraft to ferry VIPs and deliver urgent mail. Their role developed into ferrying planes and pilots around the country to the front-line squadrons so that the younger, fully trained pilots could be used for operational flights.

Ancient and tattered airmen?

Some of these ATA pilots were decidedly neither ancient nor tattered: they were young women, experienced as civilian pilots, now proudly wearing their dark blue service uniforms with the "wings" emblem. Their role was to deliver new craft from the factory, take damaged planes for repair or breaking-up and return others to their operational units. At first, because of a degree of prejudice amongst the male ATA, the women flew only non-operational planes. By 1941, though, the desperate shortage of male pilots enabled them to fly aircraft destined for the front line.

Each day could involve a bewildering sequence, flying up to four different planes to a variety of destinations around the UK. They had learned, in less than a year, to fly as many as a hundred and thirty different makes and models of plane but the highlight for all of them was to fly a Spitfire. The risks of flying these wood-and-fabric planes were considerable with no radio or radar and sometimes not even a cockpit cover - just a map and compass, simple instrument panel and excellent eye-sight!

About a hundred women flew with the ATA, mostly British with a few Americans, French, Poles and Anzacs. Among their number was Amy Johnson, the first woman to fly solo to Australia, who died ironically on an ATA mission over the Thames estuary. A few progressed to flying the largest of the four-engined bombers such as the Blenheims and some flew the first jet-engined plane, the Meteor, produced by the Gloster Aircraft Company.

Probably their most difficult time was during the Battle of Britain, flying replacement fighters to the airfields of southern England under constant threat of day-light attack from the Luftwaffe. By 1944, as the Allies moved into Europe, the ATA followed, eventually ferrying some 300,000 planes.

Finding a way to return to base after delivering a plane could be a problem. Peggy Lucas once found herself needing to return from Cornwall and was offered, without the correct papers, a Spitfire which was meant to be returned to Aston Down. She flew it here only to be told that the authorities would not receive it.

...a pretty hazardous way to serve your country.
A Spitfire IIB at Aston Down in January 1943

Having crashed in France six months before, it no longer officially existed. Eventually, she found an airfield in Hampshire prepared to take it.

The explanation of the puzzle was that this "ghost" plane had been stolen from a German-held airfield by a British pilot stranded in occupied France and then dumped in Cornwall after his escape across the Channel.

The airfield saw its share of drama and bravery. In 1941 a Miles Master burst into flames on landing, trapping the pilot in his cockpit. Leading Aircraftsman Payne eventually released him, earning the George Cross.

It enjoyed, too, its share of pranks. In 1943 three pilots were reduced to the ranks after flying their planes under the Severn railway bridge. Perhaps the most bizarre aspect of Aston Down's war was the use made of all the airfield's grass: by 1942 it had built up a flock of 600 sheep.

After the war ended, planes were brought back to Aston Down from all over the world. At one stage more than 1000 were stored here and for £25 you could have acquired a Spitfire of your own[1]. If you had restored it to working order it would sell today for about £75,000. The airfield was officially closed in 1960 and it is now the home of the Cotswold Gliding Club.

Try if you can to experience the memorable sight and sound of a Spitfire in flight. There are 27 still flying in Britain, 16 of which flew together at the 60th anniversary celebrations at Duxford. You may see one at the local air displays at Fairford or Staverton.

---

[1] Some of these crashed planes were melted down to make panels for more than 100 "prefab" bungalows, known to their residents as "B2s", and built in the late 1940s around Stroud to help overcome the post-war housing shortage. Now badly corroded and with leaky windows, they are to be demolished. English Heritage is to save one of these unique homes and preserve it in the National Housing Museum.

Aim a little left for a sleeper with a Y↑ marking yet another stone stile.

Take the clear path through the crops, through a wide gap in the hedge and on across the next field to a stone post with Y↑. Take the narrow gap through the hedge and over the stile. Keep left of the wall till you reach a metal gate. Then cross the field diagonally to find a stone step stile with Y↑. Aim then for a wooden stile to the right of the dutch barn and cross another stile with Y↑ to lead on to the access lane to Tobacconist Farm.

Follow this to a metalled road, turn left and in 100 yards you reach the main road. Turn left on to Tetbury Street which leads to the evocatively named Woefuldane Bottom. Before you begin to picture this sad Scandinavian, remember that in the Cotswolds the word "dane" comes from dene, meaning valley.

Just past the cattle grid turn right off the road on to the footpath. When the lane turns left to some stables continue on the path. A stile brings you out into a field. Follow the path down gently left to the valley bottom. Pause at the end of the farm's garden to admire the feature created around a spring.

Cross the well-chewed wooden stile to head up the other side. The path becomes a stony track leading up to a stile and gate to a lane. Follow this for nearly ½ mile to reach Gatcombe Farm. Don't be too surprised to see a uniformed policeman patrolling, apparently in the middle of nowhere. Turn left to follow the farm access road out to the Minchinhampton-Avening road. Turn right.

Gatcombe Lodge Barrow

This barrow is of the Cotswold type, similar to Belas Knap, with a false doorway between stone horns and with thin stone walling surrounding the mound. First to explore it was a poor woman called Molly Dreamer who dug it in vain for treasure.

Later in the 19th century a burial chamber was discovered formed by six huge stones inside which was a crouched skeleton. There may be a second chamber just west of the barrow beneath a large stone slab.

The Long Stone

This is the best-known of Gloucestershire's standing stones, comprising two stones in the corner of a field. One stands upright, seven foot nine inches high and 18 inches thick, pierced by two large holes; the other has been incorporated into a stone wall as a stile. They lie 34 feet apart so might well be the remnants of a long barrow. Three stories are told about the stone:

- Children with rickets were passed through the holes in the hope of curing them
- At the stroke of 12 midnight, the Long Stone runs around the field or alternatively,
- The stone visits the spring at Minchinhampton to drink at 12 midnight on Christmas Eve. But if you should try to steal the crock of gold hidden at its base, the Long Stone will return to crush you.

Contd: page 159

Gatcombe Park

Gatcombe Park was bought by the Queen as a home for Princess Anne and Captain Mark Phillips in 1976. The house was built 200 years earlier for Edward Sheppard of Uley, one of the most prosperous of the cloth manufacturers who produced many of the "Uley blues".

The scale of his enterprise is illustrated by the fate of his son, Philip. In 1812 the business became bankrupt. More than 1000 people lost their jobs and Philip escaped his creditors by fleeing to Dunkerque. He sold the house to David Ricardo MP who will be known to any student of economics as one of the earliest writers of economic theory.

The house remained in the Ricardo family almost up to the Second World War when an offer of £22,500 was made to buy it on behalf of the Gloucester Lunatic Asylum. It passed instead into the hands of the politician, RA Butler.

Gatcombe Park has been described as *a well-proportioned and spacious mansion*. It has a very large conservatory and, of course, is well endowed with stables.

Appropriately, there is a ghost - a huge black dog known as The Hound of Odin.

De tour

Nether Lypiatt Manor

If you'd like to see the complete trio of Cotswolds Royal Residences, then detour to Nether Lypiatt Manor, home since 1980 of the Prince and Princess Michael of Kent. It lies near the Brimscombe end of the Toadsmoor Valley that runs down from Bisley (and makes a lovely walk) in a secluded area of old farms and manors.

The house stands behind formidable tall wrought-iron gates. They were commissioned in 1717 by Judge Charles Coxe, a Gloucester MP, who entirely rebuilt the original 13th century manor. The result is tall and thin: there is a cellar floor, an above-ground "basement", a floor for living rooms, a bedroom floor, all of which is topped with an attic. Sir Sacheverell Sitwell said *...no house could compose so beautifully for a glass transparency.*

Nether Lypiatt Manor

The house has the ghost of a blacksmith who rides his white horse through the gates at midnight each 25th January. Coxe tried the blacksmith for sheep stealing and instead of a death sentence offered the man a reprieve in return for making gates for the house. The gates were made in the stipulated fortnight but the judge reneged on the deal and put him to death. In the woods below the splendid formal gardens is a stone obelisk in memory of Judge Coxe's horse, Wag, who lived to the age of 42.

You now have ½ mile of road to skirt Gatcombe Park. Pass the lodge at the start of the drive to the house and at a grassy triangle keep right. Another 400 yards brings you to Steps Lane (unmarked) on the right which will lead you the mile into Avening.
As you walk notice:

The Tinglestone

This slab of oolite stands six feet high at the end of the long barrow which is well preserved in a grove of beech trees. Legend has it that at the stroke of 12 midnight the Tinglestone...behaves just like the Long Stone!

➤ just before the second barn, glimpses of Gatcombe Park nestling at the head of the valley. The view of the house, which is long and low, improves each time you glance back

➤ Steps Lane is criss-crossed with jumps designed by Captain Mark Phillips to intimidate the world's best riders in the Gatcombe Park Horse Trials in mid August. The hilly parkland is ideal for posing all sorts of technical problems for both horse and rider. They look formidable obstacles to a mere pedestrian.
Captain Phillips farms 1000 acres adjacent to the estate where the Princess Royal still lives and he now coaches the American riding team

➤ after Steps Barn the lane becomes sunken as it drops down towards the village of **Avening**.

The lane becomes a road and when it forks, go right and cross the road, heading for Avening church.

➤ The church has a small museum. It includes a model of the tombs unearthed from the field called the Norn, just above Nag's Head hamlet, and models of the church itself in various stages of its development - Norman, Early English, Decorated, Perpendicular and Modern.

➤ Avening celebrates Pig's Face Sunday on the first Sunday after 14th September. This bizarre ceremony may commemorate the killing of a wild boar that had been terrorising the area in the 18th century. A brawn made from pig cheeks, together with apple dumplings, were carried up to sustain the ringers in the belfry. Today, the feast has evolved into a pig-roast and a model pig-making competition for the children!

Cross Inn

A pleasant village Wadworths pub, just off our route. Old village photos in the bar include the pub in its Stroud Brewery days. The Stroud Brewery owned about 100 pubs in the Cotswolds and Forest of Dean but ceased production in 1957 when Whitbread took over.

Bell Inn

Marstons, Wickwar, Bob & Uley beers. Stone-built pub which holds a beer festival each Easter and August bank holiday. An attractive pictorial map of the Cotswolds illustrates all of our route.

Avening Burial Chambers

Avening has a curiosity in the form of burial chambers set into the hillside. They were probably taken from the long barrow at Nag's Head and moved here in 1806 by the then Rector who had excavated the barrow finding 11 skeletons. One chamber has an odd porthole entrance made by cutting semi-circles in adjacent upright stones large enough to pass a body through. This entrance is unique in England.
Dyer describes three chambers but I can only find two, beside the road leading to Old Quarries, a home run by the Home Farm Trust. The overriding impression is of their very small scale for housing so many bodies, the largest dimension of a stone being little more than six feet.

The sculptor, William Simmonds, made this theatre and its lovingly detailed puppets for the children at Rodmarton. In the 1920s and '30s he toured the country performing playlets he had written based on a mixture of folk stories and his own imagination. His wife Eve made the costumes and often played a musical accompaniment to the story.

The Last Great Country House

Rodmarton Manor is a truly remarkable 20th century monument and it may never be possible to bring together again in Britain the money, the materials and the craftsmanship that created it.

Built for a City banker, the Honorable Claud Biddulph, the building work spanned 1909-29, designed and supervised till his death in '26 by Ernest Barnsley. His brother Sidney, and then Norman Jewson, completed the enormous project. The scale of the house is huge. Biddulph intended to spend £5000 each year for a number of years but, like Topsy, the undertaking grew. It began with the kitchen court at the east end and kept extending in a westward curve, slowed a little during the war, and ended in a chapel topped with balconies fit for a Romeo and Juliet production, at the west end 20 years later. Despite the long facade and the reputed 365 windows, Rodmarton is just one room and a corridor deep.

Barnsley's design is based on Cotswold vernacular just a little romanticised with curious chimney stacks and lead drainpipes decorated with animal motifs. The techniques used are traditional and carried out to a very high standard of craftsmanship. The attention to detail encompasses not just the Cotswold stone of the house but also the furniture, fabrics, and fittings and the landscaped gardens.

"Juliet's" balcony

The stone and slates were quarried on the estate, transported by farm cart and cut and laid by local masons; the timber was felled in the estate woods, much of it by use of a double-handled saw over a traditional saw-pit; chair legs were shaped on a lathe powered by the estate's own stream!

Most of the furniture was specially made by the Sapperton Craftsmen while the estate workers provided most of the labour. The local blacksmith made all the door and window fittings and a local man laid out the gardens. The Rodmarton Women's Guild made appliqué curtains for the chapel and wall-hangings based on themes such as Archery and The Village Green to designs by Hilda Sexton, born in Minchinhampton. Alfred and Louise Powell from nearby Tarlton hand painted much of the pottery, a service they normally provided for Wedgwood.

The involvement of the local community was so complete that while the building work progressed, the drawing room was used to hold cabinet-making classes.

The interiors are simple with white walls, oak doors and exposed beams but the textiles and furnishings give it surprising colour and richness. The exterior design ensures that the house looks timeless. The gardens, set out in "rooms" as at Hidcote, are separated by walls and hedges and rather narrow paths. The oldest and most formal are near the house and all were developed extensively by Mary Biddulph after the neglect of the war years.

Just a selection of Rodmarton's 365 windows!

The "rooms" include an enchanting "Troughery" which mixes topiary with alpine-planted troughs, many raised on staddle stones, and the "Long Garden" focusing on Barnsley's delightful clematis-clad stone summerhouse. The garden is still evolving: part of a former tennis court is now a splendid Rockery with a splendid size of rock.

This masterpiece was Ernest Barnsley's greatest achievement, bringing together local materials and skills and is a wonderful monument to the impact of the Arts and Crafts Movement. In "The Spirit of the Cotswolds", Susan Hill describes her year-long quest to identify the atmosphere that makes the Cotswolds special. The spirit certainly eluded her at Rodmarton. She writes:

...I came to the small village of Rodmarton. There isn't anything very remarkable here.

For me, the building of this wonderful house, evidence of a continuing, living tradition, gets very close to the true spirit of the Cotswolds.

The little roads are warm roads
And fine to house within;
They grow great trees, escape the breeze
And nurse the homely inn;
The high roads are dry roads
For many a thirsty mile,
But their wind and rain I will face again
As I have done many a while.

JH

12
Avening to Westonbirt
9 miles

And I'll sing as I tramp by dusty hedges
Or drink my ale in the shade
How Gloucestershire is the finest home
That the Lord God ever made.

WH

Avening to Westonbirt

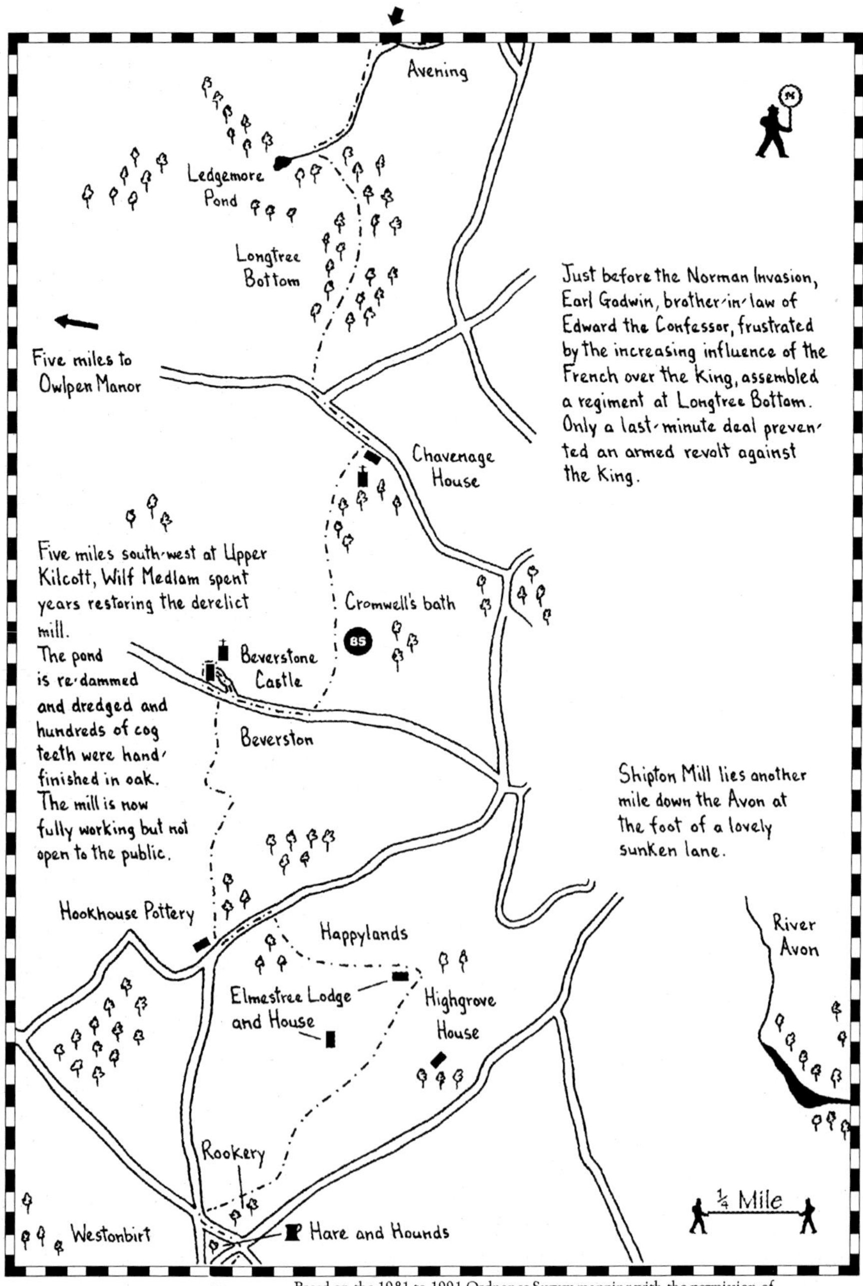

Take the footpath to the right of the churchyard. A stone stile with Y↑ takes you into a field. Cross it, passing through a wooden kissing gate, to reach a double stile with a Y↑ by a footbridge. Keep left of the stream to another stile with Y↑. Climb a little to reach the next stile and then head for the gate in the top corner of the field. Take the steps over the wall to the road. Turn right.

Follow the road above the pleasantly tree-lined stream. Cross the stream and take the lane to the left of Orchard House. Pass the cottage, go over the stile by the gate with Y↑ and cross the stream on the stone path. Go through the next gate with Y↑ and take care to turn left to reach the field boundary. Follow this and the stream, through a gateway to a stile with Y↑ just past a damaged willow. Pass through a small young plantation and beside a (sometimes) noisy little water pumping station. Go over a stile with Y↑, keeping the field boundary on the left.

Keep above a spring to a gate with Y↑. Go another 100 yards to pass through a gate with Y↑ and turn sharp left to contour round the hill through the scrubby trees. Pass through a gate by a pumping station on to a track through the wooded Longtree Bottom. This is a quiet secluded valley disturbed only by the wing claps of startled pigeons. A beautifully mossy decaying stone wall marks the entire length of the valley. You will find some log piles suitably placed for taking a rest.

The muddy track leads you steadily upwards, out of the trees to a gate a little short of the unfenced road. Turn to the left to aim for the diagonal corner of the green. Leave it via a double railed gateway by **Chavenage** Green Cottages. At the main road turn left along the road lined with beech to reach a large cattle shed on the right. Keep on the road past solid 17th century farm buildings to gain a splendid front view of the entrance to Chavenage Manor.

Turn right at the bridleway sign just past the cattle shed into an unsurfaced lane. To the left, notice the tower of the chapel, built originally as an 18th century folly, an eye-catching but pointless adornment to the property. After a few hundred yards the route follows the field boundary and then again becomes a narrow path to drop down a little to the left of the valley bottom.

Pass through a gate with B↑ and Intriguing Gate Fastening Mechanism Number 5 and aim just left of the stone wall ahead to climb the field. Follow the fence but take a pause for breath on the way up to look back at Chavenage Manor.

Pass through a gate at the top. Notice the tumulus shown on the Ordnance Survey map just to your left has been ploughed almost out of existence. Follow the field boundary across a field and then a grassy lane to reach the main road, passing good views of Tetbury, the tall, slender spire of St Mary's to the left and Beverston Castle to the right.

Turn right on to the road and take care walking into **Beverston**. Just past the first trio of cottages take the footpath right. Cross a small green, spotting turkeys to the right, on to the road leading past the 14th century Pilgrims Barn to reach the castle and church. The supported tree is a walnut.

➤ I have often quoted from David Verey whose encyclopaedic pair of Gloucestershire volumes in the Buildings of England series provides a wealth of information for the architectural historian.

Contd: page 169

Chavenage

One of the finest sights in all the Cotswolds is the beautiful facade of Chavenage viewed from the entrance to its drive. You could be gazing at the template of the Cotswold vernacular building design which has lasted through 400 years. The eye is drawn to 18 narrow windows to the left of the entrance porch which light the two-storey hall, flanked on either side by the wings of the traditional Tudor E-shaped house.

The nucleus of the house was a farm built by the Prior of Horsley to oversee his monastic properties. Soon after the Dissolution, the lands passed into the hands of the Stephens family who built the oldest parts of the present house in about 1576. The centrepiece was the Great Hall with its minstrels' gallery and windows that recycled various pieces of medieval glass, such as St James with his scallop shell symbol, taken from redundant local Church buildings.

The two most striking rooms are those with Civil War connections, Cromwell's and Ireton's Rooms. Cromwell is said to have visited during the Civil War - a well in a field behind the house is called Cromwell's Bath. Rather better documented is the visit of General Henry Ireton, Cromwell's son-in-law. Colonel Stephens was influential in the Parliament and Ireton was despatched to persuade him to support Cromwell's intention to execute Charles I. He eventually agreed but brought a curse upon himself from his daughter.

The perfect facade of Chavenage Manor

The two bedrooms are sumptuous with 17th century tapestries entirely covering the walls, one room with a complex forest theme, the other showing Biblical scenes. The sheer quantity of meticulous work required to create these tapestries is astonishing. When they were taken down recently for cleaning in London they were found to have been fixed to the walls with nails.

Rooms have been added over the years, the most recent being the Ballroom with its sprung floor, now used for dinners and society wedding receptions.

If any part of the house looks familiar it may be because its archetypical Elizabethan appearance has been used as the backdrop for many films including "Barry Lyndon" and Agatha Christie's very first Poirot story, "The Mysterious Affair at Styles".

Another contemporary use is by The Gloucestershire Drama Association who, for the last decade, have staged just one outdoor production for a few evenings each year in July on the Jacobean lawn, performing in recent years, Shakespeare's "The Winter's Tale" and "The Merry Wives of Windsor". The 550 who make up the audience at least get the benefit of being able to sit under the shelter of a marquee.

I'll leave you to visit and hear for yourself the Lord of the Manor of Horsley, David Lowsley-Williams' masterly guided tour which will explain the fate of an unlucky ANZAC aviator, how the capital was raised to re-roof the entire house with hundreds of tons of stone and why the Civil War militiamen tied tassels on their pikes. The present incumbents were fortunate indeed to be given the house as a wedding present; it is sad that their inheritance is now under threat from a new bypass around Tetbury.

Beverstone Castle

We pass only one castle on our route and this is it, built in about 1220 by a junior branch of the Berkeley family. It is now a rather romantic ruin and, although the building does not open to the public, the gardens do on a few days each year. Our route provides a complete circuit giving a fine view of the shaded, spooky moat, dry now at the foot of the towering castle walls. Originally there was a second moat which followed the line now taken by the main road and the farm buildings.

Maurice de Gaunt's original castle must have been an imposing sight rearing up on this flat stretch of country with a circular drum tower at each of its four corners and a drawbridge over the moat in front of the Gatehouse. In the 14th century the domestic accommodation was improved by Thomas, Lord Berkeley, at one time suspected of the murder of Edward II at Berkeley Castle. He turned one of the towers into the huge square one we see today with access from the three storey octagonal turret that reaches up beside it. Look closely near the top and you see a massive iron chain preventing turret and tower from parting company.

The improvements included a new first floor stone-vaulted chapel which was accessible from the ground floor hall, from the owner's new suite above and also from the outside. Verey amusingly describes the solution to this three dimensional puzzle as being achieved by *...a series of interlocking levels that only a 14th century designer could have conceived...*

Beverstone Castle's Berkeley Tower

Three times during the Civil War Beverstone was besieged and eventually fell to Colonel Massey's Roundheads while the master of the house was across the fields visiting his mistress at Chavenage House. Her family supported Cromwell and she had managed to weedle out of him sufficient about the secrets of Beverstone's defences that at the third attempt it was captured and blown up. The more recent living accommodation, essentially a farmhouse, dates from this time.

If you pick the correct few days each year, when the 3½ acre garden is open to the public, you can get a better feel for the antiquity of the building. The aged beeches, yews, walnuts and weeping ash speak for themselves; the 18th century gazebo with its pyramid roof offers a splendid view over the moat with its bridge supported by a weirdly distorted stone arch, linking the terrace with the rest of the garden; two enormous beeches screen an ancient nut walk; a fig tree grows in the shelter of the walled kitchen garden and two glasshouses house a magnificent orchid collection.

Sheltered by an antique yew, the most beautiful part of the garden lies between the house and the moat; plants bursting out of gaps in the stone-slabbed terrace make crossing it in high summer like a game of hop-scotch. To stand here, dwarfed by the Berkeley Tower, is to travel back in time with the privileged feeling of experiencing something that few have seen.

And if you visit at Easter, you will see that most elusive of Cotswold flora, the pasque flower.

So Many Pauls

Highgrove House was built in the 1790s for a man with the confusing name of John Paul Paul. The Paul family specialised in Christening their children with odd names, choosing such Biblical rarities as Nathaniel, Josiah, Obadiah and Onesiphorous.

The rather box-shaped Highgrove as it appeared in 1825. Most of the interior was destroyed by a fire in 1893.

Mary, the sister of Walter Paul who owned Highgrove, married in 1835 yet another Paul, Sir John Dean Paul Bart, becoming Lady Mary Paul (née Paul).

Sir John was a banker who was found to be fraudulently disposing of his clients' assets. For this he was sentenced to 14 years penal servitude in Australia. After his transportation, Lady Mary followed him down under and bought a beautiful house in the Sydney suburbs. The story ends neatly with Lady Mary applying to the Government for her own husband's services and then actually employing him as an "assigned servant".

So it is pleasing to note that here in Beverston is a pair of houses he designed in 1954 - Beverston House in Queen Anne style and its cottage in the style of the Cotswold tradition.

Three Megaliths

Sullivan cannot find these. No more can I! An article in the 1950 Archaeological Record describes two six foot stones sticking out of a field and in 1973 three stones were noted. They seem to have disappeared while clearing or ploughing the field.

Pass in front of the churchyard and turn left into a lane leading back to the main road, circumnavigating the castle. Turn left at the main road and after 100 yards turn right on to a road that brings you to Park Farm with its weather vane, bell and clock. Continue past the farm buildings to reach a walled lane. This becomes a sunken lane with high banks bursting with flowers in summer. Follow it as it turns sharp left and at a T junction of lanes, turn right.

Notice Oldown house in trees to the left, nestling above the dished shape of the fields. Notice too, the surface you are walking on which was presumably an old road, surfaced before the days of tar macadam. A gate brings you into a field. Keep to the boundary till you reach a gate leading on to the road at **Hookhouse.**

➤ In the garden to the right you may well see some traditional "gypsy" caravans. They belong to a horse-drawn caravan holiday firm whose circular Cotswold route passes through Hookhouse.

➤ The Hookhouse Pottery has been established for 20 years. Christopher White trained at Michael Cardew's Winchcombe Pottery. He hand throws a range of traditional domestic ware - patio pots, distinctive tableware and attractive one-off items with geometric designs. You are able to watch him at work and on open days in early July try your hand at the wheel. Several times a year he holds exhibitions of local craft work together with that of visiting craftsmen from Brittany. You will find beautiful pots, ceramics, leatherwork, wooden bowls, drawings and paintings and, possibly, the local blacksmith at work.

Turn left on the road for 450 yards and take the footpath right into a field. Keep to the field boundary and pass to the left of Hare Covert spinney which may be awash with bluebells. A tiresome detour from the right of way then takes you round the rough edge of the next field - be consoled by passing closer to the extraordinarily-named hamlet of Happylands! At the point you would have reached by crossing the field turn left through a gate with Y↑ by an oak with a huge girth.

A post with Y↑ points along the field boundary. Follow it to the second gate with Y↑ (not as shown on the Ordnance Survey map). Through the gate, skirt the new tree planting and aim for the gate to the left of the house. Turn right at Elmstree Lodge, following the footpath through the white gate and then a second gate. As the track to Elmstree House bears off to the right, keep straight ahead across the parkland making for a gate in the iron fence. If you try very hard you can make out the buildings of Highgrove House through the trees on the left, although, whichever side you try from, you won't get a good view of the house.

Keep straight on to the point where the post and wire fence meets the trees by a pond. It is impossible to tell where the parkland of Highgrove House meets that of Elmstree House but the latter does allow you some superb views. Pass through two gates with Y↑.

From the derelict house by the pond, keep straight to cross the house drive. As you do, look left to see a fanciful gate-house. Bear a little right to reach a stile in the post and wire fence. Cross the next field, still going straight, aiming for a field jump which you...well, jump. Keep right of the hedge to cross the next field, walk through (!) a neatly maintained short section of wall and follow the post and rail fence for 200 yards.

Past another field jump, go left over an unmarked stone stile. Follow the path through the crops to another stone stile. Go straight to reach the corner of the next field and cross the stile. Turn right and follow the hedge to the gate in the corner that leads into a lane beside a rookery[1].

Follow the lane through a couple of gates, noticing the way the wall has literally been undermined by badgers, and turn left on the road passing the grounds of the Hare and Hounds.

At the cross roads, cross to the kissing gate. Aim across the field for a gate nearer the wood than the buildings of Home Farm. This brings you again on to parkland. Keep straight to reach a gate and kissing gate. The elaborate gate-house on the right is an entrée to the view of Westonbirt House, emerging on the left.

Keep just right of the clumps of trees to cross the drive and continue on a paved road. Drop down to the cattle grid, turn right by the church and follow the line of cottages which comprise **Westonbirt** village.

➤ The village was moved to this fold in the Cotswolds to make way for the building of Westonbirt House and to hide the cottages from its view. It's a pretty comprehensive village, too: in the row you'll spot a village hall, post office and what was the school house. The front gardens are pretty and it's worth a look to see what has been done with the very steep slopes of the back gardens.

Hare & Hounds
Public house and hotel.
Wadworth, John Smith & Smiles.
If you have several thousand pounds seeking a green investment, come here for a Forestry Commission auction and buy a stand of growing timber anywhere in the country. It would incur, though, quite some responsibilities - in addition to felling the timber and hauling it away, you must replant in a way that enhances the local environ-

[1] Helpful hint: you may have difficulty distinguishing rooks and crows because both are essentially large black birds. The easiest way is to remember that if you see two or more crows together then they are rooks; conversely, a lone rook is invariably a crow. Take care, though, not to confuse either with jackdaws (large black birds). Gloucestershire wisdom has it that you must *always take your hat off to a jackdaw* or else you're in for a run of bad luck.
For more helpful information about birds see Appendix D.

Contd: page 173

Robert Holford's portrait which hangs in the Hall of Westonbirt School

Westonbirt village to the Arboretum

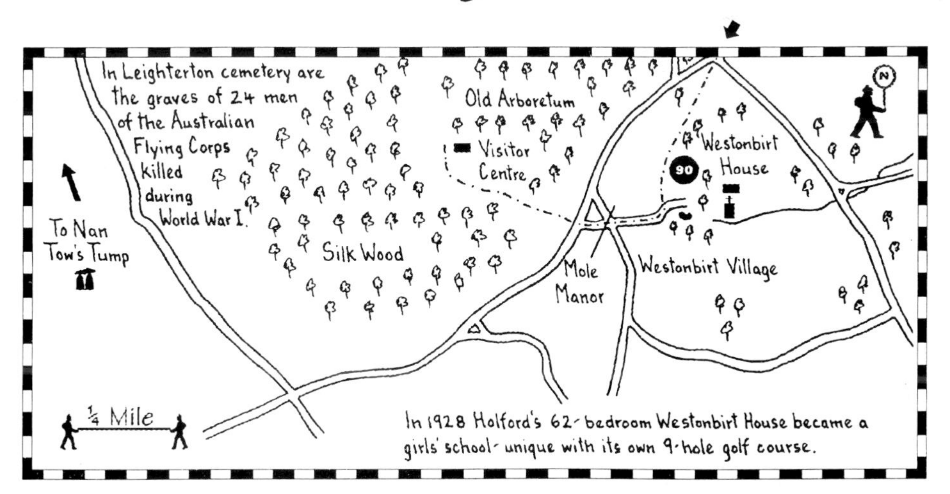

Organic Lambs and Duchy Originals

The Highgrove Estate was bought as the home for the Prince of Wales in 1980 and since then he has been converting its 1100 acre Home Farm to run organically, its substantial profits going to the Prince's charities.

An early venture was the Highgrove Loaf, sold in its thousands by Tesco. Since 1992 much of the oats and wheat are used to make the oaten biscuit, Duchy Originals. The cereal is milled at the nearby Shipton Mill and baked in Scotland. After some hundred experiments, a recipe was developed producing a crunchy, nutty cross between an oatcake and a digestive biscuit. The process involved is a carefully guarded secret, closer to a craft process than modern mass bakery production. Although the price is set high, demand is outstripping supply, helped along by the smart packaging displaying the biscuit, embossed with the coat of arms of the Duke of Cornwall which includes two choughs[1].

These biscuits have now been joined by Duchy Originals Gingered Biscuits made from malted wheat and chunks of stem ginger. Their fame is quickly spreading, taking them to more than 700 outlets in the UK, the Middle East, North America and even the grand Paris food hall, La Grande Epicerie. The latest Duchy Original enterprise is the bottling of estate spring water for sale as Herb and Fruit Blend drinks.

The original Duchy Originals

The Prince's earliest organic endeavour was with the 500 sheep kept on Home Farm. The farm complies with the rigorous Soil Association standards, uses no artificial fertilizers and avoids dipping the sheep in potentially harmful chemicals which can drain away into streams and reach our water supplies. The farm's clover and ryegrass produce lamb that is sold through some of the Q Guild butchers (Q for Quality) and is of a standard that has won gold medals at the Smithfield Show.

For some years the origin of this excellent quality meat was kept secret but now with the publication of "Highgrove: Portrait of an Estate", the secret is out. We can read of the one acre kitchen garden with its medlars and quinces, and the reed bed that acts as a sewage garden, the lily pond with its rare great-crested newts and the pond of Koi carp, a gift from Sir Yehudi Menuhin.

The absence of fertilisers and pesticides has allowed the environment here to revert to its former diversity. The wildflower meadow beside the drive is alive with poppies, buttercups and the rarer white campion and yellow rattle. The field hedges, which are up to 1000 years old, are a dense habitat for dragonflies, weasels, and voles.

We can read about this bold ecological experiment but most of it we cannot see. It hides behind a 20 foot brick wall and, from whichever direction you approach it, you won't penetrate the privacy of Highgrove House.

---

[1] Choughs are large black birds! Sadly, these aerial acrobats, once thought to be exclusive to Cornwall, have not been seen over Cornish cliffs for some 20 years. Elwes called the chough *the most graceful in its flight, and most pleasant in its cry, of all the crow tribe.*

➤ If you turn right at the crossroads, in a few yards you see what little there is to be seen from the outside of Mole Manor - not much more than its front door leading into the hillside. The house was built underground in 1987 to be the last word in energy saving design. The rooms radiate from a large circular atrium, lit from above by a huge glass dome, its roof supported by Doric-style columns. This eccentric home was recently on the market for £¼ million.

St Catherine, patron of

- knife grinders
- millers
- rope makers
- craftsmen who work with words
- librarians
- philosophers
- preachers
- swordsmen
- lady students

Cross this road and after 250 yards cross the main road on to the bridleway leading into Silk Wood, part of Westonbirt Arboretum. With the car park of the Visitors Centre up to the right, you reach Skilling Gate where you take the gate that leads you straight on. Keep more or less to the valley bottom and continue past Waste Gate. To the right is the Visitor Centre, the end of our journey.

Nan Tow's Tump

This is one of the largest round barrows in the Cotswolds, eight feet high and about 95 feet in diameter. It was allegedly the burial place of a witch, Nan Tow, who was buried in a standing position. Quite possibly the legend has its roots in mob action taken against witches. The name tump is given to many Gloucestershire barrows.

Detour to Didmarton

To round off the theme of black birds, try the King's Arms at Didmarton shortly after 12th May. Duff Hart-Davis has described a recently innovated tradition of the Rook Pie Supper, inaugurated at the pub as a joke in 1994! Rook pie was a traditional country dish made in the spring when the rookeries were thinned out.

The birds are shot on the Duke of Beaufort's Badminton estate. The dark breast meat is removed, marinaded for two weeks and cooked with beef, producing a gamey and apparently delicious result.

This unlikely event has proved tremendously popular so you probably need a local connection if you want to taste a piece of the pie.

Westonbirt

When, at the age of 31 in 1839, Robert Holford inherited £1 million from an uncle and the Westonbirt estate from his father, he was in a position to put his plan into action. Throughout his twenties he had been devising the changes he would make to the estate which eventually transformed a flat, unpromising 300 acres of Gloucestershire into what is now the country's premier arboretum.

He began to put his wealth and energy to work in the 1840s by rebuilding all the estate farms. In the 1850s he built a new Westonbirt village and demolished the original one with the exception of the church. In the 1860s he demolished the Regency mansion, built just 40 years before by his father, and replaced it with the sumptuous house with its 63 bedrooms that is now Westonbirt School. And whilst all this was going on, he developed the 40 acres of "Pleasure Grounds" around the house into what has been described as a Victorian plantsman's delight.

Before all this, in 1829, Holford began planting a bare site with the avenues and rides which have become the arboretum, taking care early on to plant hardy native trees which would shelter later plantings of more exotic tender species. These were obtained from all over the world, from plant hunters, nurseries, botanical gardens and fellow fanatics. The resulting collection is not only famous for its sheer quantity of species, about 4,000, but also for the care and foresight put into their siting and spacing, their relative sizes and textures and their changing appearance through the seasons. Planting saplings just a foot or two high, Holford had to consider the visual effect a couple of hundred years later when the trees matured. There were a few notable miscalculations resulting in trees up to 30 feet high being moved in a specially-adapted cart.

A Wellingtonia and a Blue Atlas Cedar

The corkscrew hazel is a curiosity that grows in the demented fashion suggested by its name and was first discovered in a local hedgerow in 1863. Both Holford and his rival, the Earl of Ducie who was creating an arboretum at nearby Tortworth[1], thought they had the only specimen. The two landowners jealously guarded their new acquisitions in carefully hidden nurseries, little knowing that their Head Gardeners frequently drank at the same pub, enthusiastically exchanging plants. Once the secret was out, the Scottish music hall comedian, Sir Harry Lauder, put a length to good use as his stage walking stick.

---

[1] The Tortworth Chestnut can still be seen today, a 900 year old specimen which stands in Tortworth churchyard.

In-between-times he collected and hybridised the newly-introduced amaryllis, building a special glasshouse as home to 2000 specimens; and he started work on cultivating orchids which enabled his son, George, to win innumerable awards with hybrids grown in his 21 orchid houses.

Now owned by the Forestry Commission, Westonbirt holds the national collections of willow and Japanese maples which, in the Acer Glade, are an absolute gem. A fascinating feature, amongst all the exotic forms of lumber life, the Native Species Collection tells the story of how Britain has been colonised by trees since the end of the last Ice Age.

Around 40 acres are managed as hazel coppice, continuing at least 600 years of tradition and providing full-time work for three people. Just a few generations ago every farm had its own small hazel coppice. The hazel bushes are cut back to ground level every third winter which encourages the growth of straight new stems. During the rest of the year the harvested hazel rods are made into traditional products like hurdles, fences and trellises. In fact, hand-finished furniture made from coppice hazel has become very fashionable.

Young's Weeping Birch

Something you may miss in the profusion of trees is the care that has gone into the design of the pagoda-like Visitor Centre. The roof of western red cedar shingles is supported by a frame of Douglas fir from the Forest of Dean; inside, the ceiling is Baltic pine, the floor a tropical hardwood called Angelique; the information desk is Californian nutmeg and the beam above the fireplace was cut from a home-grown oak. So even the Visitor Centre becomes a celebration of the world's trees.

Arthurian themed carving

The arboretum has a constant stream of other attractions:

➤ For the last three years nine local wood carvers have had just one week to work on portions of wind-damaged oaks and redwoods, creating sculptures as diverse as a 12 foot barn owl, dancers and a charcoal burner. The auctioned carvings raise money for Tree Aid, a small British charity which plants indigenous trees like eucalyptus and mesquite in sub-Saharan Africa, preventing soil erosion, and providing fuel and leaves for animal feed.

➤ For several weekends Roger Winfield has set up an "orchestra" of Aeolian harps made from larch and decorated with pennants in amongst the maples, leaving the breeze to play their strings.

This random, unearthly music is then picked up, mixed and amplified to produce unique sounds like nothing you have heard before.
➤ Sections of a 2000 year-old small leaved lime were distributed to carvers around the world and the resulting display included a rocking horse.
➤ Turner or "Bodger", Mike Abbott, can sometimes be seen with his very "low-tech", environment-friendly pole lathe shaping legs to incorporate in his entirely hand-crafted chairs.
➤ During some October evenings a mile-long section of the autumn trail is illuminated, providing an extra dimension to the riot of colour.

Westonbirt, probably the greatest collection of trees in the northern hemisphere, is a triumph of nature arranged by man. The Arboretum now contains more than 18,000 trees and shrubs with 109 "champions", that is the largest British specimen in terms of height or girth. It is best visited in spring, summer, autumn and winter but if you must choose just one, make it autumn: the amazing array of colours of the Japanese maples, ranging through scarlet, crimson, yellow and gold, is a sight you are unlikely to forget.

The Legacy of Bartholemew de Olepenne

Including Owlpen as a detour is sheer indulgence - it is some way from our route. This tiny hamlet lies in one of the steep, narrow valleys that cut into the western, scarp edge of the Cotswolds. It is a perfect cluster of manorial buildings nestling near the head of the Ewelme valley. Positively vibrating with 700 years of history in its house, tithe barn, mill and formal gardens, Owlpen is one of the most romantic sights in the County, hiding away in its beautifully secluded setting. The Prince of Wales has called it *the epitome of the English village*.

The barn and part of the house's east wing were built by the 12th century de Olepenne family. Most of the house, though, dates from the mid 16th century. In the 1720s the interior was classicised with panelling, and the terraced lawns and enormous yews were planted. Owlpen's story then starts to take strange twists.

For 90 years up to 1840 the house was hardly occupied, felt to be insufficiently grand by its industrialist owners. Instead, they built Owlpen Park a mile away on the lip of the Cotswold edge. During this "Sleeping Beauty" period, the Manor was relegated to the role of family picnic site with a caretaker to maintain the gardens, while the mill became a water pumping station for the new house.

The house viewed from the formal gardens

In 1925 the derelict Manor was bought by Norman Jewson, the pupil of Gimson and the Barnsleys, and was sensitively altered and restored using local stone and oak and handmade nails. Jewson sank a lot of money into the project but could not afford to live there. He re-sold it in 1927. Then in 1955 the story twists again with the demolition of the Park, too expensive to maintain in the mid 20th century.

Since 1974 the Manor has been in the hands of the Mander family who have opened the house and gardens to the public and converted the barn into a restaurant serving European, especially Swedish, dishes. Visit, and you will be captivated but you'll be hard pressed to capture the beauty on film - the lie of the land and the yew trees conspire to keep you at bay.

The enormous cider press in the Cyder House Restaurant

➤ The house is beautifully "wonky", the result of additions and demolitions over the centuries and window frames that have slid from the vertical. The chimneys are Tudor and the gutters and water shutes are the original lead. The restoration by Jewson in the '20s included plaster animals and motifs on the walls, furniture by the Barnsleys and a William Morris curtain. The Manders have assembled a splendid collection of Arts and Crafts furniture, mostly acquired from the Arlington Mill Museum.

➤ The medieval tithe barn was converted to a cider mill in the 18th century. The donkey-powered press is enormous - its uprights are whole trees 20 ft high. The barn is now the Cyder House Restaurant.

➤ The corn mill certainly stood in the 15th century. It was rebuilt in 1726 and given its central cupola with weather vane and circular leaded window. It is now a holiday cottage with its sack doors replaced by toughened glass to give a view from the ground floor right up to the cupola. It has a well-kept pond and a well-rusted mill-wheel.

➤ The gazebo is a little banqueting house where the Lord of the Manor may have held court.

➤ The church is medieval but its best feature is the intricate mosaic work dating from its Victorian-Edwardian restoration.

➤ The gardens have a very old feel. There are few flowers. The interest lies in its formal structure of terraces, walls and steep steps, its parterres and "ballroom" created with sentinel yews. Vita Sackville-West wrote *yews that make rooms...dark secret rooms of yew hiding in the slope of the valley.* Sir Geoffrey Jellicoe believed it to be the oldest surviving English domestic garden.

➤ A recent discovery is that a tall chimney, covered in ivy and hidden in trees, known to the Manders children as the "witch's house", is actually a mid 19th century private gas works which may well be unique in the South West.

➤ Naturally there is a ghost and a distinguished ghost at that - Margaret of Anjou, wife of King Henry VI, is said to have slept in the Tapestry Room on the eve of the Battle of Tewkesbury. In the eventual battle, her Lancastrian son Edward died, confirming the deposed Edward IV as king. Guests have even reported a ghostly smell of medieval spices.

If the house looks familiar, it may be because it was used as the setting for the television adaptation of Ngaio Marsh's Inspector Alleyn stories.

David Linley Furniture Ltd

It is cheating only a little to include David, Viscount Linley as a fourth Cotswold Royal resident. Whilst his furniture showroom is in Pimlico, all of the furniture sold is made by 20 craftsmen working in a Cirencester workshop who, by a happy quirk of fate, actually link back to the Sapperton craftsmen. Let's make him an honorary Royal resident.

At his public school, Bedales, David Linley was taught the basics of woodwork by David Butcher in one of the most respected design departments in the country where he learned the importance of quality of workmanship. He then spent two years in the small community of students at Parnham House School for Craftsmen in Wood in Dorset, the country's premier woodworking academy run by the very appropriate-sounding John Makepeace (he actually changed it from the rather less striking, Smith). The course there, focuses not just on a very fine standard in woodworking technique but also on design, business management and marketing as well as developing an aesthetic and environmental sensitivity.

The shop in Pimlico

For a short time after that Linley worked as a craftsman, then opened his first shop and switched to designing. More recently he finds his time is best spent seeking commissions for his design and woodworking teams to complete. The company's work is true to the spirit of William Morris, of Ashbee and of Sapperton: hand-made furniture built from fine timber to the highest standards of quality, described by Sir Roy Strong as *antiques of the future*. Their imaginative and eye-catching designs carry forward many of the features of the Arts and Crafts movement, combining them with both classical and modern, often with the intricacy and visual impact of a painting.

Predictably, their pieces are mostly very expensive one-offs, tables and cabinets, staircases, screens and "accessories", that find their way into the homes of rock stars and into corporate foyers.

A beautiful marquetry screen made from various woods depicting the Castle is a striking feature of the Drawing Room at the Queen Mother's childhood home, Glamis Castle in Angus. A gauge of the company's success is an annual turnover in the region of £½ million but if your pocket does not stretch to an expensive commission, you could always buy a pencil in walnut or sycamore which will only set you back £1!

And the link between David Linley Furniture Ltd and the Sapperton Craftsmen? The teacher at Bedales, David Butcher, learnt his craft working alongside Edward Barnsley, the son of our Sidney Barnsley, who died in 1987 and is buried in Sapperton churchyard alongside his father and uncle. They would all, I believe, feel gratified to find their design ideas and standards of work being upheld after an interval of almost a century. Perhaps here we have found Susan Hill's elusive "spirit of the Cotswolds".

Yea, we who live in Cotsall
Know that our breed is good,
And of our folk so hale and fair
We just a few can sometimes spare
To send to London - with a prayer -
And lend it lustihood.

JH

Appendices

Appendix A - The Poets

Ivor Gurney was born in Gloucester in 1890. He studied at the Royal College of Music and was beginning to establish a reputation as both a poet and composer of genius when he joined the Gloucester Regiment as a private in 1915. He was gassed near Passchendaele in 1917, repatriated and released from hospital with "deferred shell shock".

He had continued to write during the war and over the next four years his published output of poems, songs and music rose to a peak. He studied under Vaughan Williams and supported himself precariously as a cinema pianist and as a farm hand on Crickley Hill. He spent a lot of time walking or riding his rusty bike, often at night, when he would arrive unexpectedly at a friend's house to "camp out" on the living room floor. His increasing mental instability took him, in 1922 to an asylum, first in Gloucester and later in Kent.

He died there of TB in 1937 and is buried at Twigworth. None of his work is dated later than 1933. His poems, celebrating the Gloucestershire countryside and describing his war experiences are often discussed in the same breath as those of Owen, Brooke and Sassoon. An Ivor Gurney Society was launched at the 1995 Three Choirs Festival in Gloucester and a recently built pub in Gloucester has been named "The Turmut Hoer" after one of his poems.

The act of writing is a distraction in madness

FW (Will) Harvey was a Gloucestershire man, born in 1888 at Murrell's End, Hartpury, and was a contemporary of Gurney's at the King's School in Gloucester. He too joined the Glosters and won the DCM for capturing a German listening post in France while on reconnaisance. A year later, in 1916, he was captured in a foolhardy attempt to repeat the feat and was held captive for two years in seven different prisoner-of-war camps. Much of his time there he spent writing nostalgic poems about Gloucestershire and some powerful war poetry. He tried once to escape by jumping from a train. When Gurney first entered the asylum, Harvey dedicated these lines to him, recalling the times they spent walking together:

This hawthorne hedge will bank its snow
Spring after Spring, and never care
What songs and dreams of long ago
Within its shade were fashioned fair
Of happy air.

He lived for a time at Cranham and in converted railway carriages in the Forest of Dean. He worked most of his life as a solicitor in the Forest, growing famous as a local cricketer and producing a steady flow of poems, a number of them in Gloucester dialect. He died at Yorkley in 1957.

John (Jack) Haines, 1875-1960, was a Gloucester solicitor who employed Harvey after the First World War and developed a reputation as a poet and a botonist. He was a hockey player, chairman of the Gloucester club and a member of the England selection committee. He frequently visited Robert Frost, Lascelles Abercrombie and Rupert Brooke in 1914 when "the Dymock Poets" lived briefly in the north west of the County and was a friend of Edward Thomas. A good friend, too, to Gurney, he took him on long walks in the Cotswolds and the Black Mountains, trying to ease his mental trials.

...for something like a year we (Haines and Frost) met and wandered over May Hill, the Leadon Valley, and the ridges of the Cotswolds, hunting flowers together, and talking ceaselessly of poets and poetry...

Frank Mansell was descended from 20 generations of Cotswold farmers and for a time he farmed in the traditional way near The Camp. He gradually became disillusioned with raising animals for food and with bloodsports, ceased farming and became a vegetarian.

He worked for the GPO and was famed locally as a fast bowler for Sheepscombe who play home matches on an extraordinary pitch shaped *like a pony's back* and bought for the club by Laurie Lee. He was also a teller of horoscopes in which he had an unshakeable belief. Though a secretive man, he became well-known as a broadcaster and his deceptively simple verses, especially the "Cotswold Ballads", have been set to music by several hands and recorded. He died in 1979.

Appendix B - Rattleskull

3lb gooseberries - if frozen, allow time for thawing
1 bag sugar
1 Campden tablet
1 tsp yeast nutrient
1 tsp pectolase
1 sachet or ½ tsp wine yeast

➤ Sterilise all equipment and containers before use, with a solution of sodium metabisulphite.

➤ All the equipment and unusual ingredients can be obtained from home-brew shops or chemists such as Boots.

➤ The recipe makes 1 gallon; for larger quantities increase all ingredients in proportion.

Day 1

Crush the gooseberries in a fermenting bin so that each is split.
Add the Campden tablet dissolved in a little water.
Add the pectolase powder.
Fill the bin to the 1 gallon mark with cold water.
Leave in a warm place - beside a radiator or a sunny window.

Day 2

Add the sugar, nutrient and yeast. Stir well and leave in the warm. Fermentation will start within a few days. Once fermenting, the fruit will keep rising to form a dense mass. Stir daily to break it up and release carbon dioxide.

After about a week of fermenting
Strain through muslin or a nylon bag into a demijohn. Top with a rubber bung and airlock containing a sodium metabisulphite solution. Store in a warm place - an airing cupboard or over a boiler is ideal.
About 6 weeks later
When bubbles are no longer passing through the air-lock and the wine is clear, rack it, i.e. syphon off the wine into a clean demijohn taking care to disturb the sediment as little as possible. A stocking over the neck of the demijohn will catch any sediment that passes through the tube. Fit a plastic cap which will allow gas to pass through and leave in a cool place such as a garage.

The wine is now drinkable although it will be "rough" and will contain some very fine particles of the ingredients. I suspect this is the true Rattleskull.

A more refined approach would be to top up with water and leave it three more months. Then, rack it again into another demijohn or 6 wine bottles, again topping up with cold water.

It will be a smoother drink by the six month point and it will keep improving for several years.

Appendix C - Tyndale and Shakespeare Answers

The answers to the puzzle are:

1. Salt of the earth - Tyndale
2. The scales fell from his eyes - Tyndale
3. In my heart of hearts - Shakespeare
4. What a piece of work is man - Shakespeare
5. The fat of the land - Tyndale
6. To thine own self be true - Shakespeare
7. Tush, ye shall not die - Tyndale
8. Fight the good fight - Tyndale
9. The evil that men do lives after them - Shakespeare
10. Eat, drink and be merry - Tyndale
11. The milk of human kindness - Shakespeare
12. Blessed are the peacemakers - Both!

Appendix D - Twitcher's Guide for the Ornithologically Challenged

Baffle your bird-watcher friends by coining a bird of your own.
Select one name from each column moving left to right to create, for example, the Tufted Herring Pipit or the Arctic Sand Warbler.

Greater	Crested	Gull
Lesser	Black-headed	Warbler
Slender-billed	Short-toed	Oystercatcher
White	Golden	Plover
Long-tailed	Bearded	Stork
Siberian	Spotted	Wren
Black	Ringed	Crow
Great-Northern	Garden	Duck
Tufted	White-backed	Hoopoe
Little	Black-eared	Kite
Arctic	Herring	Pipit
Ringed	Sand	Skua
Hooded	Pygmy	Nuthatch
Pied	Tawny	Tit
Common	Meadow	Flycatcher

Three Local Trusts

The Gloucestershire Wildlife Trust

(The Gloucestershire Trust for Nature Conservation)

The Trust is a volunteer organisation which for 25 years has worked to protect Gloucestershire's countryside and the wildlife living there. It operates nearly 80 nature reserves throughout the County - on the Cotswolds, in the Severn vale and in the Forest of Dean, nearly all of them open to members at any time.

Its reserves must be as varied as it is possible to find within one County - wetlands, woodlands, grasslands, hills, valleys, rivers, ponds and even former quarries, railways and canals. These sites provide protection for threatened plants such as Adder's Tongue Spearwort and fast-disappearing butterflies like the Pearl-Bordered Fritillary. Attempts are being made to re-introduce the Large Blue, extinct in Britain, and the rare Adonis Blue. Better managed woodlands will encourage the continuing increase in numbers of coal tits and blackcap tits.

As well as maintaining and expanding the reserves, the main thrust of the Trust's efforts is in resisting planning developments which would endanger habitats within 800 identified Key Wildlife Sites and in educating children - the people who will inherit the Gloucestershire we choose to leave behind.

Our route has passed through or passed by several of the reserves and others are open on at least one specified day each year to non-members.

Details of the Trust's work and of membership can be obtained from:

The Gloucestershire Wildlife Trust
Dulverton Building
Robinswood Hill Country Park
Reservoir Road
Gloucester
GL4 9SX.

Cotswold Canals Trust

The Trust dates back to 1972 and aims ultimately to rejoin the Severn and the Thames by restoring the Stroudwater Navigation and the Thames and Severn Canal, not this time to attract commercial craft, but to promote Cotswold tourism. Limited sections of the canals have been reopened, extensive lengths of tow-path have been cleared and locks, bridges and portals restored. Of particular interest to walkers is the intention to restore the towpath as a long-distance right of way.

The Trust has won a certain amount of commercial sponsorship and received local authority grants but relies heavily on fund-raising and voluntary support.

An interesting booklet and membership details are available from:

Stroudwater-Thames & Severn Canal Trust Ltd
1 Rowcroft
Stroud,
Gloucestershire.

Cotswold Farm Park

The farm park has now been established for more than 20 years at Bemborough Farm near Guiting Power. It was set up and is still run by Joe Henson and John Neave who turned a hobby interest in rare breeds into an important scientific and commercial enterprise when Whipsnade Zoo was forced, in 1969, to disperse its small group of endangered sheep and cattle. They were added to the collection already assembled at the farm and attracted 20,000 visitors in the first year of opening. The collection is now visited by about five times that number each year and embraces the full range of British rare farm animals - cattle, horses, sheep, goats, pigs and poultry, in fact the most complete collection in this country.

The scientific aspect of the farm is the breeding of these animals in order to maintain as diversified a gene pool of farm animals as possible. Wildlife species are currently being lost at the rate of some 30,000 each year so there is no knowing whether, in the future, we may desperately need this genetic material for cross-breeding. The outbreak of BSE has been a reminder of this work's importance.

Joe Henson was the founding Chairman of The Rare Breeds Survival Trust in 1973 which has extended the farm's work by, for example, buying an island in the Orkneys to protect the sea-weed-eating sheep of North Ronaldsay. Another success was saving the Norfolk Horn breed of sheep when it was down to its last four representatives and helping it back to a more healthy 200.

The Trust supports more than 40 endangered species and since its formation no British domestic breed has become extinct. The only breeds it has been unable to assist are those without a bona-fide history, such as the delightfully-named Blue Albion cow, or those with insufficient numbers for breeding as in the case of Norfolk grey hens.

Joe's presidency of the Gloucester Cattle Society marks his particular support for the well-being of the Gloucester Cattle.

The farm park opens from April to the end of September. Full details from:

Cotswold Farm Park
Guiting Power
Cheltenham
Gloucestershire

The Rare Breeds Survival Trust
4th Street, NAC
Stoneleigh
Warwickshire

Tourist Information

Tourist Information Centres will help you to arrange accommodation on the route and will supply telephone numbers for local taxis.

From north to south there are offices close to our route at:

Stow-on-the-Wold	01451 831082
Stroud	01453 765768
Tetbury	01666 503552

Bibliography

Barrett, Bridgeman, Bird - AM & SWJR Album Vol 1, 1872-99 - 1981
Boden, Anthony - FW Harvey Soldier, Poet - 1988
Bradley, Ian - William Morris and his World
Briggs, Katharine M, - The Folklore of the Cotswolds - 1974
Brill, Edith - Cotswold Ways - 1985
Brill, Edith - Life and Tradition on the Cotswolds - 1973
Brill, Edith - Cotswold Crafts - 1977
Brill, Edith & Turner, Peter - The Minor Pleasures of Cotswold
CAMRA - Real Ale in Gloucestershire - 1993
Catling, C & Merry, A - Shell Guide: Gloucestershire, Hereford and Worcester - 1990
Chandler, Keith - Ribbons, Bells and Squeaking Fiddles - 1993
Clifford, Elsie - Bagendon: A Belgic Oppidum - 1962
Crosher, GR - Along the Cotswold Ways - 1976
Darvill, TC - Prehistoric Gloucestershire - 1987
Darvill, TC - The Megalithic Chambered Tombs of the Cotswold-Severn Region - 1982
Delderfield, Eric R - West Country Historic Houses and their Families Vol 3
Delderfield, Eric R - The Cotswolds - 1961
Derrett, JDM - Prophecy in the Cotswolds 1803-1947
Dixon, Reginald - Cotswold Curiosities - 1988
Douglas-Home, Jessica - Violet - 1996
Dunn Euan - Windrush Water-meadows, in The Countryman, Christmas 1993
Dyer, C - Transactions of the Bristol and Gloucestershire Archaeological Society - 1987
Dyer, J - The Penguin Guide to Prehistoric England and Wales
Elwes, HJ - Memoirs of Travel, Sport, and Natural History - 1930
Exell, AW - Joanna Southcott at Blockley and the Rock Cottage Relics - 1977
Finberg, J - The Cotswolds
Garne, R - Cotswold Yeomen and Sheep - 1984
Gibbs, J Arthur - A Cotswold Village - 1984
Gissing, A - The Footpath Way in Gloucestershire - 1924
Goodwin, Jill - A Dyer's Manual - 1982
Guinness, Jonathan with Catherine - The House of Mitford - 1984
Hadfield, C&A, - Cotswolds: a New Study - 1973
Hansell, P&J - Dovecotes - 1988
Harris, Mollie - Where the Windrush Flows - 1989
Herbert, Nicholas - Road Travel and Transport in Gloucestershire - 1985
Hill, Susan - The Spirit of the Cotswolds - 1988
Hopkins, Andrea - Knights - 1990
Hopkins, James K - A Woman to Deliver her People - 1982
Household, Humphry - The Thames and Severn Canal - 1983
Hughes, Graham - Barns of Rural Britain
Hutton, Edward - Highways and Byways of Gloucestershire - 1936
Jewson, Norman - By Chance I Did Rove - 1973

Jones, Anthea - The Cotswolds - 1994
Kingsley, Nicholas - The Country Houses of Gloucestershire Vol 1 1500-1660
Lucas, YM - WAAF with Wings - 1992
MacCarthy, Fiona - The Simple Life - 1981
Maggs, CG - The Midland and South West Junction Railway - 1980
Mee, Arthur - Gloucestershire - 1966
Mills, S & Riemer, P - The Mills of Gloucestershire - 1989
Mourton, S - Steam Routes around Cheltenham - 1993
Murray, AD - The Cotswolds - 1934
Naylor, Gillian - The Arts and Crafts Movement
Ordnance Survey - Cotswolds - 1993
Palmer, Roy - The Folklore of Gloucestershire - 1994
(Miss) Pinnell - Village Camera - 1990
Rance, Patrick - The Great British Cheese Book - 1982
Rennison, John - Wings over Gloucestershire
Ryder, TA - A Gloucestershire Miscellany - 1951
Sales, John - West Country Gardens - 1980
Sanders, G & Verey, D - Royal Homes in Gloucestershire - 1981
Scott, Shane (Ed) - The Hidden Places of the Cotswolds
Shaw, Nellie - Whiteway: a Colony on the Cotswolds - 1935
Smith, Brian - The Cotswolds - 1976
Smythe, Pat - Jump for Joy - 1954
Smythe, Pat - Leaping Life's Fences 1994
Stout, Adam - The Old Gloucester - the Story of a Cattle Breed - 1980
Sullivan, DP - Old Stones of Gloucestershire
Tann, Jennifer - Gloucestershire Woollen Mills
Thacker, Joy - Whiteway - 1994
Turner, Mark - Folklore and Mysteries of the Cotswolds - 1994
Verey, D - Gloucestershire: the Cotswolds - 1991
Wright, L & Priddey, J - Cotswold Heritage - 1977

...and articles in the Saturday Independent by Duff Hart-Davis, an excellent writer on country matters who lives hereabouts, gleanings from the Gloucester Citizen, Cotswold Life and BBC Radio Gloucestershire.

Acknowledgements

The author and publisher wish to thank the following for permission to reproduce illustrations: Anne Chambers, 4; Cheltenham Art Gallery and Museums, 12, 139 and photographed with their permission, 134, 135; Mary Greensted, 13t; The Blockley Antiquarian Society, 19, 21; Lord Moyne, 24 (from The House of Mitford by J and C Guinness, Hutchinson); Hon Desmond Guinness, 25 (from Nancy Mitford by Selina Hastings, MacMillan); The English Folk Dance and Song Society, 31; Keith Glover, 32; HWG Elwes, 44b, 50, 95t, 95b; Simon Tupper, 45; The Lee Manor Society, 55; The Master and Fellows of Corpus Christi College, Cambridge, 56; Roger-Viollet, Paris, 58; Marjorie Blamey, 67 (from The Wild Flowers of Britain and Northern Europe, HarperCollins); The Gloucester Citizen, 89; The National Trust, 90 (adapted from S Gibson's original drawing); Hugh Ballantyne, 92; J Dagley-Morris, 93; Heffers: Booksellers and Stationers, 108 (from Bagendon by Elsie Clifford); The National Trust, 111 (from Ernest Born's original drawing); Maj Tom Wills, 120; Lucy and Monica Koechlin, 121; Mirror Syndication International, 122; The CW Daniel Company Ltd, 124, 125t (from Whiteway by Nellie Shaw); from a model on display in the National Waterways Museum, Gloucester, 148; Geoff White Ltd, 149, 151; Oxford University Press, 150 (from The Woad Plant and its Dye by Jamieson B Hurry); The Rennison Collection, 155; The Imperial War Museum, 156; Simon Biddulph, 160; D Smith, Gloucestershire County and Diocesan Archivist, 168 (from Brewer's Delineations of Gloucestershire); Westonbirt School, 171. The author would be pleased to hear from the owners of any copyright illustrations he has been unable to trace.

Extracts from poems are published with the permission of: Penny Ely for Cotswold Ways, Walking Song, Old Times, The Companions, The Elements, Chance to Work and Song by Ivor Gurney; Pam Haines for A Ballad of Cotsall, The High Road and Paradise by John Haines; Patrick Harvey for On Birdlip, To Ivor Gurney, The Contrast, In Flanders, Song of the Road and After Long Wandering by FW Harvey; Freda Hastings and Brenda Mansell-Skey for Autumn Ploughing, I'd Sooner Go Hedging, When the Fine Rain and Stone Wall by Frank Mansell.

Text extracts are published with the permission of: Sir Peter O'Sullevan for his commentary, 11; Sutton Publishing, 131, from J Arthur Gibbs' A Cotswold Village and 148/9, from E Temple Thurston's The Flower of Gloster; Columbia University Press 136, from the Letters of John Masefield to Florence Lamont.

The main text of this book uses a font called Cheltenham Book which sounds as if it should have a local connection. In fact, the original Cheltenham font was designed by an American architect, Bertram Goodhue, in the late 1890s. The font saw a revival in the 1970s with some adaptations made by Tony Stan. The name actually refers to the Cheltenham Press in New York.

Special thanks to Clare Bailey, Vicky Barrow and Martin Bennett, and to Ken Langsbury for his last-remaining copy of The Songwainers

KNITSKRIEG!
A call to yarns

Main cover photo: Actress Mary Pickford knits a sweater between scenes for the 1926 film Sparrows. She donated the sweater to the American Red Cross for a disabled war veteran. (Library of Congress)

KNITSKRIEG!
A call to yarns

A HISTORY OF
MILITARY KNITTING
FROM THE 1800S TO
THE PRESENT DAY

First published by Uniform, an imprint of
Unicorn Publishing Group
101 Wardour Street
London W1F 0UG

A catalogue record for this book is available from the British Library

5 4 3 2 1

ISBN 978-1-910500-33-0
ISBN PDF 978-1-910500-35-4
ISBN epub 978-1-910500-34-7

Cover design Unicorn Publishing Group
Typeset by Vivian@Bookscribe

Printed and bound in Slovenia

ACKNOWLEDGEMENTS

I would like to thank everyone who contributed including being photographed for this book.

Vivian my editor and Unicorn Publishing Group.

The uniform wearers: the 79th Cameron Highlanders Quartermaster, Greg Jackson, with the US Civil War socks and Graham Hill at the Army Reserves, Millbrook, Southampton.

My friend Janet Arnold who has put up with me for the last year and agreed to be the WI woman in the scarf and a special thanks for Wayne Bachelor for doing me some great photos and putting them in the correct context. My WW1 knitting would never be the same without Wayne wearing it.

Lastly, to Neil who kindly came to see me and put on the stump warmer. I must say he is the only person who has ever offered to take his leg off for me.

I hope that all my readers will enjoy this book and have the same fun reading it as I did knitting it.

Joyce Meader 2016

'Whenever I think I've done enough knitting for a bit
they go and call up another age group . . .'

CONTENTS

SECTION FOUR – ANTI-WAR AND PEACE MOVEMENT IN KNITTING

SECTION FIVE – KNITTING PATTERNS

INTRODUCTION

Before you stifle a yawn, I would like you to read beyond the first paragraph so that you may be enthralled, as I am, about the long and intricate history behind military knitting. From the 19th century battles at Crimea, the American Civil War and the Boer War right up to the modern-day conflicts in Iraq and Afghanistan, you will learn what garments were issued to our soldiers, why they wore it and who made it for them.

I hope you will find this book a fascinating insight into what comforts soldiers wanted, from the standard issue, the essential items from home such as socks and vests to the more bizarre items like knitted splints, smoking caps and stump warmers. The original patterns for many of these articles have been included and the final section includes modern versions of these should you wish to have a go yourself. I never believed I would actually write a book about my passion, but piqued by my own long history of picking up a pair of needles and reproducing numerous military knitwear patterns, I felt compelled to share this with you the reader.

Military Knitting! Well, what exactly does this mean? Are we being commissioned to knit tanks, guns or helicopters? No, that isn't what it means at all. Military knitting is a way of providing non-uniform items or comforts for all serving personnel when on a campaign or away from home.

There have been knitted garments made at home by the fireside or indeed by local cottage industries for many centuries. In Great Britain, for example, there were laws passed that controlled the use and wearing of wool to certain days of the week. This law gave rise in the 16th century to the knitting of caps for all levels of society and the wide use of the Monmouth Cap by the military and sailors.

I will attempt to cover a majority of different types of garments and items knitted over the years and give you, the reader, useful and often amusing, snippets of information regarding the pieces mentioned. My vast collection of knitting patterns and equipment has been the inspiration behind the chapters within this book.

The information given on these pages are my own thoughts along with the reminiscences of service personnel who were proud enough to wear the knitted item. Whilst attempting to knit some of the garments I had to try and interpret what the writer of the pattern actually meant, but luckily with my vast experience of hand knitting I can surmise what they intended and with a little trial and error reproduce the article as it was originally intended.

I have made reproduction knitwear for many re-enactment groups and events, television and film companies as well as supplying some of our national museums. Gleaned from my talks and demonstrations all over the country, I hope my knowledge will enlighten and inform you and also help to show how home crafts have helped to provide clothing, gifts and memories from home to those on distant shores.

Joyce Meader

Joyce demonstrating a knitted suit from a 1917–18 US pattern at a re-enactment at Fort Nelson

SECTION ONE
19th Century Wars

THE HAVERCAKE LADS

Hand knitting was used to produce hats, stockings and gloves for the military from early times. One fine example of this is the forage cap knitted for his Majesty's 33rd Regiment of Foot. This regiment had its origins in Yorkshire, in northern England and was closely associated with the Duke of Wellington. They were considered to be the backbone of the British Army and were made up of ordinary rank and file men, or private soldiers who fought alongside the Duke at the Battle of Waterloo.

By the time of the American War of Independence it is known that the regiment had established a considerable link with the West Riding and it is around this time that they were given the nickname 'The Havercake Lads'. What is a 'Havercake' you may ask? It is a traditional Yorkshire Oat (hafer) cake and the name is a corruption of 'have a cake lad' from a promise of an oatcake to try and tempt new recruits into the regiment.

The knitted forage cap, as mentioned earlier, was an item of working uniform for soldiers to wear when they were not on the battleground. It was designed to be both practical and comfortable, perfect for wearing when foraging for food, fuel for their fires, or food for the cavalry horses. They were hand knitted and then filled (felted) to make them feel thicker and also made them more hard wearing.

Recruiting party for the 33rd Regiment of Foot

During the Napoleonic Wars, British infantry soldiers wore a stiff cap called a *shako* when actually in physical combat, marching or on parade, but these were heavy and uncomfortable and the soldiers couldn't wait to get into something more comfortable. The knitted, woollen forage cap was introduced in 1812, and became the term used for all uniform caps worn when soldiers were off duty.

They became so popular they were worn when the soldiers were guarding the camp at night or during any activities that did not involve military duties such as cleaning or cooking. Warmer and more comfortable they became the favoured form of headwear and also meant that their dress caps remained clean and undamaged. Considering the soldiers had to buy replacement caps out of their own wages, this was definitely in their own interest. A dress cap, for example, would have cost two to three shillings to buy and, at that time, a private soldier was only paid one shilling per day. For this reason they were well worth preserving.

CRIMEAN WAR

The first book of military knitting patterns published in any number that we know of was written by Mlle. Riego de la Branchardière and published by Simpkin, Marshall and Co. of London. This small booklet was entitled *Comforts for the Crimea or, The Fourth Winter Book, in Crochet and Knitting* and contains a pattern, amongst others, for a knitted Guernsey to be worn over clothes or as an undergarment.

COMFORTS FOR THE CRIMEA;

OR, THE

FOURTH WINTER BOOK,

IN

CROCHET AND KNITTING:

BY

MLLE. RIEGO DE LA BRANCHARDIERE.

LONDON:
SIMPKIN, MARSHALL, AND CO.,
ACKERMANN & CO., STRAND; OLIVER AND BOYD, EDINBURGH;
AND ALL THE BERLIN WAREHOUSES.

1854.

Entered at Stationers' Hall.

MADEMOISELLE ELEONORE RIEGO DE LA BRANCHARDIERE

Mlle Riego, as she preferred to be known, was born in England in 1828 to an Irish mother and a French father. From a young age she was fascinated by anything to do with needlework, knitting, crochet, tatting and netting and is believed to have published her first book at the age of twelve. She is believed to have introduced the art of crochet and her work was so superior it appeared in the Great Exhibition and won the Prize Medal for 'the skill displayed in the imitation of old Spanish and other costly laces.' By the time she died, Mlle Riego had published a staggering 72 books on various needle arts.

The conditions for the soldiers were appalling and the need for warm clothing was essential. Lord Ellesmere started up the 'Crimean Army Fund' asking for personal contributions, a request which was received enthusiastically. On 2 December 1854, Lady Charlotte Bridgeman of Weston Park wrote in her journal:

> *We are all better with the desire to do something for the poor soldiers in the Crimea & hearing that Lord Wilton, Lord Ellesmere & some others are fitting out a yacht with warm clothing & other comforts, which is to start in a fortnight, we have all frantically begun knitting muffetees & comforters, have written to ask several people to do the same & Lady B. has been buying flannel for the schools to make up & stockings to be knitted.*

THE PATTERNS

The pattern for the helmet cap or Guernsey is made in both knitting and crochet and looks very much like a modern-day balaclava. It also has the appearance of chain mail. This shows that the women designing these garments used historical paintings and drawings for reference.

The *Comforts for the Crimea* booklet – a copy of which can be seen in the Hampshire Museum

Service Collection – also contains patterns for mitts with cuff, gloves, travelling caps, a knitted comforter and a crochet maud or plaid. Many of these items are still knitted today but are known by different names. For example, a comforter became a muffler and is now more commonly known as a scarf. A maud or plaid is simply a long, but narrow blanket or, to an American, an Afghan.

Unfortunately, the price of these patterns was out of the reach of most women costing as much as 1s to 1s 6d, so they were mainly bought by women of means. These women also had more time to knit items to be sent overseas to offer some comfort to the brave men fighting for their country.

Maud or Plaid

One of the problems I have come across when reproducing these patterns is that the instructions are very different from the ones we use today. The original patterns are written in paragraphs and not by individual row, or even a graph, as the more modern versions. The abbreviations used are also different and so it often means you are unpicking and restarting so it is really a matter of trial and error. I find that you can unpick the work up to three times before the garment looks correct. If there is a drawing of the garment in the pattern book, make sure you look at it with a sceptical eye, as it was often drawn by a non-knitter who had actually never seen the article in its finished form.

One final point of interest before we move on to an actual pattern is that it was possible to buy tickets and visit the Crimea for your holiday during the time of the War. I always imagine these women sat on the hills above the battlefield knitting furiously for the men fighting just below their feet.

Crochet Mitt and Cuff

PATTERN FOR KNITTED MITTEN

(VERY SIMPLE)

Materials – ½oz. of 4-ply Fleecy, or double Berlin wool; 2 Knitting Pins, No.15, Bell Gauge.

Cast on 56 stitches.

1st row. – Slip the 1st stitch, knit the rest plain.

2nd. – Slip 1, pearl 13, knit the rest.

3rd. – Slip 1, knit 41, pearl the rest.

4th. – Slip 1, knit the rest.

Repeat these 4 rows 20 times more.

85th. – Slip 1, knit 15, cast off 10 stitches, and knit the remaining 31 stitches.

86th. – Slip 1, pearl 13, knit 17, cast on 10 stitches to correspond with those cast off, and knit the remaining 16 stitches.

87th. – As the 3rd row.

88th. – As the 4th row.

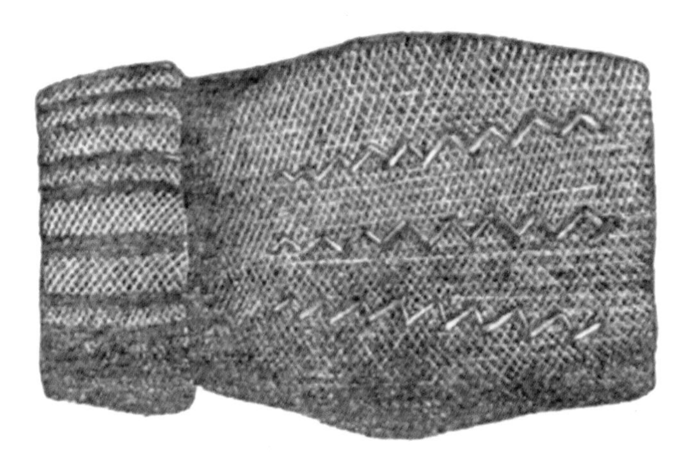

Then repeat the 1st 4 rows, 4 times, and cast off.

Sew the foundation and the last row together.

Work the other mitt the same, and down the back work 3 rows of hem stitch.

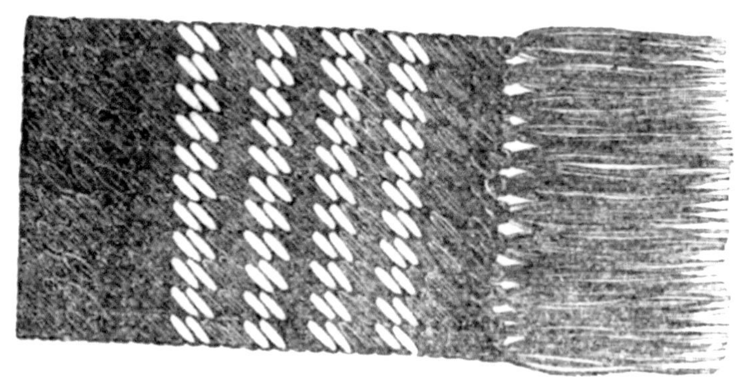

PATTERN FOR KNITTED COMFORTER

Materials – Double Berlin wool or 4-ply Fleecy. Colours – For the stripe, violet, white, scarlet, amber, and black. 2 skeins of each, and for the ground, 4 ounces of dark green, or Sultana wool may be used; 2 knitting pins, No. 8, Bell Gauge.

This scarf can be worked in only one or two colours, if wished.

Cast on with the black wool 74 stitches, that is 3 stitches for each pattern, and 2 over for the edge stitches.

1st row. – Bring the wool in front of the pin in the right hand, then turn the wool quite round the pin so as to bring it in the front again, and pearl 2 stitches together; * the wool will now be in the front; turn it round the pin so as to bring it in the front again, pass the needle down the next stitch, and take if off without knitting it; then pearl the next 2 stitches together, and repeat from * to the end of the row.

2nd. – Bring the wool in front of the pin and turn it round as before, then pearl 2 stitches together; * turn the wool round the pin, bringing it in the front; then slip the next stitch, thus put the pin down at the back of the stitch, and, bringing the pin in the front take off the front part of the stitch without knitting it, this stitch slipped is a long loop; then pearl the next 2 stitches together and repeat from * to the end of the row.

All the rows are the same as the second.

Work 4 rows of black, 4 rows of violet, 4 rows of white, 4 rows of scarlet, 4 rows of amber, 4 rows of black, 4 rows of amber, 4 rows of scarlet, 4 rows of white, 4 rows of violet, 4 rows of black, which finishes the stripe. Then 20 rows of green; repeat the 1st stripe; then work 1 yard of green, and repeat the stripes, to correspond with the other side; finish with a green fringe looped in the same manner as in the crochet comforter.

THE 79TH CAMERON HIGHLANDERS

We are a collection of people who are dedicated to living history and re-enacting life as it would have been in the 79th Cameron Highlanders Regiment during the Peninsular wars and leading up to up to the Battle of Waterloo. We try to recreate as authentically as possible the everyday life for the soldiers and their families within the regiment, using costume, muskets, drums and food cooked to authentic recipes and day to day routine life in the camp.

The regiment meets regularly at Fort Amherst, Chatham, Kent, a genuine Napoleonic Fort and is one of the best preserved Napoleonic fortresses in England; it was designed and built to protect Chatham Dockyard which is situated on the banks of the river Medway during the threat of invasion by our enemies.

Our uniforms, much of which we make ourselves and the drill are based on the regiment before the Battle of Waterloo in 1815. We participate in various re-enactments both in the UK and in Europe, organised by the Napoleonic Association plus other events organised from within by us or by other re-enactment units or localities.

We are proud of our living history which aims to provide an insight into the camp life of a regiment of that period; and we were one of the first Napoleonic groups to do this. This aspect of our group provides opportunities to persons who may not want to portray the life a line infantryman, but still be actively involved in the group using their own unique skills.

Furthermore we also have our own Pipers and Drummers, in their distinctive reverse coloured tunics. We welcome any interested musicians, whether they are experienced players, or just wishing to learn.

Many of us have participated in Film and TV work, and have attended educational visits to local schools and at Fort Amherst and other locations in the UK.

Our unit caters for every member of the family, whether you would like to be a soldier, partisan, a camp wife or a musician, there will always be a place for you within the 79th.

www.the79thcameronhighlanders.co.uk

The Crimea War 'gansey'. Note how small it is and the gusset under the arm allowed for easy movement; each of the ribs on the garment are three stitches.

Our Diagrams for **ARMY SOCKS** *having been found useful, we herewith submit one for* **ARMY MITTENS**

Those who may be disposed to knit **MITTENS** *for the* **ARMY**, *may forward them through the Women's* **CENTRAL RELIEF ASSOCIATION**

Diagrams may b

by applying to

JOHN J. HINCHM

Dealers in Hosier

26 & 28 Vesey S

New-York.

Directions for **ARMY**

Use Grey or Blue mixed Y

or Coarser; any color but wh

The pair should weigh

3 ounces.

Use needles No 15.

Length of Mittens 11

inches.

Width over palm 4 ¼

4 ½ inches

May be knitted or Crocheted at option.

---

22 Stitches on each needle of No 20 Yarn, or more or less in proportion, if the Yarn be finer or coarser to make the **MITTEN FULL SIZE of PATTERN**

Rib 2 & 2 – 2 ½ inches for Cuff.

for seams

en seams

d until

A

Seam

hes at B

ches to

C

8

th

D *Begin to narrow keeping the width well to the end*

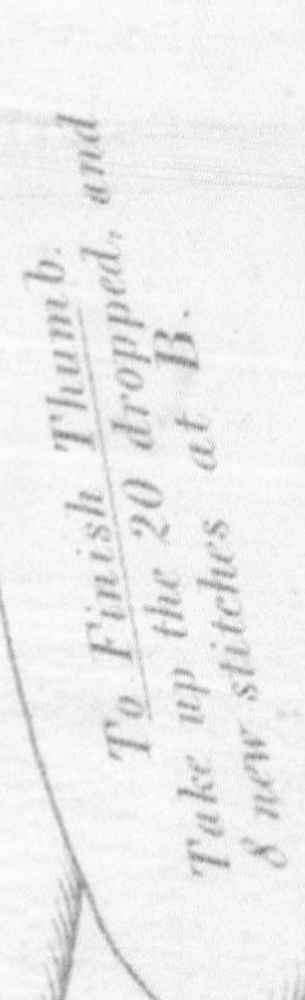

To Finish Thumb. Take up the 20 dropped, and 8 new stitches at B.

To Finish Finger. Take up the 16 dropped, and 8 new stitches at C.

AMERICAN CIVIL WAR

By the fireside, cosily seated,
With spectacles riding her nose,
The lively old lady is knitting
A wonderful pair of Hose.
She pities the shivering soldier,
Who is out in the pelting storm;
And busily plies her needles,
To keep him hearty and warm.

The lines written here are part of a poem found in a bundle of socks sent to an American military hospital in Philadelphia, dated 22 December 1863.

Although knitting for the troops was not a new idea, with each new conflict came a new set of rules or, as some would like to describe it, propaganda. The Civil War began on 12 April 1861 and became a pivotal event in the history of America. Without doubt hand knitted garments were more highly sought after than the inferior machine-knitted versions of say socks or stockings, as the latter survived the rigours of long marches and infrequent washing. Because of their longevity the call for hand knitted socks went out through America. Considering that nearly half of the nation's young men volunteered or were conscripted into military service, it is not surprising the womenfolk back at home felt compelled to play their part. As they heard harrowing stories of their men marching barefoot or suffering from blistered, swollen and infected feet from wearing boots without stockings, they were spurred to take up their knitting needles regardless of age.

LEFT: Greg Jackson has been a member of the Southern Skirmish Association (SoSkAn) since 2001, re-enacting Federal impressions with the 18th Missouri Veteran Volunteer Regiment and the Union Battalion Staff. Formed in 1968, SoSkAn is the oldest American Civil War Re-enactment Society outside of America. The Association has performed in numerous venues around Britain, Europe and the United States.

During the early months of the American Civil War many confederate women answered the call and immediately set to knitting for the soldiers. Some of the women with time on their hands vowed to knit as many as one hundred garments which included hats, socks, mittens, gloves, scarves, nightshirts, undergarments, bandages and even mattress covers, all of which were in great demand. Classes were introduced for young women who had not been taught to knit, but who were only too pleased to learn. Wives, mothers and sweethearts sent packages to their loved ones, while women's organisations filled boxes full of food, books and hand knitted clothing.

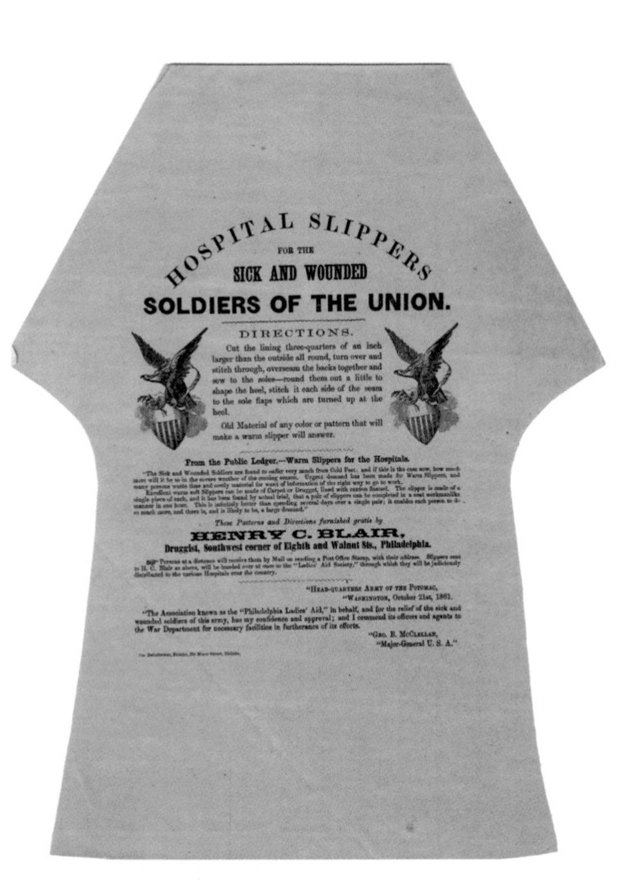

HOSPITAL SLIPPERS FOR THE SICK AND WOUNDED

SOLDIERS OF THE UNION.

DIRECTIONS.

Cut the lining three-quarters of an inch larger than the outside all round, turn over and stitch through, overseam the backs together and sew to the soles—round them out a little to shape the heel, stitch it each side of the seam to the sole flaps which are turned up at the heel.

Old Material of any color or pattern that will make a warm slipper will answer.

From the Public Ledger.—Warm Slippers for the Hospitals.

"The Sick and Wounded Soldiers are found to suffer very much from Cold Feet; and if this is the case now, how much more will it be so in the severe weather of the coming season. Urgent demand has been made for Warm Slippers, and many persons waste time and costly material for want of information of the right way to go to work.

Excellent warm soft Slippers can be made of Carpet or Drugget, lined with cotton flannel. The slipper is made of a single piece of each, and it has been found by actual trial, that a pair of slippers can be completed in a neat workmanlike manner in one hour. This is infinitely better than spending several days over a single pair; it enables each person to do so much more, and there is, and is likely to be, a large demand."

These Patterns and Directions furnished gratis by

HENRY C. BLAIR,

Druggist, Southwest corner of Eighth and Walnut Sts., Philadelphia.

Persons at a distance will receive them by Mail on sending a Post Office Stamp, with their address. Slippers sent to H. C. Blair as above, will be handed over at once to the "Ladies' Aid Society," through which they will be judiciously distributed to the various Hospitals over the country.

"Head-quarters Army of the Potomac,
"Washington, October 21st, 1861.

"The Association known as the "Philadelphia Ladies' Aid," in behalf, and for the relief of the sick and wounded soldiers of this army, has my confidence and approval; and I commend its officers and agents to the War Department for necessary facilities in furtherance of its efforts.

"Geo. B. McClellan,
"Major-General U. S. A."

Children as young as three were encouraged to knit and many were made to knit three inches in length on the socks before they were allowed out to play.

The patterns shown here demonstrate just how few instructions were published with the patterns – there isn't even a needle size with the one for the sock.

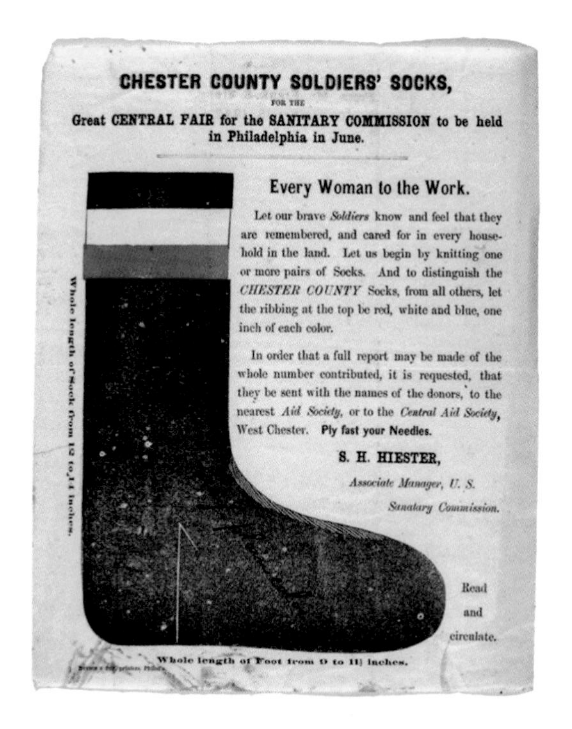

CHESTER COUNTY SOLDIERS' SOCKS,

FOR THE

Great CENTRAL FAIR for the SANITARY COMMISSION to be held in Philadelphia in June.

Every Woman to the Work.

Let our brave *Soldiers* know and feel that they are remembered, and cared for in every household in the land. Let us begin by knitting one or more pairs of Socks. And to distinguish the *CHESTER COUNTY* Socks, from all others, let the ribbing at the top be red, white and blue, one inch of each color.

In order that a full report may be made of the whole number contributed, it is requested, that they be sent with the names of the donors, to the nearest *Aid Society*, or to the *Central Aid Society*, West Chester. **Ply fast your Needles.**

S. H. HIESTER,

Associate Manager, U. S. Sanatary Commission.

Whole length of Sock from 13 to 14 inches.

Read and circulate.

Whole length of Foot from 9 to 11½ inches.

A variation on the Winter Sock

WINTER SOCK

(pattern taken from *Godey's Lady's Book and Magazine*, January 1860)

Materials – Six ounces of lambswool; 4 pins, No. 18

Cast one 38 loops on each of three pins.

Knit two plain, one pearl in every row. Knit till the work measures nine inches, narrowing five times in that space by knitting two stitches together on each side of the back seam; divide the loops in half, and form the level thus: Plus one half of the loops on one pin for the heel, the remainder on the two pins for the instep. Knit the loops on one pin for four inches, narrowing twice; knit to the back seam, divide the loops and cast off. Pick up the loops at each side of the heel, knit these with those for the instep. In the first round make a stitch after every third on the two side pins; in the next round, narrow by knitting the last on the side pin and the first on the instep. Next round, plain. Repeat these two rounds; after which, narrow for the toe. Narrow three times at each side of the pins in every other round, till the whole are narrowed off the sole of the foot, and the last sixty rounds must be plain knitting.

John L. Hayes, a devout lobbyist for wool, called knitted socks '. . . the class of clothing the most indispensable for the health and comfort of our soldiers.'

An officer from West Point who commanded one of the finest regiments commented that '…woollen mittens for soldiers will be greatly needed when the cold weather begins.' It has been said that there were more soldiers disabled by frost bite than from any other cause.

KNITTED MITTENS

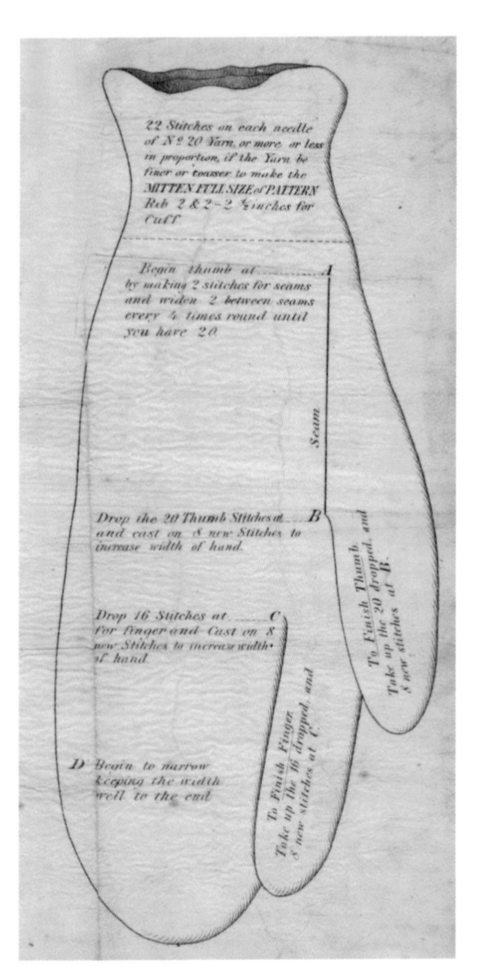

John J. Hinchman & Co, dealers in hosiery based in New York, included diagrams with their knitting patterns as can be seen by the mitten illustrated here.

The following instructions accompanied this pattern:

Our diagrams for ARMY SOCKS having been found useful, we herewith submit one for ARMY MITTENS.

Those who may be disposed to knit MITTENS for the ARMY, may forward them through the Women's Central Relief Association, No 814 Broadway, New York.

Directions for ARMY MITTENS.

Use Grey or Blue mixed yarn No. 20 or courser, any colour but white will do.

The pair should weight at least 3 ounces.

Use needles No. 15

Length of mittens 11 to 11½ inches

Width over palm 4¼ to 4½ inches

May be knitted or crocheted at option.

GENTLEMAN'S SHOOTING MITTENS.

REQUIRED, 2½ ozs. of fine fingering or speckled wool. Four steel knitting needles, No. 16, or for a small hand No. 18. Knit first the left-hand mitten. Cast 20 stitches on each of three needles, 60 stitches in all. **1st round**—Knit 2, purl 2, and repeat. **2nd round**, and following rounds, the same, till 20 rounds are knitted. (This part, which is for the wrist, can be knitted longer if wished.) Knit three plain rounds. **24th round**—Knit 1, make 1, knit 7, purl 2, knit 5, purl 2, knit 5, purl 2, knit 35, make 1, knit 1. **25th round**—Knit 9, purl 2, knit 5, purl 2, knit 5, purl 2, knit 37. **26th round**—The same, and note that the purled stitches will always be in the same place in every round, and will form the three seams on the back of the hand. **27th round**—Knit 2, make 1, knit 7, purl 2, knit 5, purl 2, knit 5, purl 2, knit 35, make 1, knit 2. **28th round**—Knit 10, purl 2, knit 5, purl 2, knit 5, purl 2, knit 38. **29th round**—The same. **30th round**—Knit 3, make 1, knit 7, purl 2, knit 5, purl 2, knit 5, purl 2, knit 35, make 1, knit 3. **31st round**—Knit 11, purl 2, knit 5, purl 2, knit 5, purl 2, knit 39. **32nd round**—The same. **33rd round**—Knit 4, make 1, knit 7, purl 2, knit 5, purl 2, knit 5, purl 2, knit 35, make 1, knit 4 **34th round**—Knit 12, purl 2, knit 5, purl 2, knit 5, purl 2, knit 40. **35th round**—The same. **36th round**—Knit 5, make 1, knit 7, purl 2, knit 5, purl 2, knit 5, purl 2, knit 35, make 1, knit 5. **37th round**—Knit 13, purl 2, knit 5, purl 2, knit 5, purl 2, knit 41 **38th round**—The same. **39th round**—Knit 6, make 1, knit 7, purl 2, knit5, purl 2, knit 5, purl 2, knit 35, make 1, knit 6. **40th round**—Knit 14, purl 2, knit 5 purl 2, knit 5, purl 2, knit 42. **41st round**—The same. **42nd round**—Knit 7, make 1, knit 7, purl 2, knit 5, purl 2, knit 5, purl 2, knit 35, make 1, knit 7. **43rd round**—Knit 15, purl 2, knit 5, purl 2, knit 5, purl 2, knit 43. **44th round**—The same. **45th round**—Knit 8, make 1, knit 7, purl 2, knit 5, purl 2, knit 5, purl 2, knit 35, make 1, knit 8. **46th round**—Knit 16, purl 2, knit 5, purl 2, knit 5, purl 2, knit 44. **47th round**—The same. **48th round**—Knit 9, make 1, knit 7, purl 2, knit 5, purl 2, knit 5, purl 2, knit 35, make 1, knit 9. **49th round**—Knit 17, purl 2, knit 5, purl 2, knit 5, purl 2, knit 45 **50th round**—The same. **51st round**—Knit 10, make 1, knit 7, purl 2, knit 5, purl 2, knit 5, purl 2, knit 35, make 1, knit 10. **52nd round**—Knit 18, purl 2, knit 5, purl 2, knit 5, purl 2, knit 46. Knit 2 more rounds the same. There should now be 80 stitches on the needles. **55th round**—Knit 11, make 1, knit 7, purl 2, knit 5, purl 2, knit 5, purl 2, knit 35, make 1. knit 11. **56th round**—knit 19, purl 2, knit 5, purl 2, knit 5, purl 2, knit 47, knit 2 more round the same. **59th round**—Knit 12, make 1, knit 7, purl 2, knit 5, purl 2 knit 5, purl 2, knit 35, make 1, knit 12. **60th round**—Knit 20, purl 2, knit 5, purl 2, knit 5, purl 2, knit 48. Knit 2 more rounds the same. **63rd round**—Knit 13, make 1, knit 7, purl 2, knit 5, purl 2, knit 5, purl 2, knit 35, make 1, knit 13. **64th round**—Knit 21, purl 2, knit 5, purl 2, knit 5, purl 2, knit 49. Knit 2 more rounds the same. Now to begin the **Thumb**—Knit 13, take off the next 60 stitches upon two spare pins, and let them remain for the present, cast on 5 new stitches, and knit the 13 stitches left at the end of the round, have these 31 stitches arranged upon three needles. **2nd round**—Plain. **3rd round**—Knit 14, knit 2 together, knit 2 together again, knit 13 **4th round**—Plain. **5th round**—Knit 13, knit 2 together, knit 2 together again, knit 12. **6th round**—Plain. **7th round**—Knit 13, knit 2 together, knit 12, knit 18 plain rounds, and cast off. Replace the 60 stitches again upon three needles, and also take up the other edges of the 5 new stitches cast on for the thumb, these last being at the end of the round. **67th round**—Knit 8, purl 2, knit 5, purl 2, knit 5, purl 2, knit 41. **68th round**—The same. **69th round**—Knit 8, purl 2, knit 5, purl 2, knit 5, purl 2, knit 37, knit 2 together, knit 2 together again. **70th round**—Knit 8, purl 2, knit 5, purl 2, knit 5, purl 2, knit 39 **71st round**—Knit 8, purl 2, knit 5, purl 2, knit 5, purl 2, knit 35, knit 2 together, knit 2 together again. **72nd round**—Knit 8, purl 2, knit 5, purl 2, knit 5, purl 2, knit 37. **73rd round**—Knit 8 purl 2, knit 5, purl 2, knit 5, purl 2, knit 35, knit 2 together. **74th round**—Knit 8, purl 2, knit 5, purl 2, knit 5, purl 2, knit 36. Knit 10 more rounds the same as the last. Knit 3 plain rounds. For the **First Finger**—Take off upon two spare pins 44 stitches, keeping on the needles the first 8 and the last 8 stitches of the round. Knit the first 8 stitches, cast upon another needle 5 new stitches for the part between the first and second fingers, knit the other 8 stitches, and now upon these 21 stitches knit 22 plain rounds, and cast off. For the **Second Finger**—Knit the first 7 stitches off the first spare pin, cast upon another needle 5 new stitches for the part between the second and third fingers, knit the 7 stitches from the end of the other spare pin, and pick up the edge of the 5 new stitches made for the first finger, and now upon these 24 stitches knit 32 plain rounds, and cast off For the **Third Finger**—Knit the first 6 stitches off the spare pin, cast upon another needle 4 new stitches for the part between the third and fourth fingers, knit the 6 stitches from the end of the other spare pin, and pick up the edge of the 4 new stitches made for the second finger; and now upon these 21 stitches knit 26 plain rounds, and cast off. For the **Fourth Finger**—Knit the 16 stitches from the spare pin, and pick up the edge of the 4 new stitches made for the third finger; and upon these twenty stitches knit 20 plain rounds, and cast off. This finishes the left-hand mitten. For the **Right-Hand Mitten**—Again cast on 60 stitches, and knit in ribbing the same number of rounds as before. For the hand part, knit exactly the same as the left-hand mitten, only making each round *reversely*—that is, beginning each round at the end of the instructions—thus, the 24th round of this mitten will be knit 1, make 1, knit 35, purl 2, knit 5, purl 2, knit 5, purl 2, knit 7, make 1, knit 1, and all the other rounds similarly. Knit the thumb and fingers in the same consecutive order, there is very little difference in the arrangement of the stitches, but knit each round reversely from the instructions to insure correctness. These mittens can be converted into gloves by knitting the thumb and fingers a little longer and then gradually narrowing them off to a point. If required for a lady, working with Andalusian wool and needles No. 18, will produce a nice fitting size

GENT'S SHOOTING MITTENS.

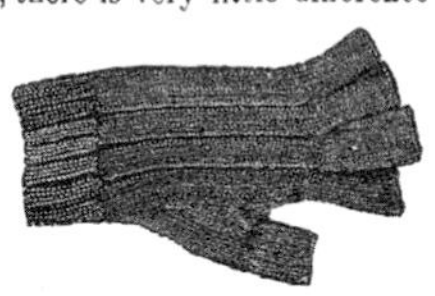

Another major obstacle was how to obtain the wool which was in short supply, along with cards, knitting needles (seen here in photo) and the tools needed to prepare the wool for spinning. Due to the shortage of wool women often had to knit with coarse cotton, but this was expensive. As stated in the *Charleston Mercury*: 'The coarsest yarn costs two dollars a pound, and a pound of yarn will not quite make five socks.' It was suggested that the women mix cotton with either cow's hair or rabbit's fur to make items of a superior quality. This last point was important because governments would always ask for garments to be made in good quality yarn only.

As the need increased for knitted items, women were able to obtain yarn and patterns from central distribution points and either sat alone in their homes or in a group, which offered support and helped take their minds off what their men were having to endure.

As long as yarn was available, women would knit, and for all classes it became more than just a pastime. Ladies associations were formed, with some suggesting that each member should be expected to knit at least six pairs of socks during a six-month period to keep their membership valid. Schools also added knitting to their curriculum and at one Tennessee women's college, the principal requested that the girls be given an hour a day to knit socks for soldiers. The patriotic knitting fervour had really taken off and girls, some under the age of twelve, started to form their own clubs. Papers throughout the South constantly reminded women 'that it was their patriotic duty to knit for the soldiers and their knitting needles were the only things standing between soldiers and the cold.' One ingenious lady even thought of knitting stump socks to fit over amputated limbs.

All women helped the north to win.

The Ladies' Repository published the following poem in 1861 to encourage everyone to pick up their needles and knit... knit... knit...

Knit – Knit – Knit
With a warm heart and a true!
Knit – Knit – Knit
The stockings warm and new.
The mittens with a finger and thumb complete,
The gloves for the drummers to beat –
And the nice warm socks for the shivering feet.

As the war raged on and the initial frenzy started to wane, patterns stopped appearing in publications but the women were undeterred and just made use of what they already had.

In January 1865, a war correspondent who worked for the *New York Times* reported that: The weather had been cold, icy and wet and that one out of four soldiers still didn't have mittens. He went on to say that the extra money spent on Christmas dinners could have been better utilised by providing the extra 50,000 pairs of mittens still desperately needed by the army.

The word mitten comes from the French word *mitaine*. As the Old French word *mite* is a pet name for a cat, it can be assumed the link is the appearance – that of a cat's paw.

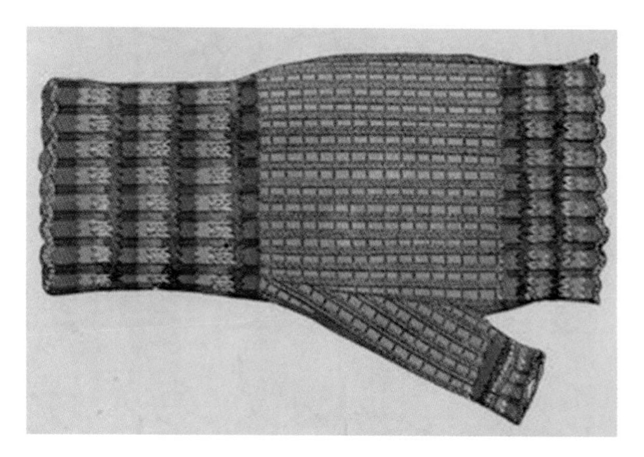

Filed March 4th 1862

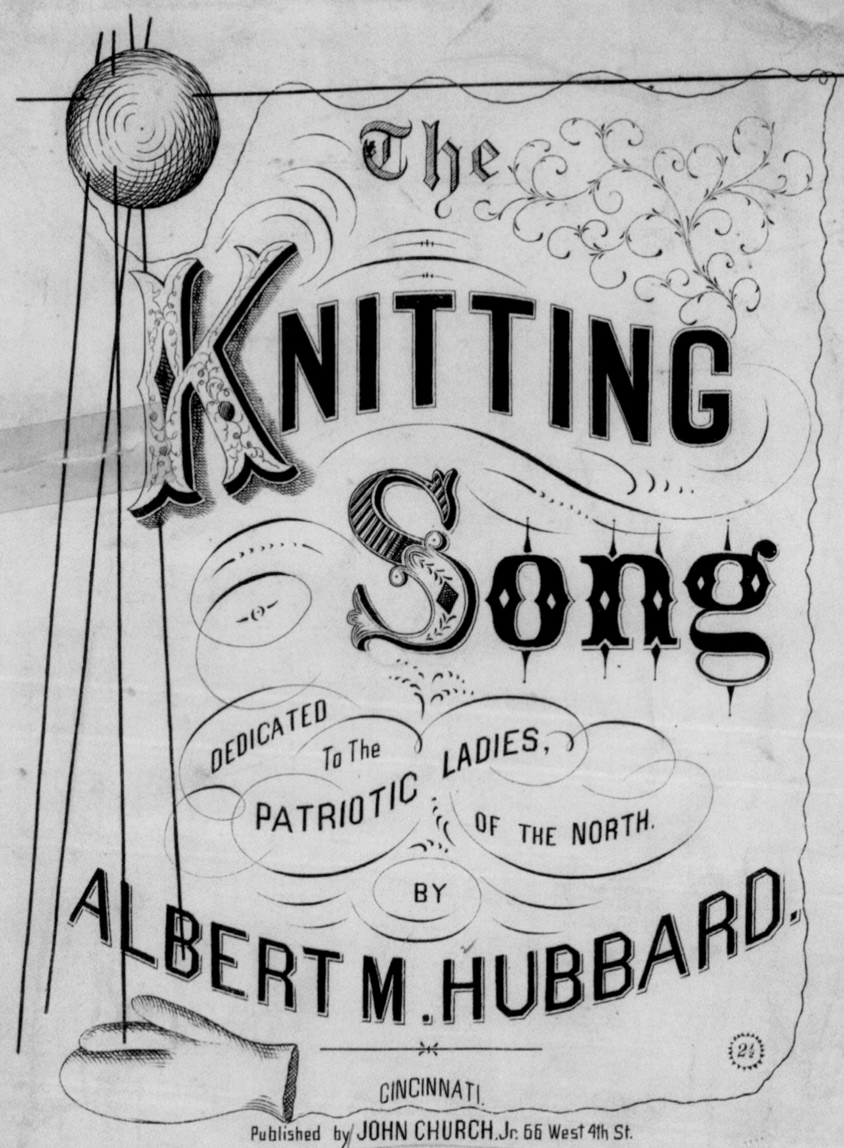

Published by John Church, Jr. 66 West 4th St.

Boston. O. Ditson & Co. | N. York. Firth Pond & Co. | Philad.a Lee & Walker.

In admiration of the women who knitted for hours on end and believed it might accelerate their speed of knit one, purl one, Albert M. Hubbard composed *The Knitting Song*:

Knit! Knit! Knit!
For our Northern soldiers brave!
Knit! Knit! Knit! While the Stars and Stripes they wave!
While they the rebels in battle meet
Be yours to fashion with fingers fleet
The nice warm socks for the weary feet
Knit! Knit! Knit!
    For our boys on Southern hills
    Our boys in Southern vales
    By the woods and streams of Dixieland
    Are feeling the wintry gales.
Knit! Knit! Knit!
The socks and mittens and gloves!
Knit! Knit! Knit!
Each one that her country loves!
Lay beside the useless, though beautiful toy,
With which you many an hour employ,
And knit, instead, for the soldier boy
Knit! Knit! Knit!

When the battle was raging at its worst, workers of the Sanitary Commission worked day and night sorting, counting, wrapping and writing letters of appreciation so that every single knitter knew they were not forgotten. Stockings were on the top of the list, but the donations also included woollen and cotton shirts, woollen and cotton drawers, handkerchiefs, slippers, slings, dressing gowns, pants, overcoats, old clothing and bandages and of course the ubiquitous knitted mittens, shawls and hats. There was a large black market for socks and for this reason the Sanitary Commission would stencil their name on the socks with indelible dye so that they could not be stolen and sold on the black market.

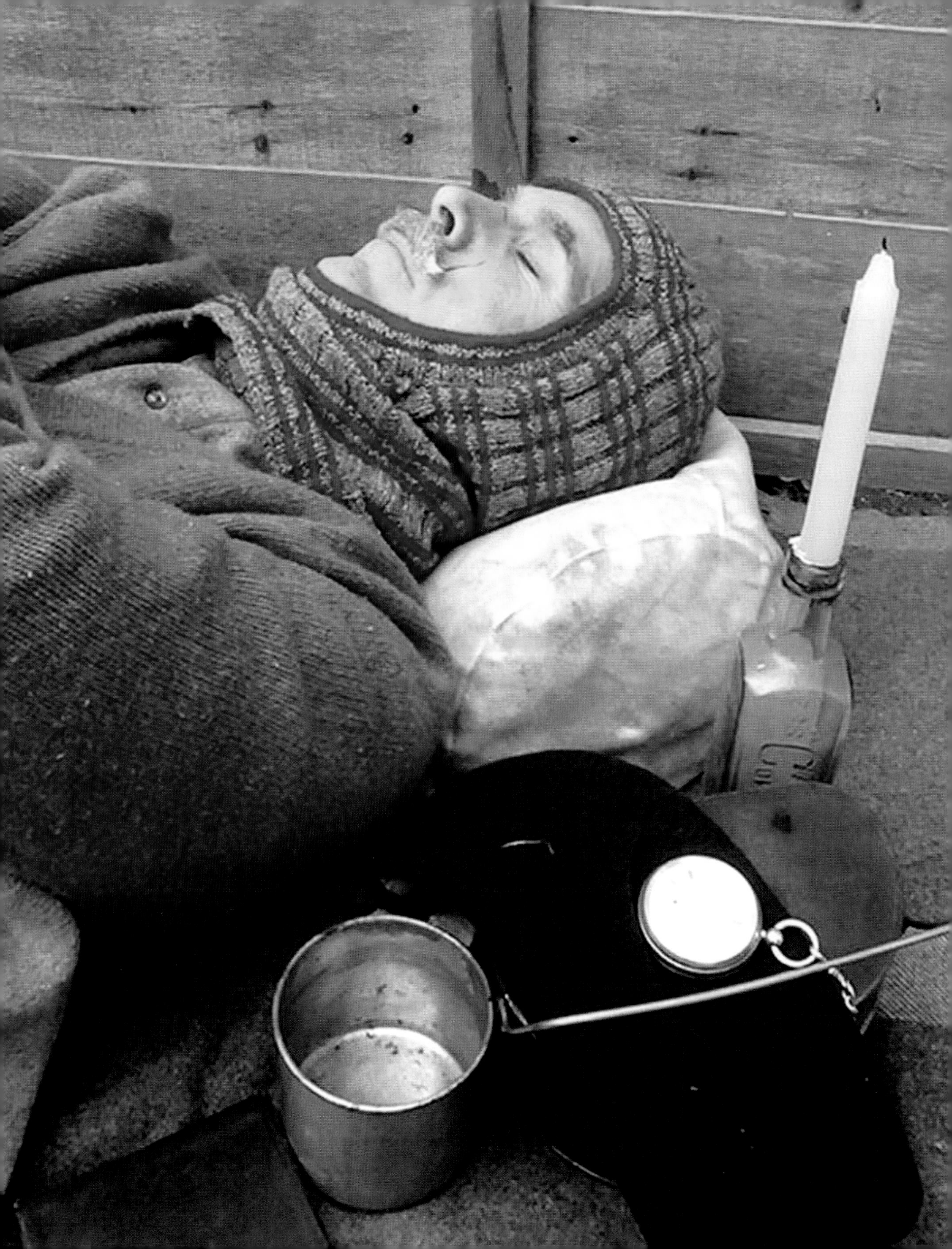

THE BOER WAR

The war in South Africa (better known as the Second Boer War) raged on from 11 October 1899 until 31 May 1902 and acquired the name 'Boer' from the Dutch Afrikaans word for farmers. Even if the little ladies left behind could not take an active part in the conflict, at least from the comfort and safety of their own homes they could knit and sew, a hobby which appealed to women in the nineteenth century. But knitting was not just confined to the home, women knitted while travelling, waiting to be served at restaurants, at work canteens and some even went to the extreme and took their needles to the theatre. A great variety of articles were required including: comforters or mufflers, caps, balaclavas, gloves, waistcoats, jumpers and body warmers, just a few of the items sent to the soldiers fighting bravely overseas. Some found the clicking of needles comforting, while others moaned that they were 'likely to go cross-eyed for life!'

The Bangor Women's Patriotic Guild received a special commendation for their work as they branched out to make mosquito nets and sunshields, but above all was the need for socks. Socks were a welcome luxury to soldiers who frequently found their feet sodden by sweat from the heat and marching in leather boots.

Of course knitting socks was not as easy as it sounds, in fact it was quite a skill to get it right, especially when turning the heel. Home knitters would be taught the 'family' heel and toe method. They only needed the number of stitches for the main body and foot and tables of numbers were published to work by. Very often socks were sent out that were either too large, too small, or simply too misshaped to be of any use. To be successful the sock needed to be stretched when completed and this would be done by using a sock-blocker or sock frame. One of the downsides to the knitted sock was that it would take so long to dry once the wool got wet.

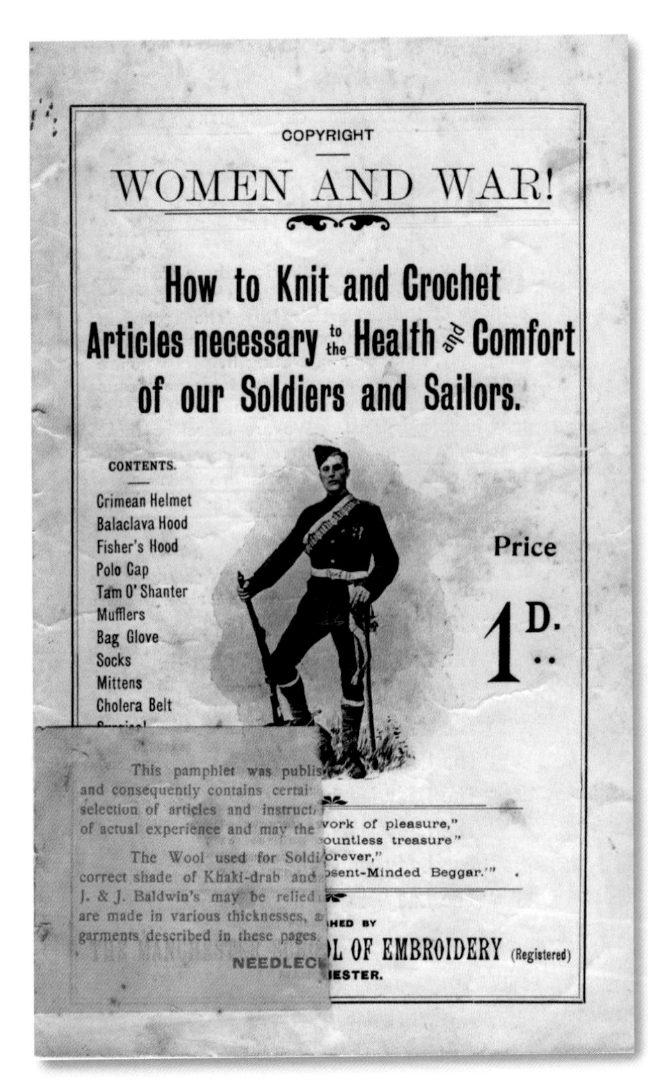
COPYRIGHT

WOMEN AND WAR!

How to Knit and Crochet Articles necessary to the Health and Comfort of our Soldiers and Sailors.

CONTENTS.

Crimean Helmet
Balaclava Hood
Fisher's Hood
Polo Cap
Tam O' Shanter
Mufflers
Bag Glove
Socks
Mittens
Cholera Belt

Price 1D.

This pamphlet was publis
and consequently contains certai
selection of articles and instruct
of actual experience and may the

The Wool used for Soldi
correct shade of Khaki-drab and
J. & J. Baldwin's may be relied
are made in various thicknesses, a
garments described in these pages.

NEEDLEC

vork of pleasure,"
ountless treasure"
orever,"
osent-Minded Beggar.'"

HED BY
L OF EMBROIDERY (Registered)
IESTER.

Of course knitting for troops was not a new occupation for those left at home. Florence Nightingale had a team of nurses who sorted through assorted knitted items during the Crimea War, many of which had patriotic messages or simple blessings tucked inside and the enthusiasm was no less for the war in South Africa. Magazines and newspapers published numerous patterns or the knitters referred to the publication as *Women and War* just priced at 1d.

Ladies who wanted to knit Stockings, Socks, Mufflers, Tam O'Shanters, Nightcaps and other woollen articles to be sent out to the troops fighting the Boer War, were requested to send a free sample, or so the advertisement for Providence Mills Spinning Company in *Lloyd's Weekly Newspaper* suggested. The advertisement was headed GIFTS FOR OUR SOLDIERS IN SOUTH AFRICA, informing the dutiful ladies that they stocked all the regulation shades of khaki that they would ever need.

In fact, khaki (the Indian word for sand) became a fashion statement for women during this period and an advertisement in the *Illustrated London News* appealed to the 'new woman' with:

KHAKI! KHAKI! KHAKI!
All Wool Serge Khaki as made for the Government

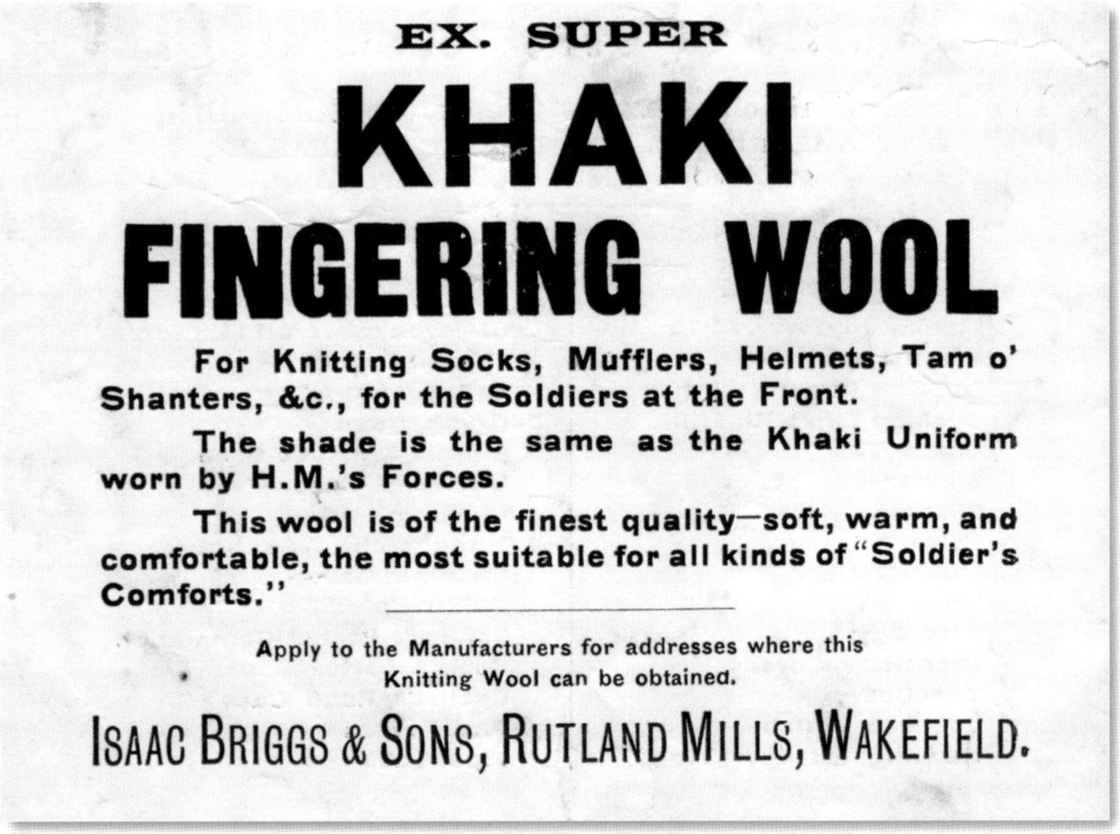

EX. SUPER

KHAKI

FINGERING WOOL

For Knitting Socks, Mufflers, Helmets, Tam o' Shanters, &c., for the Soldiers at the Front.

The shade is the same as the Khaki Uniform worn by H.M.'s Forces.

This wool is of the finest quality—soft, warm, and comfortable, the most suitable for all kinds of "Soldier's Comforts."

Apply to the Manufacturers for addresses where this Knitting Wool can be obtained.

ISAAC BRIGGS & SONS, RUTLAND MILLS, WAKEFIELD.

The advertisement continued…

Most fashionable as well as most suitable material for cycling, shopping, golfing, holidaying, racing, and for everyday wear.

This move to freedom and increased mobility for the feminine race did not go down too well with the male gender. They saw the adoption of the khaki as a copy of their martial dress code and an intrusion on their masculinity. It was still considered that the 'little lady' should be at home doing their rightful duties, not gadding about enjoying themselves on their bicycles.

Despite all the propaganda and shortage of yarn, the knitting mania continued and many women received letters of thanks from soldiers who had found comfort in say a pair of mittens, to try and alleviate the discomfort of frostbite during the night.

QUEEN VICTORIA

Even royalty was not exempt from this mania. Queen Victoria herself wished to honour the bravery of soldiers fighting in the Boer War. She wanted to let them know she was thinking about them and to send a token of her own respect. For this reason she knitted eight scarves in khaki-coloured Berlin wool and put the initials 'V.R.I.' on one of the knots.

However, to earn one of these prestigious scarves, the recipient need to be 'the best all-round man taking part in the South African campaign.' This accolade could only be achieved if the individual soldier was voted for by his comrades as being the most brave. Four of Queen Victoria's scarves went to British units and one to each Empire (commonwealth) country who had sent troops to the conflict.

Sleeping Helmet.

With long neck, which, turned up, forms a warm wrap and comfortable support when sleeping. The repeating 3 cross bars are darker because knitted in the crimson shade of wool.

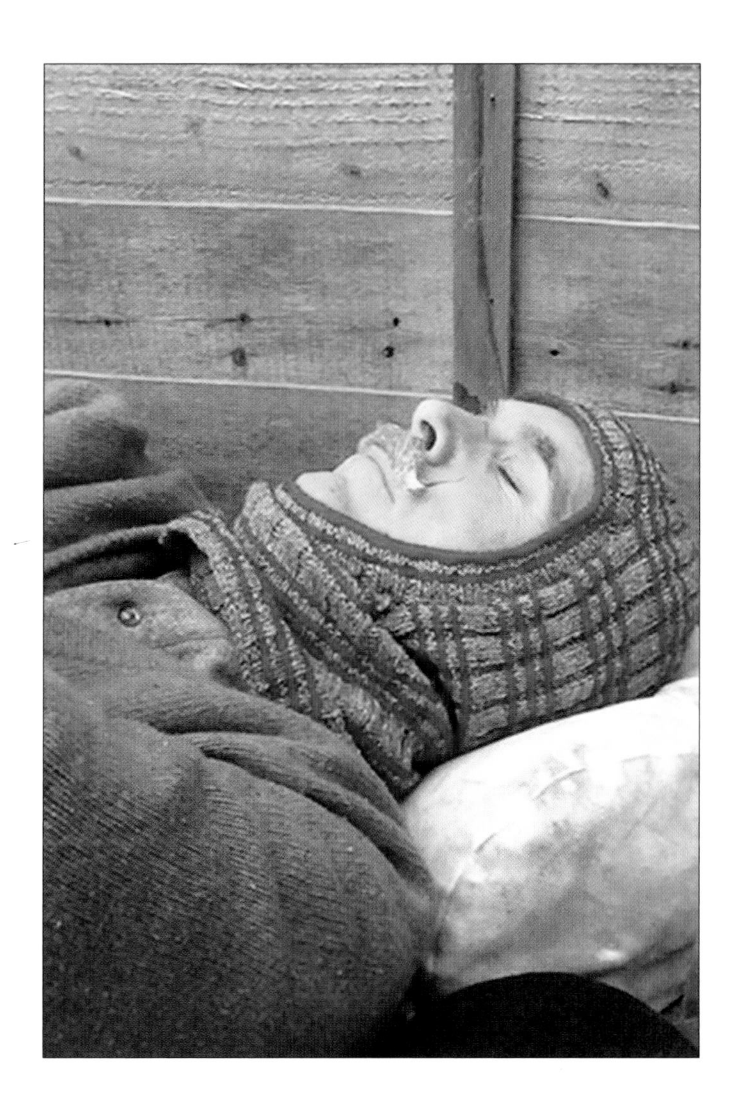

Abdominal or Cholera Belt.
This shows the pointed end and a part of Cholera Belt.

THE ABDOMINAL OR CHOLERA BELT
These were used to keep the kidneys warm; it was believed that cholera infection was harboured there. I remember my Grandma saying when I was a child, "Don't get your kidneys cold, you'll catch your death" and she was born in 1905.

This garment merely consists of a long, straight piece of knitting pointed at one end. It should measure from six to eight inches in width, and from two and half to three yards and upwards in length according to the proportions of the wearer. This piece of knitting is wound round the body thrice in a slightly spiral direction, and is fastened at the point with a small safety pin. It always fits closely, and remains comfortable as long as it lasts.

The most suitable stitch for a belt of this kind is a dice pattern (see illustration). Isaac Briggs and Son's nice soft 4 ply fingering wool and two steel knitting needles, No. 13, are suitable materials. The quantity of material depends upon the size of the belt; a belt measuring 7 inches in width will use about 1 skein of wool for each foot in length.

For a 7 inch belt cast on 60 stitches.
1st row – * Knit 4, purl 4, repeat from * ending with knit 4. 2nd row – * Purl 4, knit 4, repeat ending with purl 4. 3rd row – Same as 1st. 4th row – same as 2nd. 5th row – Same as 1st. Repeat these five rows until you have completed the length you wish ($2\frac{3}{4}$ yards is an average size), then make the pointed end as follows:– Decrease at the beginning of each row by knitting or purling together the 2nd and 3rd stitches, taking care to follow the pattern. When only 4 stitches remain cast off.

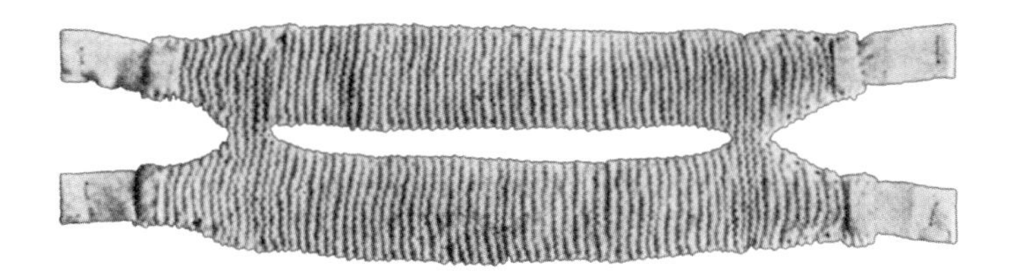

Lower Jaw Bandage

Many bandages and hospital comforts were made during this conflict – eye, lower jaw and plain bandages were made in great numbers. When casting on and off, women were asked not to use knots as it was believed these could harbour bacteria when washed.

These bandages should be carefully washed with good soap and water, and thoroughly rinsed. Nothing in the way of washing powder, soda, starch or blue should be used in making them up. The washing is necessary to remove any dressing that may be in either cotton or tape; the knitting should only be carefully dried, but the tape should be smoothly ironed out.

This pattern was printed in the *Women and War!* booklet which also contained a Balaclava Hood, Fisher's Hood, Polo Cap, Tam O'Shanter, Mufflers, Bag Glove, Socks and Mittens.

Soldier's Mitten

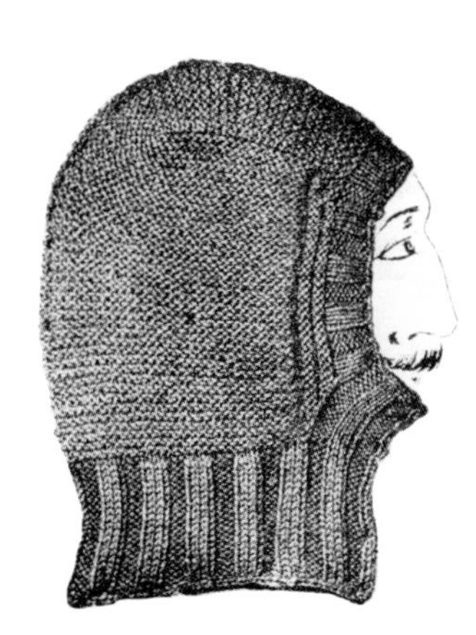

Balaclava Helmet

Knitted Muffler

SECTION TWO
20th Century Wars

FIRST WORLD WAR

KNITTING FOR KITCHENER'S ARMY

During the first months of the Great War literally thousands of women lost their jobs. The majority of these were employed in what were considered to be the 'luxury' trades such as dressmaking and millinery; services that were no longer required as shoppers reacted by pulling in their purse strings.

As the war took hold, the traditional feminine skills were in great demand as they were required to help make the items essential for the soldiers' kit bags. They made ammunition bags, sand bags, sleeping bags, they stitched straw into calico bedrolls and also machined military tents; these were just a few of the jobs they were asked to do. Although the saying goes that an army marches on its stomach, in the case of Kitchener's army they marched in the socks, boots and uniforms that were created by a workforce of unstoppable women. Whether it was in a domestic or industrial scale there is no doubt that the skills of both knitting and sewing were invaluable and it took the Great War to make people realise the value of women's work.

Lady's World announced in October 1914:

> 'When our troops marched away into the unknown, with banners waving and flags flying, they were furnished by the girls they left behind them with an abundant supply of woollen garments of all descriptions. The heroes that come back wounded can also be served by us with needles, knitting pins, and crochet hooks that ply busily for their benefit.'

THE KIT

The British soldier was only issued with two pairs of socks, so these were in great demand by the men fighting and living in the trenches. The men shared what they had and if a soldier received a new pair from home he would often simply replace the worst one and give the spare to his colleague. It was important to keep the feet as warm and dry as possible because trench foot was rife during the war. Trench foot was a fungal infection caused by cold, wet and insanitary conditions and because the soldiers stood for hours on end in waterlogged trenches, unable to remove either their boots, putties or socks, their feet would eventually go numb and the skin would turn various shades of red or blue. If left untreated, trench foot could turn gangrenous and result in amputation. It is estimated that as many as 20,000 men in the British Army were treated for this particular problem during the winter of 1914–15, so a good supply of warm, woollen socks was essential.

Of course it wasn't just socks that were supplied to the men at the front – gloves, mittens, body or cholera belts, mufflers, chest protectors, caps, balaclavas and many more garments were regularly packaged and sent out to try and afford some kind of comfort from the gruelling conditions. At the beginning of the war when soldiers were only issued with their uniform hats which offered very little protection from the wet and cold. As soon as the temperature dropped below freezing the water in their hats would freeze which made the supply of woollen caps and balaclavas a necessity.

Rudolf Hess (left), later a prominent politician in Nazi Germany, wrote home from the front thanking his family for all the gifts – especially the socks.

As communications along the front improved and telephones were being used more, a new kind of improvised balaclava was introduced with tuck-in ear flaps. This meant you could remove the flap from over your ear to use the telephone and then replace it to keep out the biting winds. A pattern could be found for this particular balaclava in the *Leach's Home Needlework Series*:

LEACH'S HOME NEEDLEWORK SERIES—No. 4 2D.

LEACH'S COMFORTS FOR MEN

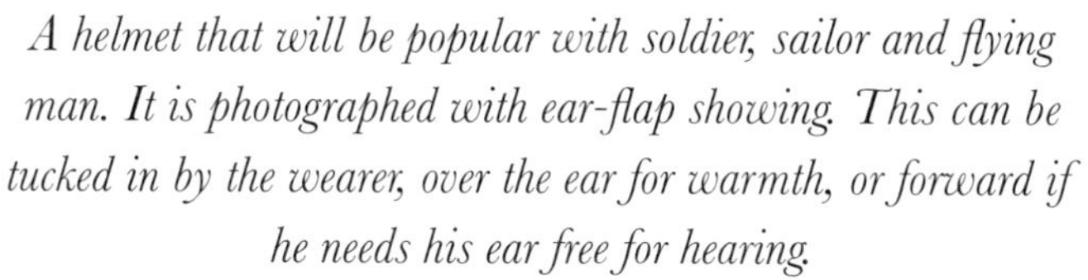

A helmet that will be popular with soldier, sailor and flying man. It is photographed with ear-flap showing. This can be tucked in by the wearer, over the ear for warmth, or forward if he needs his ear free for hearing.

Gift to the Troops at the Front
from the Queen and the Women of the Empire

Directions for HAND-KNITTED Woollen Belts.

WIDTH OF BELT AT EDGES WHEN FOLDED AND LENGTH:

SIZE II.		SIZE III.
10 inches wide	...	11 inches wide
12½ inches long	...	13 inches long

NEEDLES: Nos. 16 and 10 (four steel needles of each).

WORSTED: 4-ply fingering. Amount required, 2 to 3 ounces.

COLOUR: Natural shades.

SIZE II.

With No. 16 needles cast on 260 stitches, knit 1 plain, 1 purl, for 3 inches. Now take No. 10 needles and knit 1 plain, 1 purl, for 6½ inches. Now again take No. 16 needles and knit 1 plain, 1 purl, for 3 inches.

SIZE III.

With No. 16 needles cast on 286 stitches, knit 1 plain, 1 purl, for 3 inches. Now take No. 10 needles, knit 1 plain, 1 purl, for 7 inches. Now again take No. 16 needles and knit 1 plain, 1 purl, for 3 inches.

All Parcels to be marked "Woollen Belts," and addressed to

THE LADY IN WAITING TO THE QUEEN,
DEVONSHIRE HOUSE,
PICCADILLY.

The Size to be marked on each belt.

Because of such an urgent need for knitted items everyone was encouraged to knit. Children were given lessons as were wounded men in hospital, refugees, prisoners of war and even theatrical celebrities were not exempt from picking up a pair of needles even if it was only to knit a straight scarf or a blanket.

A PLEA FROM THE QUEEN

Amazingly, the plea to keep our troops warm during the long winter months in the trenches came from none other than our own Queen Mary. She led the movement to encourage knitting and when Lord Kitchener commissioned her to provide 30,000 pairs of socks, she was determined to fulfil this gigantic task. Ladies from all classes, spurred on by the fact that royalty had now become involved, joined in and knitted socks by the dozen. Just about every wool manufacturer and magazine either ran advertisements or provided patterns for what became known as Soldiers and Sailors Comforts. Even the Archbishop of Canterbury offered dispensation to allow women to knit during Sunday morning sermons in church.

Not only were the items sent to the front offering physical comfort to our boys they also played an important role in keeping up their morale, knowing that the item they were wearing had been lovingly made by either their mother, sister, sweetheart, grandma. Basically they were sending them a message of love in every stitch.

BEEHIVE KNITTING BOOKLETS No. 18
Lubbock & Saunders & Co.
1785
FIELD & HOSPITAL
COMFORTS
IN KNITTING
& CROCHET
Made from
J. & J. BALDWINS
REGISTERED TRADE MARK.
WHITE HEATHER
FLEECY
(OR PETTICOAT WOOL)
W.D
J. & J. BALDWIN & PARTNERS LTD. HALIFAX ENGLAND
ESTABLISHED 1785.
PRICE 2d. (or by post 2½d.)
All Rights Reserved.

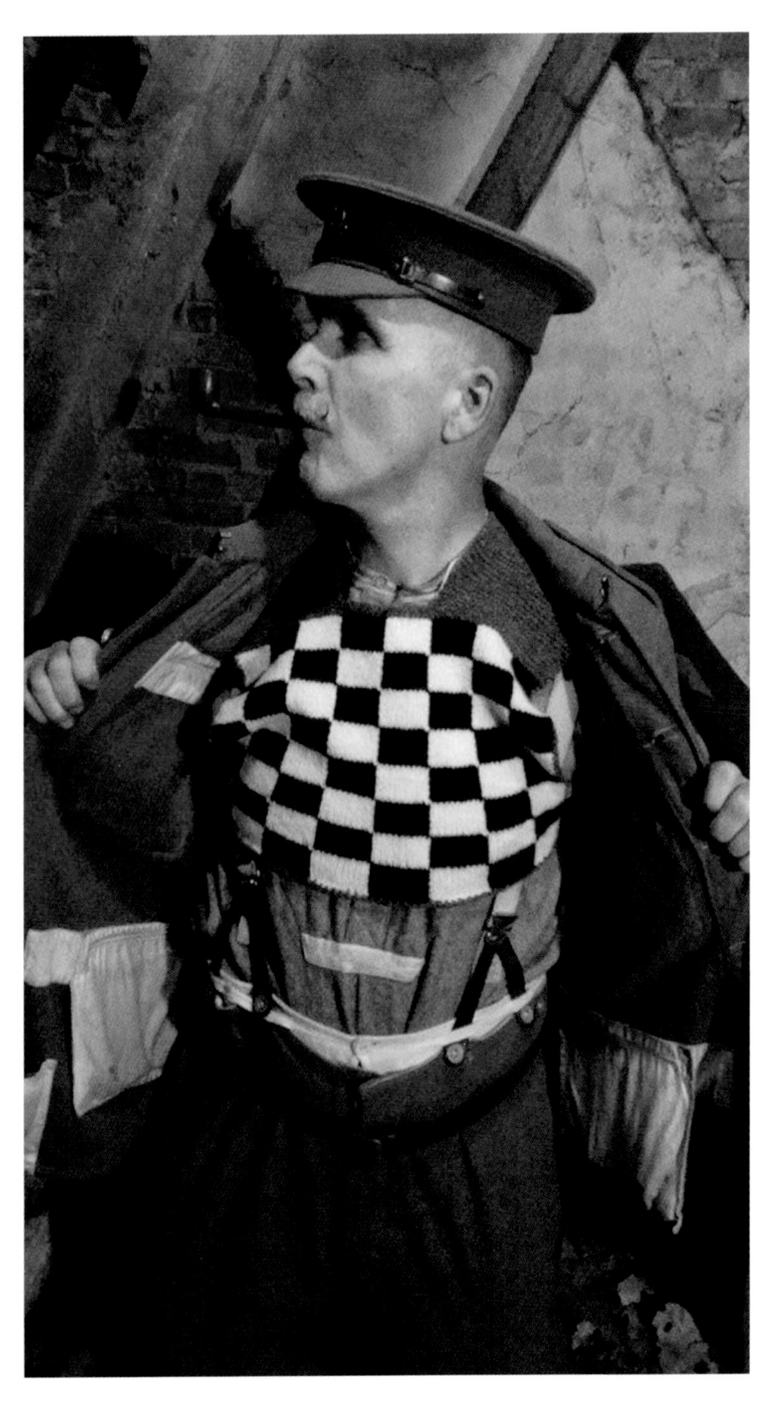

Questions were asked in parliament as women were put out of work in the machine knitting trade because of the over-production of home comforts. There were not sufficient materials for the factor and so the home workers were asked to cut down on production. The military were not happy about this as they would prefer to have free items rather than having to pay for everything.

As wool became scarce and the government had to resort to importing large quantities, jumpers that had been outgrown were lovingly unpicked and made into a new garment for the forces which included the Navy and the Royal Flying Corps as well. Although for the seaman, rather than the normal khaki, the items would be produced in dark blue and Aran white.

One of the more popular patterns was one for a Steering or Stout Glove (see pages 50–51). These were actually mittens which were made using four needles. This meant that each mitten was designed to be worn on either the left or right hand, which proved to be very useful as when one palm got a bit thin or damaged you could simply swap them over. Although socks were the main items there were more unusual items such as balaclavas with a flap for the ears so that the soldier could listen for the enemy, or a glove with a separate forefinger and thumb to make firing easier.

In addition to these there were large knitted belts to try and keep internal organs warm in the freezing conditions in the trenches and knitted eye patches to help hold dressings in place.

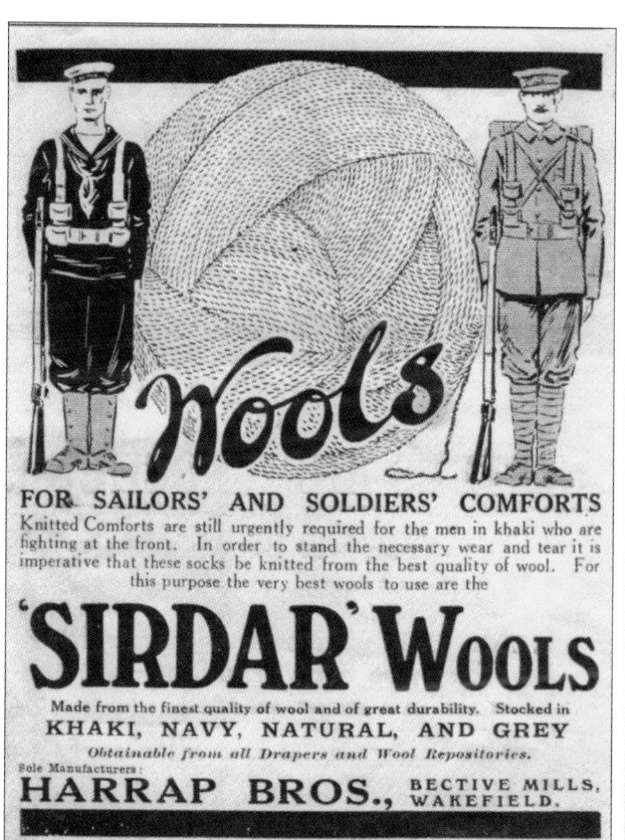

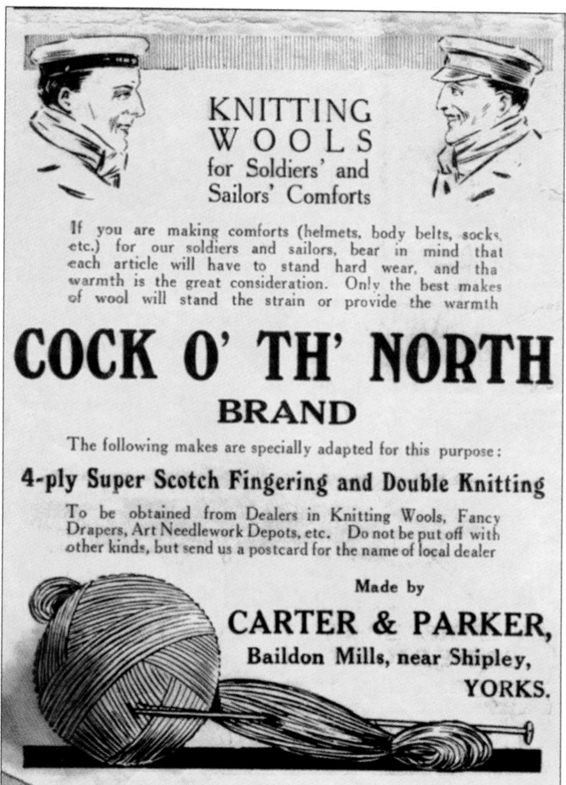

PATTERN FOR STEERING OR STOUT GLOVE

Materials required: 3oz (¾ cut) J. & J. Baldwin's 3-ply 'White Heather' Wheeling. Four No. 11 Knitting Needles.

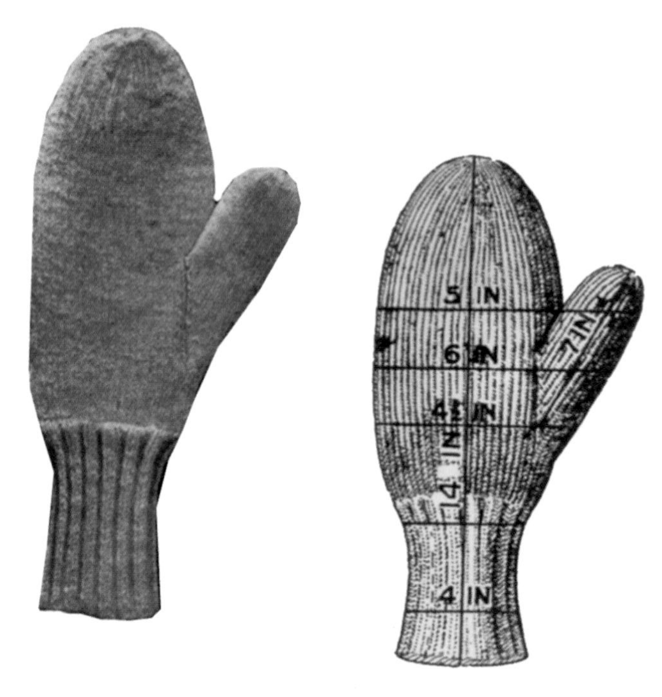

Cast on 52 stitches, 18 on each 2 needles, and 16 on the 3rd needle.
Work, in rib of knit 2 and purl 2, for 36 rounds.
Knit 10 rounds in plain knitting.
47th round – (Commence the thumb.) Purl 1, increase once in the next stitch (by knitting through the loop just underneath the stitch), knit 2, increase once in the next stitch, purl 1, knit to the end of the round. The 2 purled stitches mark the outside of the thumb.
* Knit 2 rounds plain, purling the stitches that were purled in the previous round.
50th round – Increase once on the inside of each of the purled stitches, then knit plain to the end of the round.
Repeat from * until there are 18 stitches between the 2 purled stitches.
Knit 2 more rounds without increasing; then, in the next round knit 1 (the purled stitch), put the next 18 stitches on to a thread and leave them for the thumb, cast on 4 stitches after the knit 1, follow on and finish the round.

Knit 35 more rounds in plain knitting, decreasing 4 stitches in the last round.
Knit every 7th and 8th stitches together in the next round.
Knit 5 rounds plain.
Knit each 2 stitches together in the next round.
Knit 1 round plain.
Run the thread through all the stitches on the needles and finish off very securely.
For the thumb take up the 18 stitches that were left on the thread and divide them on to two needles; with a third needle, knit up 6 stitches along the space between the 2 needles.
Knit 23 rounds in plain knitting.
Knit each 2 stitches together in the next round.
Knit 3 rounds plain. Finish off in the same way as at the top of the glove.

This jumper was made from a 1903 pattern book for sailors and was worn by Sir Ernest Henry Shackleton CVO OBE FRGS, the polar explorer who led three British expeditions to the Antarctic.

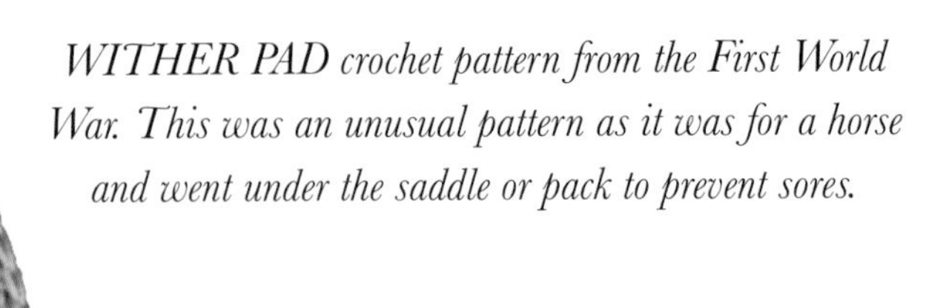

WITHER PAD crochet pattern from the First World War. This was an unusual pattern as it was for a horse and went under the saddle or pack to prevent sores.

The main problem with garments made out of wool is that the wool itself holds one third of its own weight in water. Once the garment is saturated it is unable to absorb any more water and this became a major problem for the Highland Divisions. As the war progressed, the quality of the wool cloth for kilts became poorer and subsequently would stretch considerably when it got wet. When it got cold, the water in the kilt would freeze and as they walked the ice could cut the soldiers' legs. These divisions also wore patterned and highly coloured socks. Although the men were issued with kilt covers, it was left to the home front to provide covers for the actual socks. They were requested in great numbers and looked similar to a pair of leg warmers. They were very useful as they had a long turnover at the top which could be pulled up over the knee to help keep their legs warm.

And of course the animals were not forgotten, wither pads were either crocheted or knitted to go underneath the saddle or packs to stop them from rubbing the horse's back.

In New Zealand, Her Excellency the Countess of Liverpool, had a book of patterns published. This contained all the patterns you would need to make a garment for your ANZAC. It was paid for by sponsorship and the left page carried an advertisement while the right had the printed pattern. Socks and mittens were the first patterns in the book and then came the balaclavas. It was said that more socks were knitted in New Zealand than in any other country.

To obtain wool and patterns women would join 'Comfort Groups', receiving a badge to say who they were knitting for. They had committees and these were often men and women of social rank. Garments were collected at a central point and from there sent out to the front.

Some committees were organised by specific regiments with the commanding officer's wife and some of the senior officer's wives running it. The honourable president would very often be the retired General.

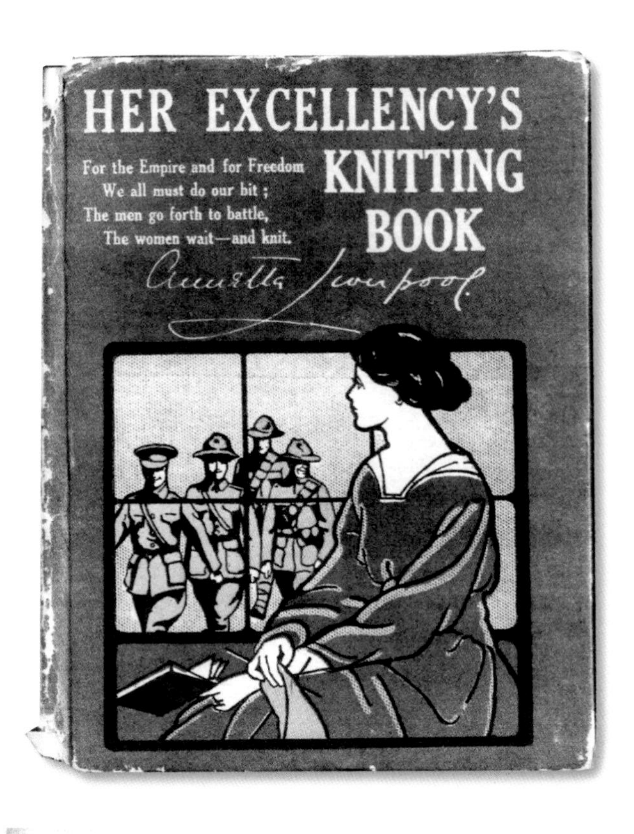

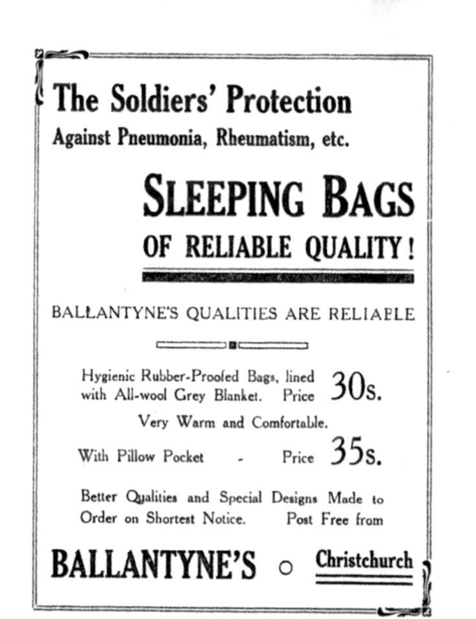

CHAPTER II.

Patterns from a Book of Army and Navy Garments.

PLAIN KNIT SOCK.

6 oz. 3-ply wheeling, 4 No. 12 knitting needles.
Cast on 60 stitches, 20 on each of three needles.
Work in rib of knit 2, purl 2, for 4 inches.
Next round.—Knit plain to within 2 stitches of the end of the 3rd needle, then pick up the loop between the 2 stitches, knit it, knit 1, purl 1. This last stitch is the seam-stitch and must be purled in every round. Knit plain, purling the seam-stitch, for 4 inches more.
To decrease.—* knit 1, knit 2 together, knit plain to within 3 stitches of the seam-stitch, then knit 2 together, knit 1, purl the seam-stitch.
Knit 7 plain rounds, purling the seam-stitch.
Repeat from * twice more.
For the Heel.—Take on 1 needle the seam-stitch and 13 stitches on either side of it (27 in all). Leave the rest of the stitches arranged on two needles for the instep, to wait till the heel is done.
On the heel needle * slip 1, knit 12, purl 1, knit 13.
Turn, slip 1, purl 12, knit 1, purl 13.
Repeat from * till 30 rows are done.
To turn the Heel.—Knit 17, slip 1, knit 1, pass the slipped stitch over, * turn, purl 8, purl 2 together.

9

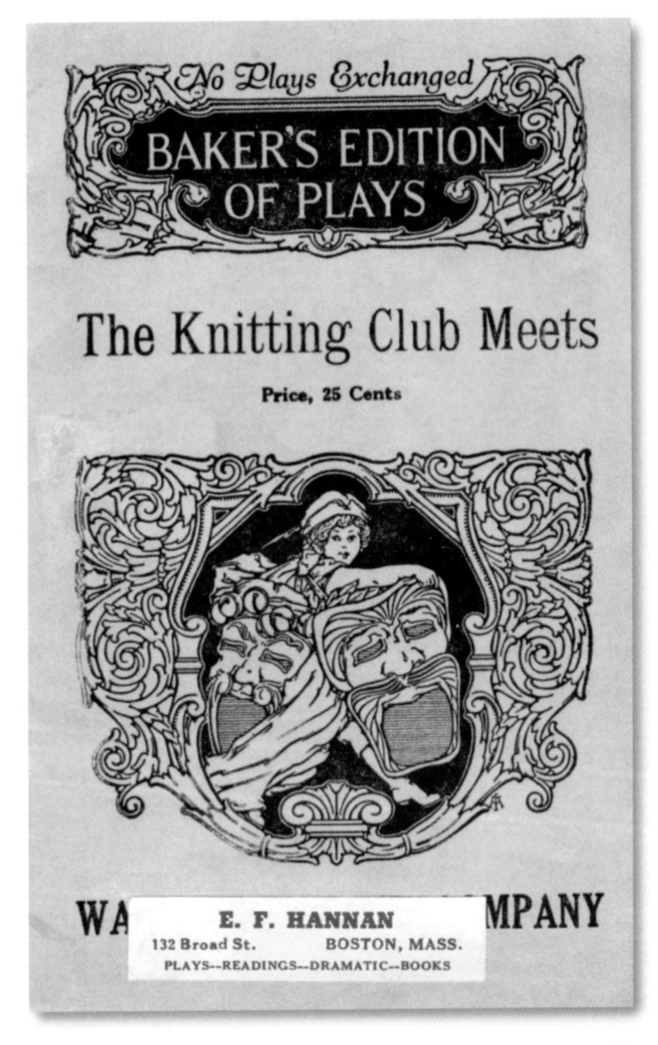

PROPAGANDA

Propaganda had a major impact on the world during the First World War because it promoted economic and industrial stability. In most people's minds was how many soldiers had been killed and injured, but due to the art of propaganda citizens worldwide wanted to help their country's cause in whatever way possible. Advertising encouraged the public to buy the company's product while promoting patriotism and knitting played its own role as can be seen by the play *The Knitting Club Meets*, part of Baker's edition of plays. This was used to raise morale bringing a little humour into the art of knitting for the soldiers on the front as the following excerpt shows:

Lydia (*smiling good-naturedly*): I dare say I am absent-minded about the time, but I don't forget my knitting as often as frivolous Lucy, or disobey the government dictates as does the daring Eleanor.

(*Takes knitting out of a shabby lawyer's bag and begins to work.*)

Eleanor: Humph! The government hadn't tried wearing nothing but khaki when it made that rule, I'm sure. The men's socks and sweaters are always underneath – can't possibly be seen from a distance – so why shouldn't they be a cheerful pink or blue instead of that dreadful, bilious no colour? Ugh!

Sometimes morale could be low, with little to occupy the minds of those left behind at home and it was a well known fact that a good singalong could lift the spirits. A lot of sheet music was published to encourage women to knit and also to help prevent a spell of the doldrums. In the United States there was Irving Berlin and Glenn Miller, while over here there was Arthur Askey and "I'm a Little Knit Wit" and "Knitting".

The Family Journal published the following song in the form of a song sheet on 2 December 1916.

THE KNACK OF KNITTING

Words by Douglas Stuart

Tempo di Polka

Some time ago, we used to know,
The way to mend a stocking,
But times have alter'd, we have falter'd
The waste of stocking's shocking;
But now you'll find in tube or bus,
No matter where you're sitting,
No one seems to care a cuss,
Who's got the taste of knitting.

Just mind your eye, as you pass by,
Someone who's needle staring,
It's simply killing, hear them filling
The air with cuss-words sparing;
So come and join this stitching throng,
No time should you be wasting,
For lumps of air with wool around
Needs lots of needle pasting.

The knack of knitting nimbly needs new needles which are nimble,
Then knit one, miss one, drop one, catch one,
Your elbows are your thimble;
For socks knit six slack sail or knots,
To keep the toes from slitting
Then take away the number you first though of,
And that's the art of knitting.

Down the side of the song sheet were the words:

SING WHILE YOU KNIT!

Show this fine song to your friends, and get them ALL to try one of our £1 prizes.

When women gathered in groups to knit they would often have someone read during the sessions. It could be a story, an article from the newspaper or a lesson from the Bible. There were also songs written about knitting and if you had a piano everyone would sing along. As these were the days before television or radio it was down to the individual to make their own entertainment.

MAN IN KHAKI FIRST WORLD WAR SOCK KNITTING KIT BOX AND INSTRUCTIONS

The Man in Khaki sock knitting kit was designed to make the knitting of socks for troops as simple and efficient as possible. The box, featuring an officer in uniform with a helmet, contained instructions, diagrams and a tape measure. The tape gave the knitter the ability to measure the length of the foot for the appropriate size boot.

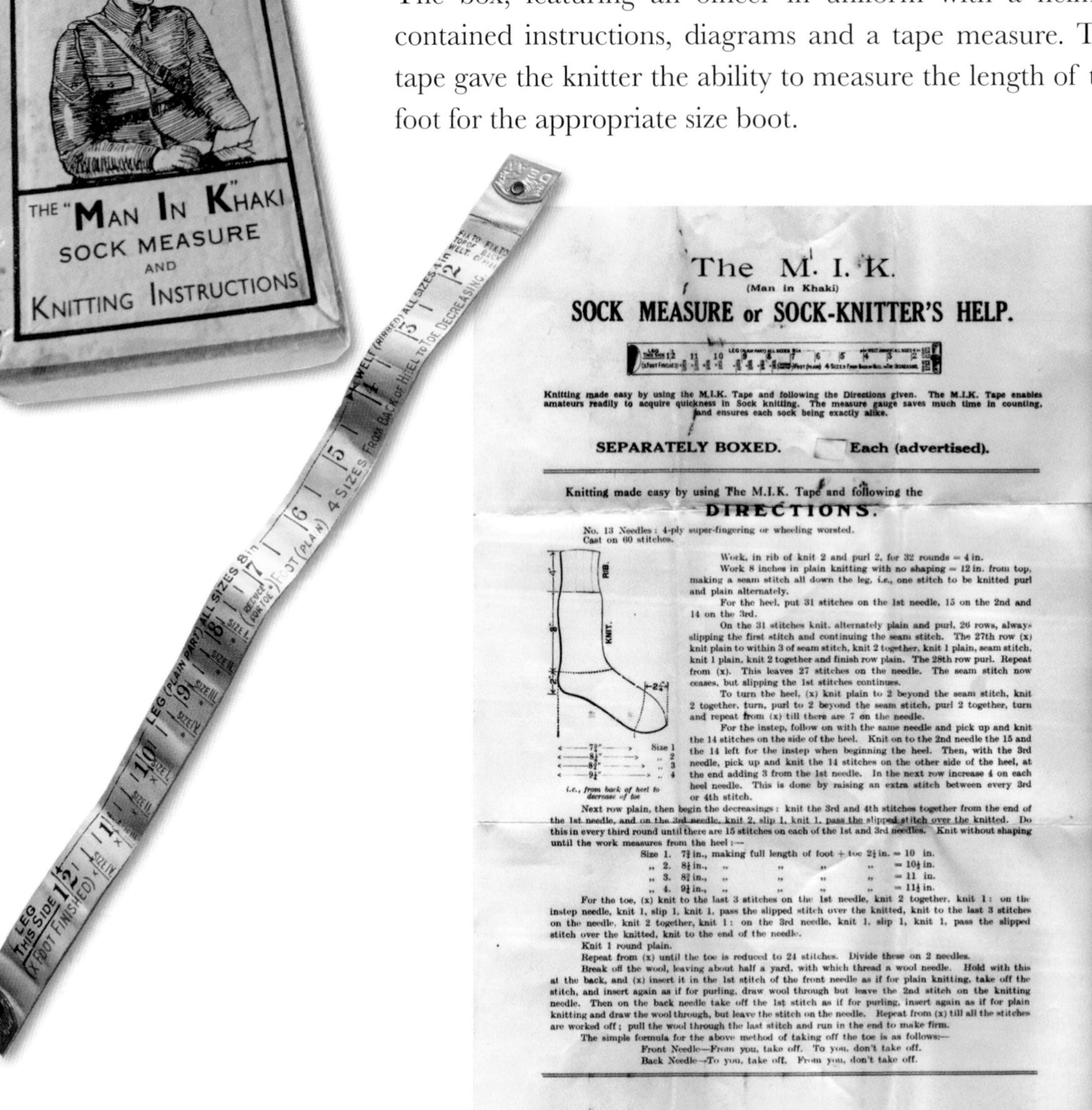

The M. I. K.
(Man in Khaki)

SOCK MEASURE or SOCK-KNITTER'S HELP.

Knitting made easy by using the M.I.K. Tape and following the Directions given. The M.I.K. Tape enables amateurs readily to acquire quickness in Sock knitting. The measure gauge saves much time in counting, and ensures each sock being exactly alike.

SEPARATELY BOXED. Each (advertised).

Knitting made easy by using The M.I.K. Tape and following the

DIRECTIONS.

No. 13 Needles: 4-ply super-fingering or wheeling worsted.
Cast on 60 stitches.

Work, in rib of knit 2 and purl 2, for 32 rounds = 4 in.

Work 8 inches in plain knitting with no shaping = 12 in. from top, making a seam stitch all down the leg, *i.e.*, one stitch to be knitted purl and plain alternately.

For the heel, put 31 stitches on the 1st needle, 15 on the 2nd and 14 on the 3rd.

On the 31 stitches knit, alternately plain and purl, 26 rows, always slipping the first stitch and continuing the seam stitch. The 27th row (x) knit plain to within 3 of seam stitch, knit 2 together, knit 1 plain, seam stitch, knit 1 plain, knit 2 together and finish row plain. The 28th row purl. Repeat from (x). This leaves 27 stitches on the needle. The seam stitch now ceases, but slipping the 1st stitches continues.

To turn the heel, (x) knit plain to 2 beyond the seam stitch, knit 2 together, turn, purl to 2 beyond the seam stitch, purl 2 together, turn and repeat from (x) till there are 7 on the needle.

For the instep, follow on with the same needle and pick up and knit the 14 stitches on the side of the heel. Knit on to the 2nd needle the 15 and the 14 left for the instep when beginning the heel. Then, with the 3rd needle, pick up and knit the 14 stitches on the other side of the heel, at the end adding 3 from the 1st needle. In the next row increase 4 on each heel needle. This is done by raising an extra stitch between every 3rd or 4th stitch.

Next row plain, then begin the decreasings: knit the 3rd and 4th stitches together from the end of the 1st needle, and on the 3rd needle, knit 2, slip 1, knit 1, pass the slipped stitch over the knitted. Do this in every third round until there are 15 stitches on each of the 1st and 3rd needles. Knit without shaping until the work measures from the heel:—

Size 1. 7¾ in., making full length of foot + toe 2¼ in. = 10 in.
„ 2. 8¼ in., „ „ „ „ = 10½ in.
„ 3. 8¾ in., „ „ „ „ = 11 in.
„ 4. 9¼ in., „ „ „ „ = 11½ in.

For the toe, (x) knit to the last 3 stitches on the 1st needle, knit 2 together, knit 1: on the instep needle, knit 1, slip 1, knit 1, pass the slipped stitch over the knitted, knit to the last 3 stitches on the needle, knit 2 together, knit 1: on the 3rd needle, knit 1, slip 1, knit 1, pass the slipped stitch over the knitted, knit to the end of the needle.

Knit 1 round plain.

Repeat from (x) until the toe is reduced to 24 stitches. Divide these on 2 needles.

Break off the wool, leaving about half a yard, with which thread a wool needle. Hold with this at the back, and (x) insert it in the 1st stitch of the front needle as if for plain knitting, take off the stitch, and insert again as if for purling, draw wool through but leave the 2nd stitch on the knitting needle. Then on the back needle take off the 1st stitch as if for purling, insert again as if for plain knitting and draw the wool through, but leave the stitch on the needle. Repeat from (x) till all the stitches are worked off; pull the wool through the last stitch and run in the end to make firm.

The simple formula for the above method of taking off the toe is as follows:—

Front Needle—From you, take off. To you, don't take off.
Back Needle—To you, take off. From you, don't take off.

Mufflers (*right*) started the war with fringes (see page 37), but as it went on these were not added. This was done to save wool and at the request of the Ministry as the felt the fringe could too easily get caught in the weapons they used and also on their kit.

Pattern books were published for both French soldiers and also the German military. If you study photographs of men in the trenches during the Great War, the home knits look the same for both sides it is just the colour of the wool that changes.

The British were very supportive of the Belgian soldiers and even published patterns for the kepi in our publications.

COMFORT FUNDS

Comfort funds were founded during the First World War and were often just for one particular regiment. The Cameron Comforts Fund ran from 1914–1918 and they gave service to all battalions of the County regiments, the Queen's own Cameron Highlanders under the able leadership of Dr Barron and Andrew Paterson, aided by a working committee. By the end of the War they had £700 remaining in the coffers, £400 of which they donated to the Cameron Association. The remaining £300 would be used to give help to retired Camerons, widows and their dependants.

At the beginning of the Second World War, they had £130 in the account and this sum was used to reactivate the association, this time under the guidance of a working committee headed by Lady Hermione Cameron of Lochrel.

British and German soldiers 1914
(IWM Q011745)

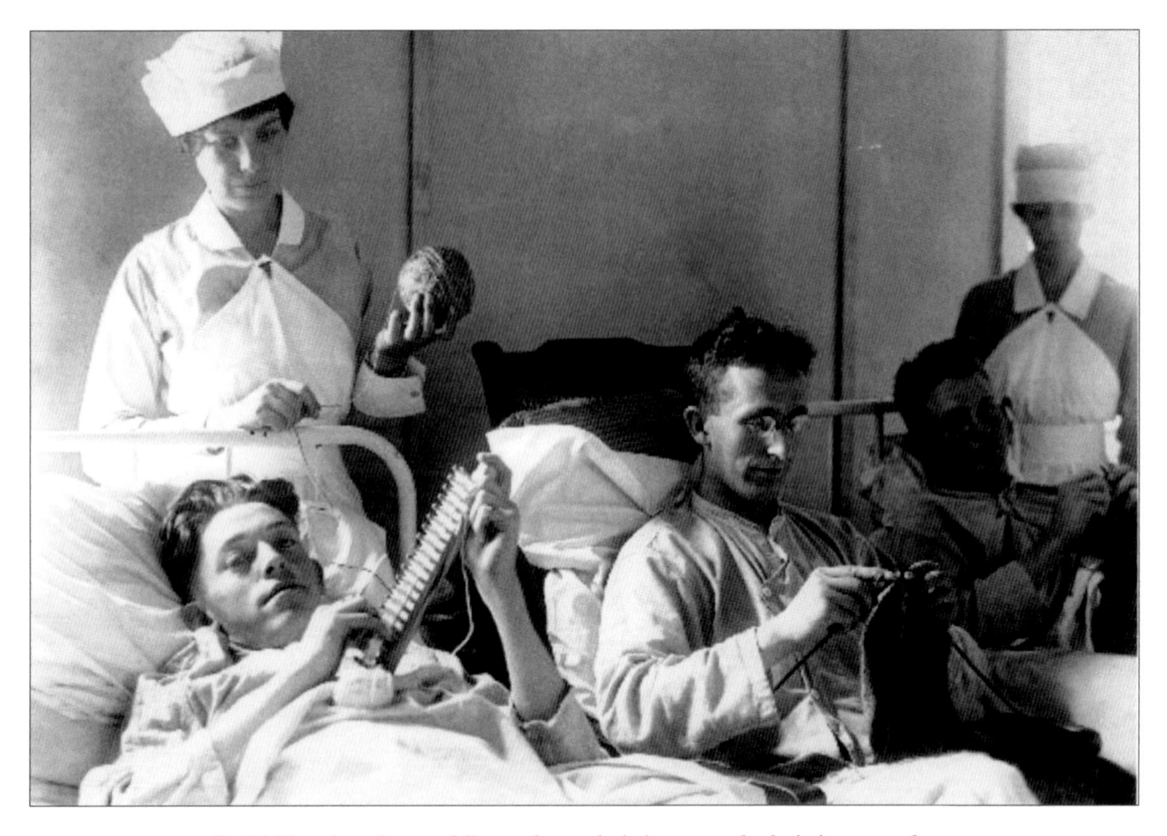

Bedridden American soldiers take up knitting, or rake knitting on a loom.

THE ARRIVAL OF THE USA

When the USA got embroiled in the conflict, their home front went into overdrive. Socks, hand knitted or made on sock knitting machines, were completed in their thousands. The US Red Cross mobilised women, children and all members of society – in fact anyone who could knit and sew – to get going with making items for the boys.

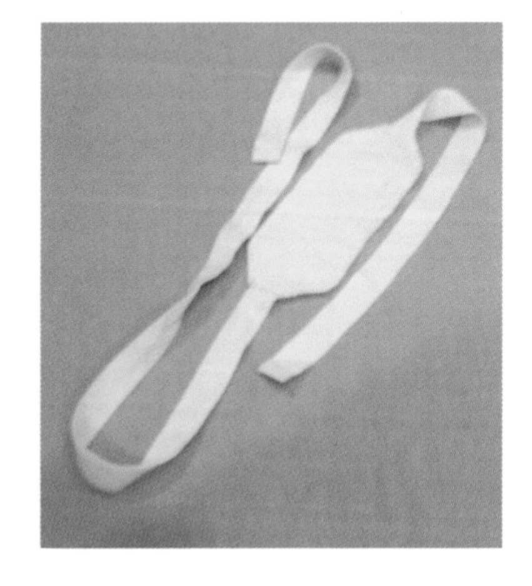

Another version of the eye bandage used during the First World War

They made 'ditty bags', which contained items from home such as gloves, soap, tobacco, a pipe, razors and, if from a Christian society, a small Bible. The patterns for these bags and the instructions to make them were published in many ladies' magazines. On the back of

Eye bandage pattern dated 1909. Handwritten and used during the First World War.

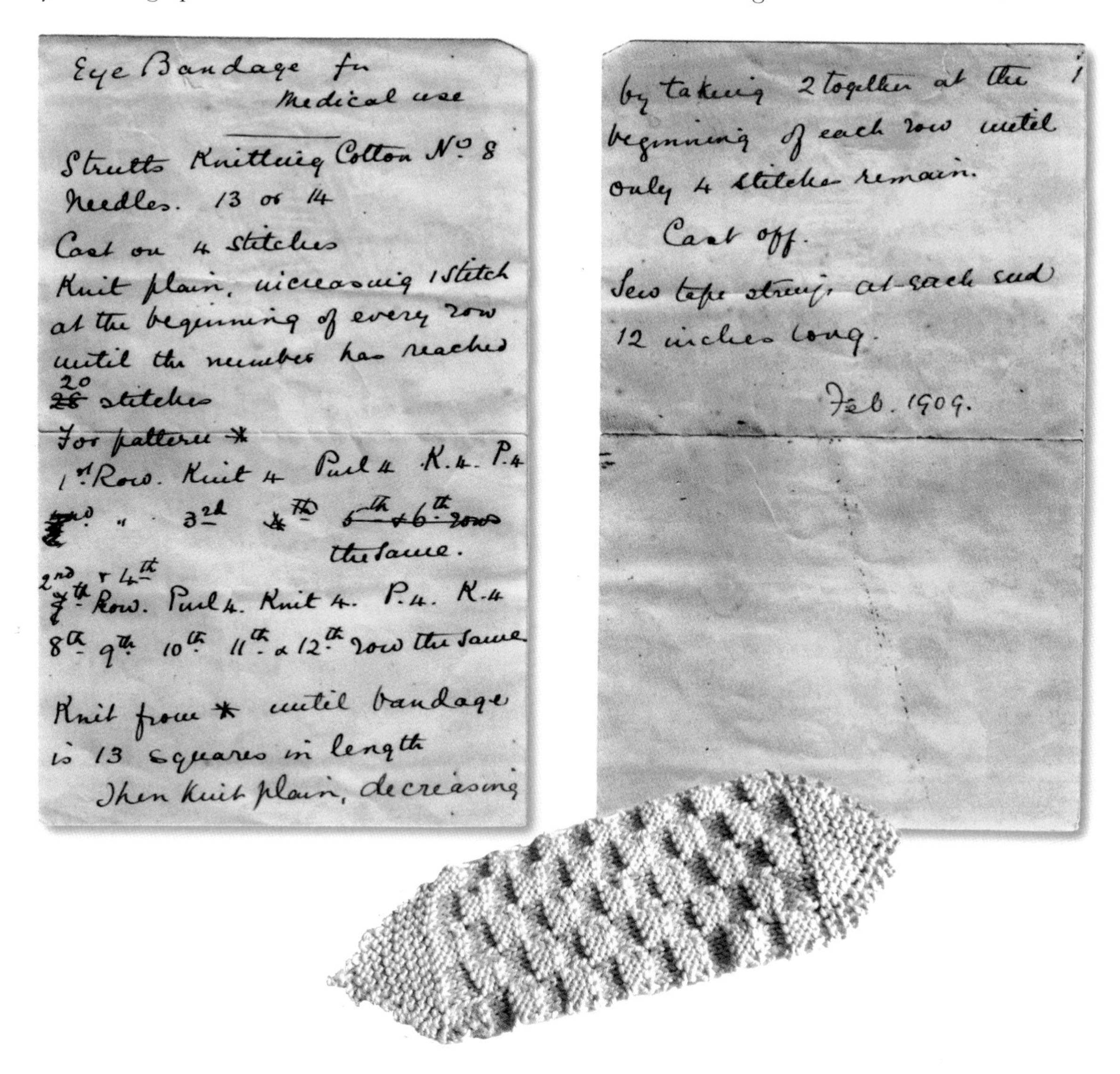

Eye Bandage for
Medical use

Strutts Knitting Cotton No 8
Needles. 13 or 14
Cast on 4 stitches
Knit plain, increasing 1 stitch
at the beginning of every row
until the number has reached
~~28~~ 20 stitches
For pattern *
1st Row. Knit 4 Purl 4 K.4. P.4
~~2nd~~ " 3rd ~~4th~~ ~~5th & 6th rows~~
the same.
2nd & 4th ~~7th~~ Row. Purl 4. Knit 4. P.4. K.4
8th 9th 10th 11th & 12th row the same

Knit from * until bandage
is 13 squares in length
Then knit plain, decreasing

by taking 2 together at the
beginning of each row until
only 4 stitches remain.
Cast off.
Sew tape string at each end
12 inches long.

Feb. 1909.

one knitting pattern from the USA there is a graphic stating that knitting needles were known as 'Women's Weapons'.

Theatre/surgical swabs were knitted in cotton. You were not permitted any knots in these items because when they were washed and boiled for re-use, the bacteria would collect in the knots and cause cross-infection. This was very dangerous during this time as there were no antibiotics to fight such infections.

The Navy played a vital role in the war. Amongst the more experienced sailors were young boys, many of whom had never been on board a boat and definitely not seen military action. All our sailors were especially vulnerable with the harsh conditions at sea. They needed special sea boot stockings which they wore over their socks and inside their long leather boots. The cuff, or top of the stocking, could be folded over the top of the boot to help keep out the cold. Gloves, sweaters and hats were also in big demand, as were all the hand knitted garments sent from home.

Trench hose

International News Service, New York:
'British Jackies interned in Holland knitting stockings and other garments to keep their minds occupied during their confinement.'

Neil Heritage wearing a Second World War stump warmer

SECOND WORLD WAR

In 1939, the £130 still in the Cameron Comforts Fund, was used to start the Second World War Comfort Fund. The committee met in the Caledonian Hotel and decided that the new fund should cover all the services, including the Scottish regiments. It was decided to rename it the Cameron and Inverness Country Comforts Association, a name which was officially adopted in 1940. When blackout was introduced, meetings were arranged to coincide with the full moon if possible, this allowed members to make their way to and from the meetings in relative safety without the use of torches, lanterns or having to turn on their car headlights.

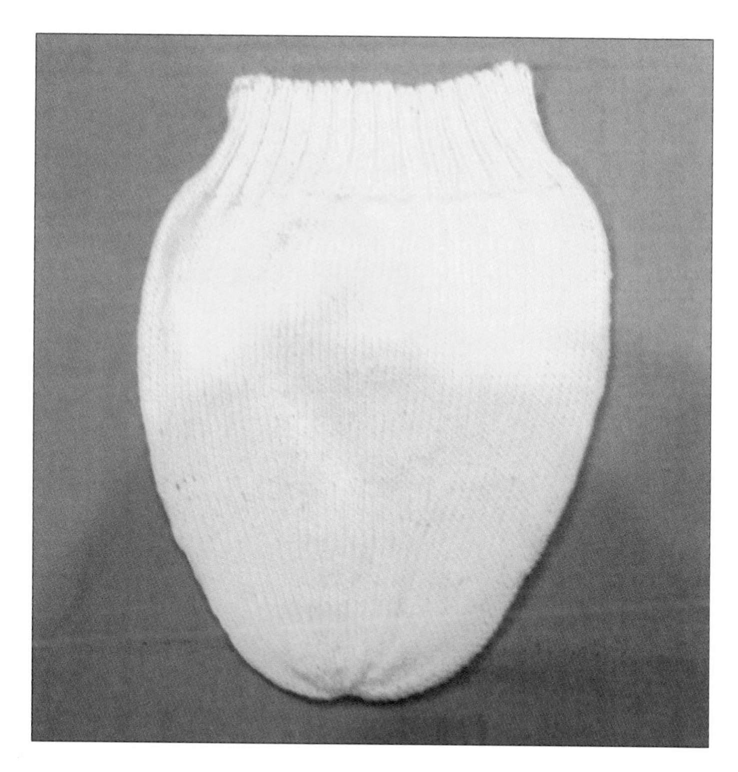

Above knee stump bandage

In November 1939, the 1st Battalion of this association asked for one thousand pairs of long hose tops which, amazingly, were supplied in just under a month.

Another job the association organised was darning and mending parties for the troops stationed in and around Inverness. Bands of ladies met weekly to repair the contents of the men's laundry and darning or replacing items when they were beyond repair. These working parties raised their own money to cover the cost of this work.

If a woman wished to knit for a loved one or a member of her family without being in a comfort's group, she would have to prove to the Board of Trade that she was knitting for a serviceman. Once she had proved this she would be issued with a chit that allowed her to obtain wool without using any of her clothing coupons. The wool would be weighed as it was given to her and weighed again when she returned the knitted garment. This was to prove that it had been made by the wool provided and if there was any yarn left over it would be taken back for future use.

BOARD OF TRADE

Name Mrs. Shenby

Address 14 Egmont Rd
Hove

is authorized to buy sixteen ozs. of knitting wool in Service colours. This voucher will serve the trader in lieu of clothing coupons to a coupon-value equivalent to that of the wool delivered.

Signed E. Vaux.
Assistant Borough Organiser

Official Stamp of Organization

Address

Date 12/1/42

(14408) Wt. 25089—7800 2000m 8/41 D.L. G. 341

Board of Trade chit

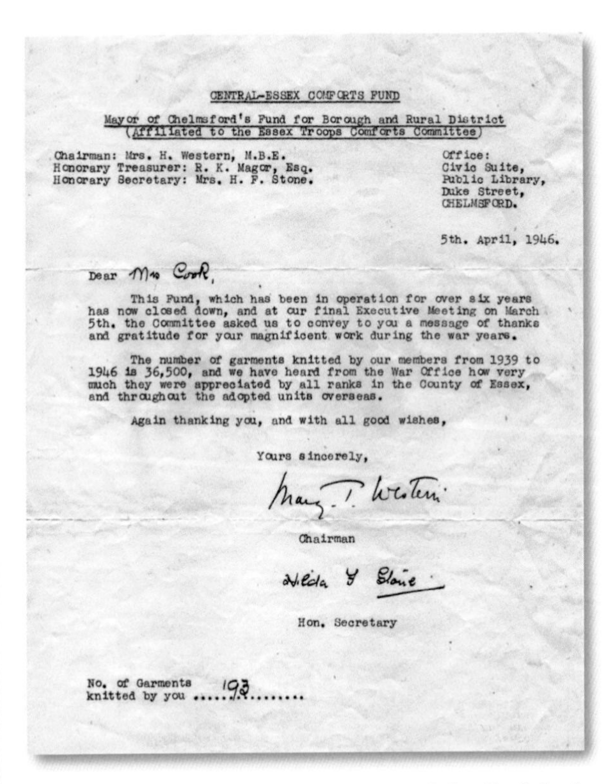

CENTRAL-ESSEX COMFORTS FUND

Mayor of Chelmsford's Fund for Borough and Rural District
(Affiliated to the Essex Troops Comforts Committee)

Chairman: Mrs. H. Western, M.B.E.
Honorary Treasurer: R. K. Magor, Esq.
Honorary Secretary: Mrs. H. F. Stone.

Office:
Civic Suite,
Public Library,
Duke Street,
CHELMSFORD.

5th. April, 1946.

Dear Mrs Cook,

This Fund, which has been in operation for over six years has now closed down, and at our final Executive Meeting on March 5th. the Committee asked us to convey to you a message of thanks and gratitude for your magnificent work during the war years.

The number of garments knitted by our members from 1939 to 1946 is 36,500, and we have heard from the War Office how very much they were appreciated by all ranks in the County of Essex, and throughout the adopted units overseas.

Again thanking you, and with all good wishes,

Yours sincerely,

Mary T. Western

Chairman

Hilda F. Stone

Hon. Secretary

No. of Garments knitted by you ......193........

Letter confirming how many garments Mrs Cook had completed for the Comforts Fund

The wool used for servicemen was of the highest quality, but yarn for the home front was of poor quality; either having been recycled or made from old rag fibres. Added to this the Ministry said that no yarn over six inches long should be discarded as it could be used to knit knee-warming rugs and blankets for injured servicemen whilst they were in hospital.

Knee cap warmers

Sirdar Hints to Knitters

No. 2

HOW TO CAST OFF AND SEW UP A SHOULDER SEAM.

When casting off, each stitch should be knitted according to the pattern in the garment. For example, if the garment has been worked in k.2, p.2 rib, continue to work knit stitches above the knit stitches and purl stitches above the purl stitches. The normal method of casting off is used except that the first stitch at the sleeve edge is knitted, but the subsequent first stitches to be cast off are slipped.

For example, 20 sts. to be cast off at the shoulder 10 sts. at a time.

1st ROW. Commencing with a knit stitch, cast off 10 sts., knit to end of row.
2nd ROW. Sl.1, purl to end of row.
3rd ROW. Commencing with a slip stitch, cast off the remaining 10 sts.

The chain stitch edges formed by the casting off at the back shoulder and front shoulder are now sewn together. With the wrong side of the work facing insert the point of the needle under both loops of the chain stitch edge on one shoulder then under both loops of the corresponding chain stitch edge on the other shoulder. Draw the wool through and sew together each pair of corresponding loops in the same manner.

Left over wool should be used for sewing up and care taken not to pull the wool tight. Working twice through the same pair of loops at approximately every 10th stitch will strengthen the seam.

A contrasting thread has been used for the sewing on the photograph and the edges of the work turned back to show the chain stitch edges.

HARRAP BROS. (SIRDAR WOOLS) LTD., BECTIVE MILLS, WAKEFIELD
W1250 Printed in Great Britain (Copyright)

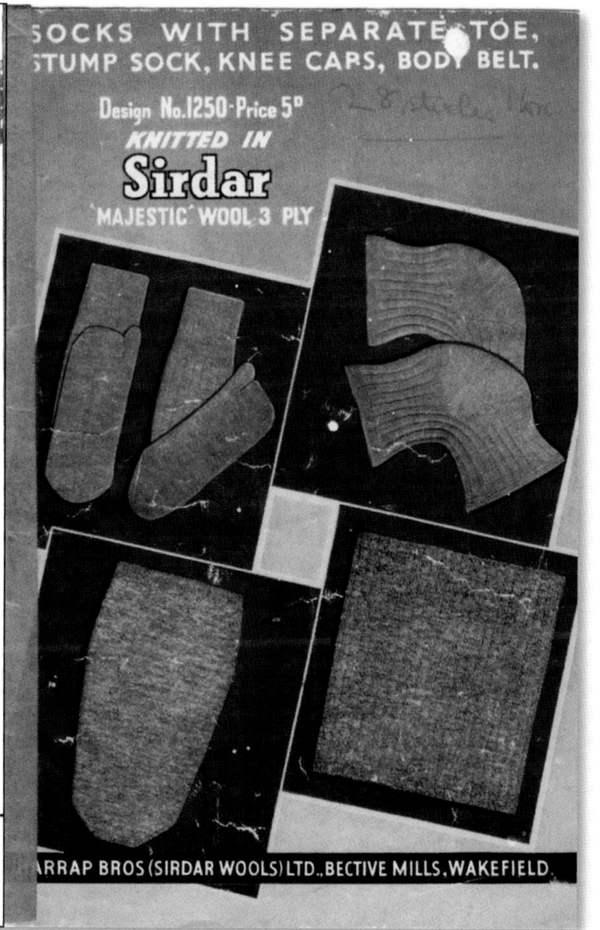

A Liberation Jumper

Hospital comforts continued to be made on the home front. Operation stockings, hot water bottle covers, arm warmers, stump warmers and jumpers for men to wear in bed were all invaluable items. Some of these jumpers had gaps in the front, and the back would be longer than the front of the garment. This meant that a wound dressing could be changed without the men having to take off their clothing which helped in keeping them warm.

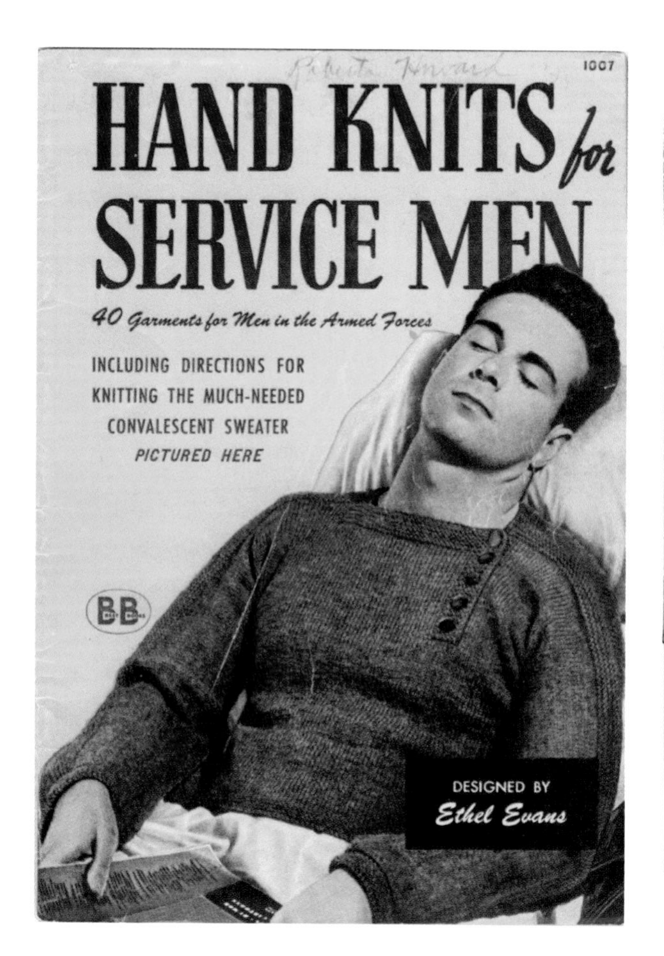

It wasn't just the Army that received knitted items, all the services were included along with the Merchant Marines and all other types of seafarers, Women's Services, Land Girls, Air Force and the Home Guard. There were printed patterns to cover all aspects of our servicemen and women.

Many women would club together to buy a pattern and would write a copy to pass on to another friend. This sometimes caused a problem, though, because if she made a mistake whilst copying it down, this mistake would be replicated in every garment made from that pattern.

Cap Muffler

My father once told me that when the men came back from Dunkirk women were knitting like mad as many items of uniform were left in France or discarded on the journey home due to damage. The garments were made in great numbers to clothe the existing service personnel and new recruits.

Many women's magazines published service patterns including *Stitchcraft, Needlewoman, Good Needlework* and *Women's Own*, to name just a few. Commercial producers of yarn and patterns also threw themselves into helping the War by publishing patterns for all the services along with the Home Front, ARP, Home Guard etc.

Needle gauge with advert

US company patriotic hat

The British Sailor's Society had their patterns sponsored and donated free by the Scotch Wool & Hosiery Co. If you knitted for the Merchant Marines via the Society, you were given the pattern but were asked to return it when it was no longer needed. The 'FANNY' would distribute the knitted items sent to them by the comfort's groups and send them on to the home front as well as to the services.

Sometimes, when I meet women who knitted during the war, they were just children or teenagers, and they all moan about the oiled wool used for sea boot stockings or jumpers for airmen or sailors. I have made a jumper from oiled Aran weight wool and have to agree with them. It was hard work as the wool does not move easily along the needles; it sticks and you have to push the stitches along the needles all the time.

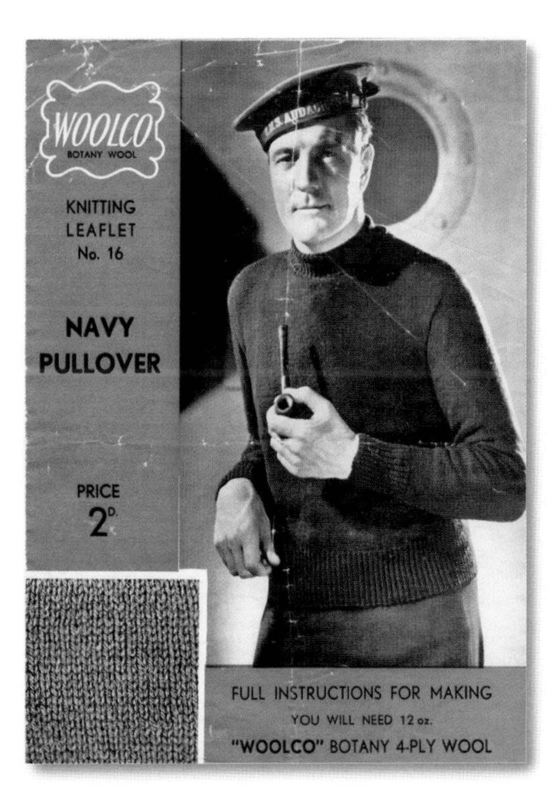

Women would be seen knitting everywhere – on buses, on the train, during their breaks, during work and even down in the underground at night when they were used as air raid shelters. Prisoners of war were also sent knitted items and some would unpick these garments if they didn't fit and knit their own. Men were often taught to knit and it covered all the social classes. The working class by mums and nans and the upper class by nannies. However, men knitting is nothing new, it has always happened and today it it is a growing hobby.

Ronald Eastman, a Second Lieutenant in the 3rd Royal Tank Regiment, was taken prisoner after the defence of Calais in May 1940. He was held in a number of prison camps in Germany and Poland for the next five years. Before the war he had been a handicraft teacher and was an expert in lettering. He put these talents to good use as a forger. He informed the Germans that heraldry was his hobby and used this as a cover to make German passes and identity cards. He made this pullover in Eichstaett prisoner of war camp (Oflag VIIA) from scrap wool.

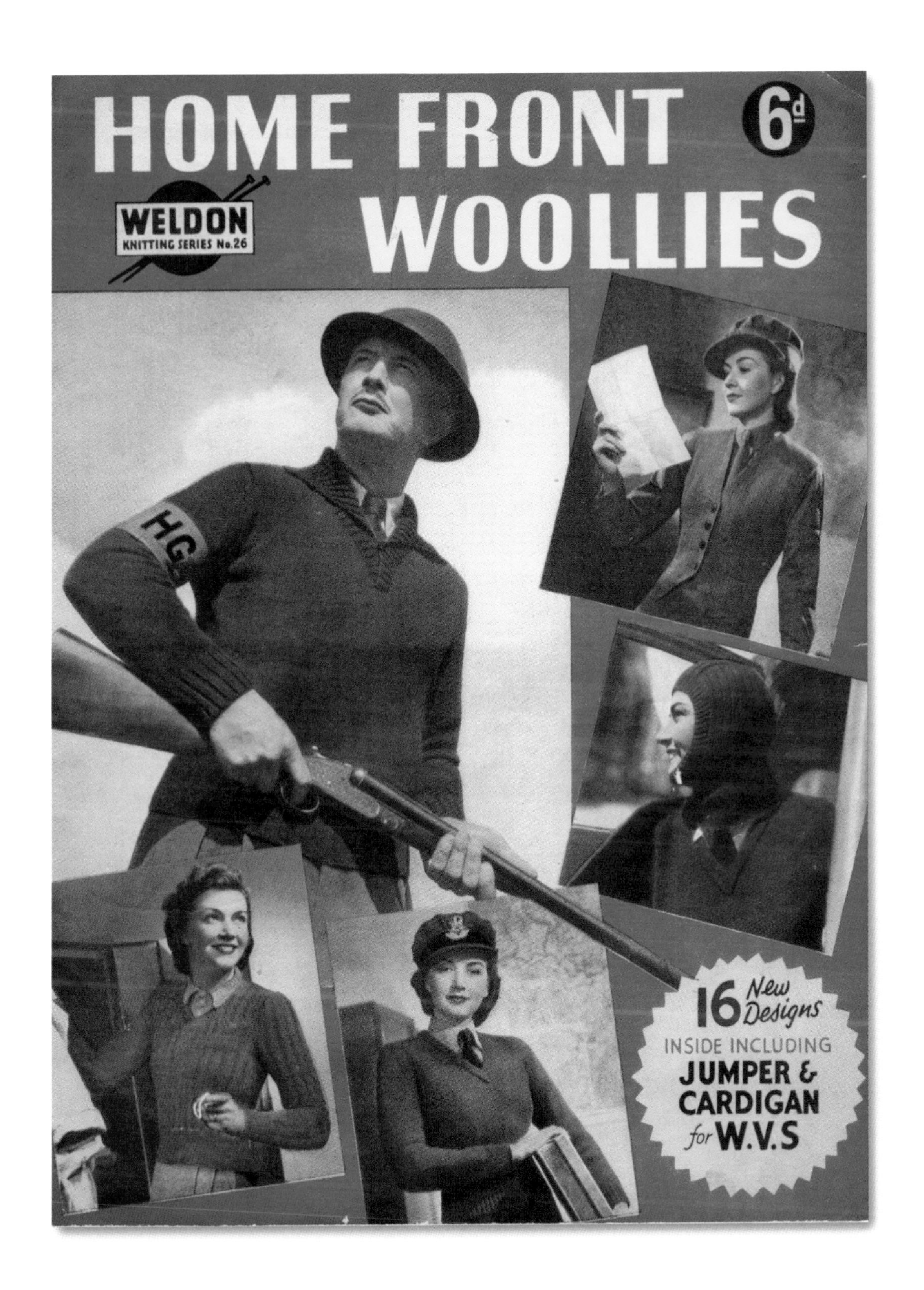
HOME FRONT WOOLLIES
6d
WELDON
KNITTING SERIES No.26
HG
16 New Designs
INSIDE INCLUDING
JUMPER & CARDIGAN
for W.V.S

Certain knitting companies would produce patterns and there is one for a jumper printed by Bachelor's Peas. In Canada, if you collected Lux packet tops you could get pattern booklets. Also in Canada, the Yellow Pages enclosed a book of war patterns.

All the yarn companies from Patons and Baldwins, to the high-class couture companies such as Jaegar and Vogue produced patterns. It was also possible to send off for yarn samples and they would come in a little wax paper bag with the type of wool – DK, Aran, etc. – along with the price printed on the front (see opposite page).

There were also patterns during the Second World War for socks to be worn in tropical areas, this meant anywhere hot. They were long socks

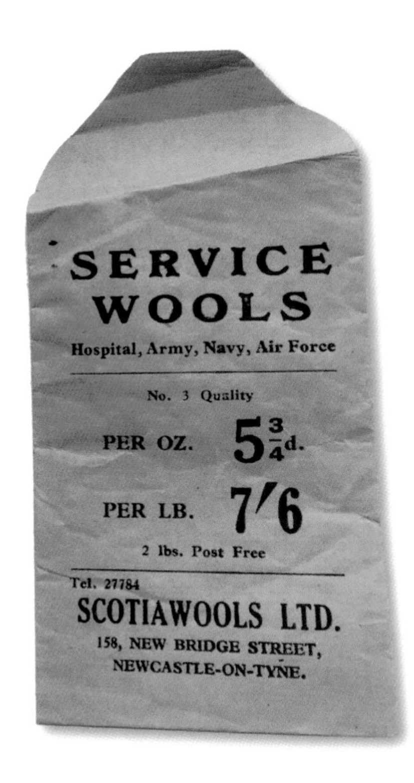

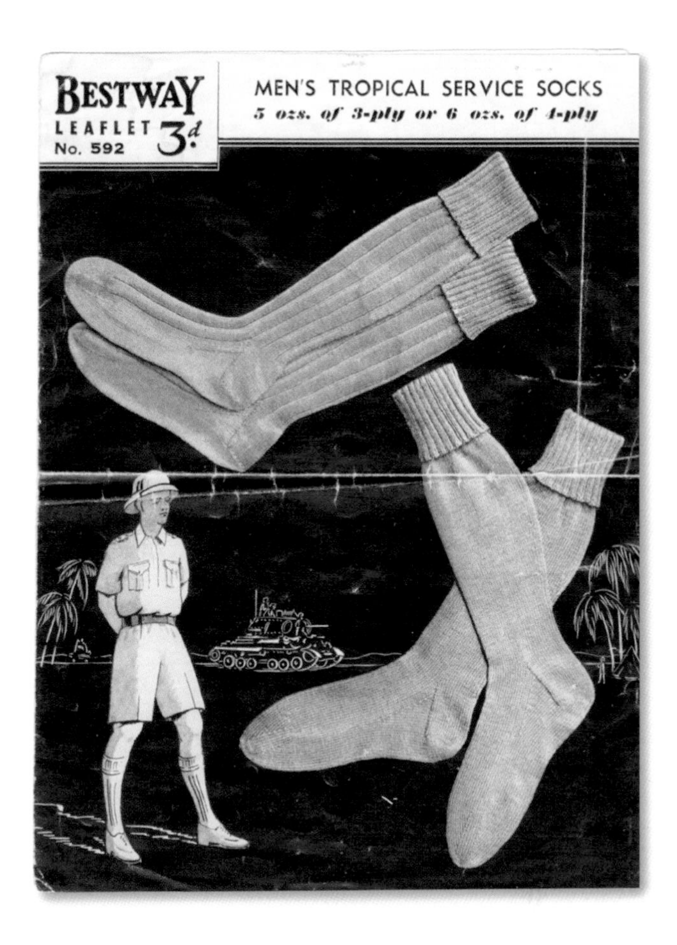

designed to be worn with the uniform shorts.

It is important to bear in mind that just as in the First World War, there was a wool shortage and the Ministry insisted you used your clothing coupons to buy 100 per cent good quality wool. They produced coupon-free yarn that could have no more than 16 per cent animal hair in it. Producers of yarn were sent instructions and the animal hairs were listed from Alpaca to Yak and all the animals of the alphabet in between. People, determined to get yarn one way or another, started to spin their own at home and very often dog and cat hair would be used as a substitute.

WOMANS KNITTING

When women joined the services they were issued with their basic uniform but no extras. Knitwear was classed as an extra, which meant the girls would have to knit their own warm clothing. The pattern companies started to produce books and patterns for them, covering all kinds of clothing including underwear and stockings. The undies needed elastic and, although it was not on the ration, it was in short supply: "There is a war on you know." When it was available, women would often sew a small button on the end and make a buttonhole at the other, which meant they could move the elastic from pair to pair when needed or when the garment was in the wash. They would have to buy their own yarn and use their coupons and this could be expensive. I have a friend who was a WAAF, Phyllis, and she told me that,"It was a cheek that they made you buy the pattern. 6d was 6d and that was a lot of money." She also said that the girls would club together to buy one pattern and share it. They could copy it but that often led to mistakes in the final knitted item.

WAAF knickers

VOGUE-KNIT SERIES No. 34
HAND-KNITS
FOR SERVICE WOMEN
INSTRUCTIONS ON PAGE 12
16 DESIGNS 9d
Reprinted from VOGUE and VOGUE KNITTING BOOKS
THE CONDÉ NAST PUBLICATIONS LTD.

BRITAIN AND HER DOMINIONS

Patterns were printed all around the Empire – Canada, Australia and New Zealand. As in the UK, women produced garments in their thousands and socks in their millions. Unlike the UK, however, Australia and New Zealand were lucky as they didn't suffer from the same shortage of wool.

Many garments were knitted in 4- and 3-ply and were worn underneath their uniforms to give many thin layers to help utilise the body's natural warmth. These layers would trap the warmth between them and prevent the soldier from getting cold.

Hats were made and the Cap Muffler – now called the Cap Comforter – was the most commonly worn. Many were made in knitting factories but because so many were needed home knitters played their part as well. This was a garment that continued to be knitted after the Second World War.

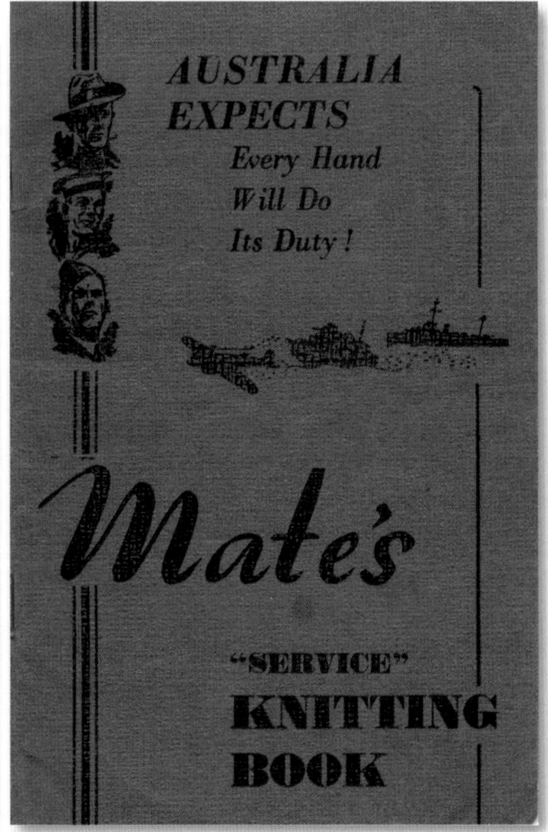

A Tribute to YOU

—the Women of Canada

FEW, including those closely connected with the work, realize the achievement of Canadian women toward helping win the war

Organized effort, represented by more than one thousand registered * organizations with total membership in the millions, shows the tremendous contribution in time, trouble and expense being volunteered by the women of Canada. In addition, there is the individual effort reaching into practically every home —representing virtually the complete mobilization of woman-power to the end that peace may come more quickly

In this splendid work, this all-out" effort, on a scale unprecedented in the history of Canada, hand knitting has played, and will continue to play, an important part in providing warm garments indispensable for the comfort of those in the service, for refugees and for our own war guests.

Hand knitting is an opportunity to express, in tangible form, care and affection for those who are dear. It is an opportunity to put idle time to profitable advantage, realizing that some airman, some soldier or some sailor (often unknown to you) will be made happier by your work—that some child or some mother driven from home by the cruelty of war may be made more comfortable by the protection of the warm wool garments you supply

This knitting book, containing a complete range of carefully chosen hand knit garments for the men and women in the service and for war victims, is dedicated to you, the women of Canada, to help you get enjoyment from your knitting and satisfaction from knowing that your time and effort are being used to best advantage.

* The "Honour Roll" of Canadian Women's Organizations registered with the Department of National Service in Ottawa, is presented on pages 24 to 27.

THE MONARCH KNITTING COMPANY LIMITED

HEAD OFFICE DUNNVILLE, ONTARIO

DESIGNS APPROVED BY
NATIONAL WAR SERVICE COMMITTEE
The Imperial Order Daughters of the Empire

Any knitted garments made in Canada were collected and distributed by the Canadian Red Cross. Various groups such as the Imperial Order of the Daughters of the Empire, the Women's Institute, church groups and other smaller women's organisations hosted knitting bees, knitting teas and also knitting showers to help with the war effort. Canadian patterns were often published by the same companies as in the UK as they would have publishing offices in the main cities throughout the British Empire.

P&B PATONS & BALDWINS' No. 132 SPECIALTY KNITTING BOOK P&B

MAN'S TUCK-IN PULLOVER—
"BRIAN" DESIGN
Instructions on page 9
PATONS ROSE FINGERING WOOL, 4-ply

MAN'S STOCKINGS (Ribbed)
(Also illustrated on page 6)
Instructions on page 18
PATONS SERVICE SOCK WOOL—NON-SHRINK

Australian patterns were usually knitted at home and the sizes differed from those in the UK. The chest size went up to 40 inches, whereas in the UK the patterns only went up to 38 inches. Interestingly, the garment patterns in the books were given names, for example, Clive, Reginald, Frank etc. Note the pattern on the left is described as 'Man's Tuck-in Pullover – "Brian" Design'.

THE UNITED STATES

The United States produced a significant number of songs during the Second World War ranging from patriotic to the sentimental, especially significant as it was the era of Big Bands. Whether on the home front or overseas, Americans would gather to listen and dance to popular bands led by Glenn Miller, Duke Ellington, Count Basie, while the knitters would tune in on their radios to help the stitches slip across their needles.

Although war broke out later in the United States, the women and children still threw themselves into making garments for the soldiers on the front line. Production patterns were produced by all the major knitting companies and these booklets often contained family patterns as well. This meant that one book could be used to knit items for everyone.

You will notice from the examples here that most of the pattern books had a very patriotic look as the covers were nearly always red, white and blue.

It was also possible to buy patriotic knitting needles and crochet hooks, in fact whole sets were produced. The Susan Bates set came with single- and double-point needles, crochet hooks, a row counter, keep pins and a tape measure. The needles were divided into three parts coloured red, white and blue.

The United States were fighting on two fronts: Europe and the Pacific. A large number of knitted items were sent to the soldiers in Europe, but naval items were also needed in the Pacific. The patterns for all services were in one pattern book.

USA knitted tank top

The Red Cross often coordinated with the collection and distribution of items. They had labels made to sew inside the garment so that the recipient knew what part of the United States the item came from.

Knitting of 'comforts' continued until after the end of the war. There is even a pattern book produced to knit items to help the victims of the atomic bomb. The Japanese cities of Hiroshima and Nagasaki were attacked with atomic bombs during the final stages of the Second World War in 1945. These two events are the only use of nuclear weapons in war to date.

I do not profess to know a lot about knitting in the United States, but there is a large community of historical knitters who make items and collect the patterns.

RAF or seaman's jumper

FRANCE

Lisette was a popular girls' magazine published during the Second World War. These cheaply printed magazines dealt with a variety of different topics of interest to children and occasionally added a knitting pattern of something fairly straightforward like a hat or bonnet.

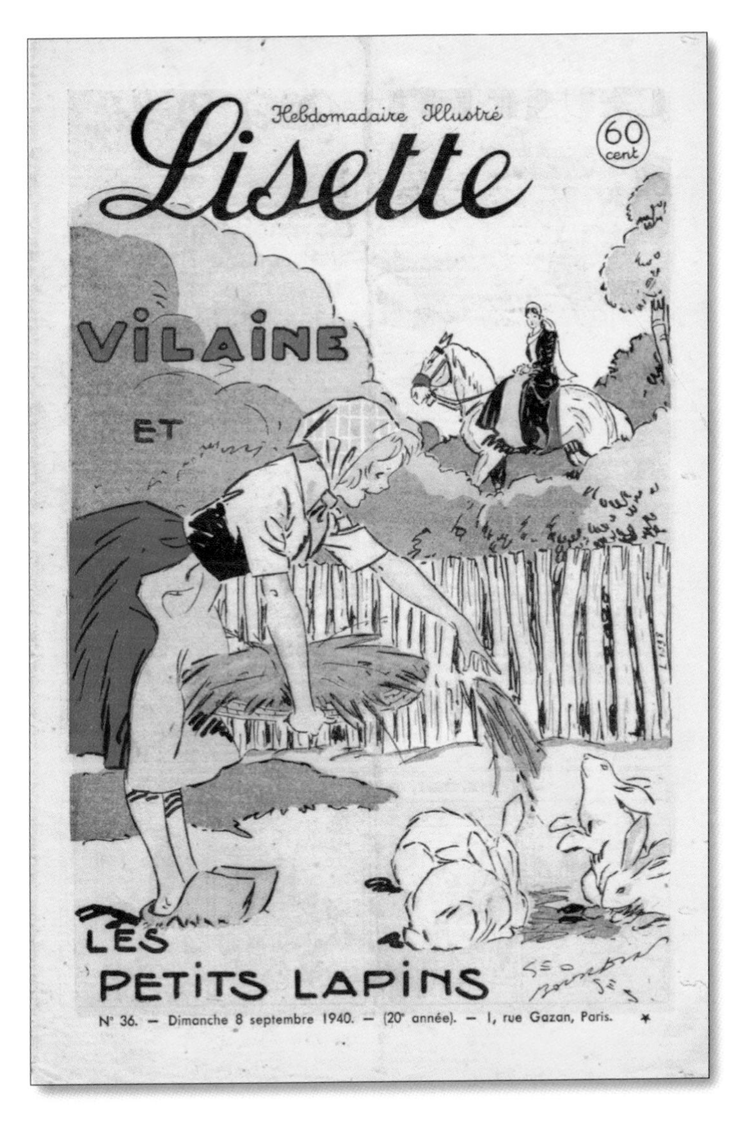

KOREA, RHODESIA & THE FALKLANDS

The need for home knitted items declined after the Second World War. There are very few patterns to be found for this period, but the Red Cross did produce patterns from 1914 onwards.

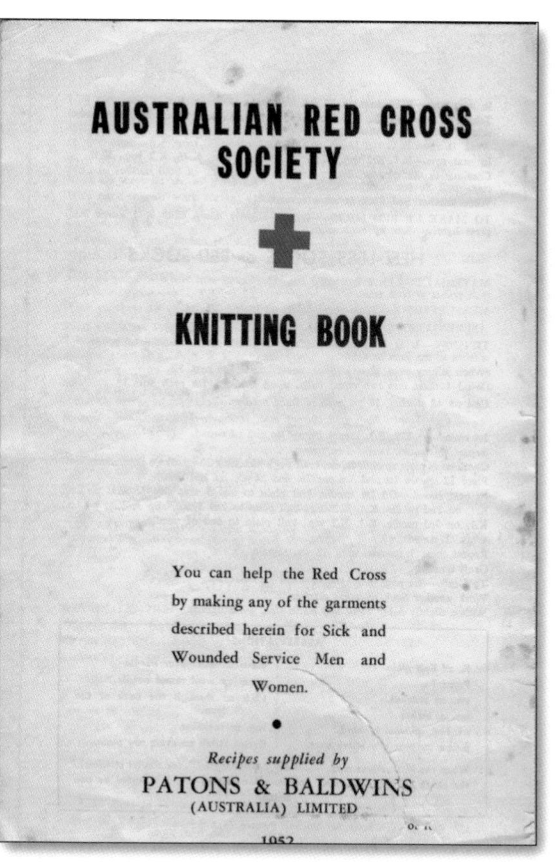

Left: Crossover scarf, Rhodesia 1965. Janet Arnold, Olivers Battery WI, made with WI yarn.

CLOTHING FOR LIBERATED EUROPE

● COATS FOR CHILDREN UNDER TWO

COAT (Boy or Girl) Fifteen months to two years. Fig. A.

MATERIALS:—5 oz. Wool. Two No. 9 Needles. Three Buttons.
MEASUREMENTS:—Length, 14 ins. Width, 23 ins. Length of sleeve (cuff turned up), 9 ins.
TENSION:—7 stitches to inch in width.
Commencing at lower edge of Right Front, cast on 50 stitches.
1st row.—K.1, (K.4, P.4) six times, K.1.
Repeat this row five times.
7th row.—K.1, (P.4, K.4) nine times, K.1.
Repeat 7th row five times.
13th row.—K.5, P.4, knit to end of row.
14th row.—K.1, purl to last 9 sts., K.4, P.4, K.1.
Repeat 13th and 14th rows twice.
Keeping a border of 2 blocks at front edge, work 26 rows without shaping.
In next row K.1, P.2, P.2 together, wool over needle (for button-hole), knit to end of row.

Fig. A.

Still keeping border at front edge, continue without shaping, making a button-hole as before in every following 36th row until there are three button-holes in all.
Work 3 rows without shaping.
Cast off 16 sts. at beginning of next row.
Work one row without shaping.
Decrease once at neck edge in every row until 26 sts. remain.
Work 6 rows without shaping. Leave until Left Front has been worked.
Work Left Front to correspond with Right Front, including button-holes and ending with a purl row.

1

P.T.O.

Patterns were re-used from the Second World War – people never threw anything away!

The only book of patterns I have managed to find from the Korean War is a Red Cross book from Australia (see page 93) and this appears to be the last of the military patterns. As in any conflict, knitters responded sympathetically to the call to produce warm clothing for Korean children, refugees and the elderly. Orphaned children in particular pulled at the heart strings, and spurred knitters affiliated with organisations such as the Church World Service, to knit like crazy. Of course the Red Cross still have knitters today who make garments for disasters all around the world.

In fact, the Korean War in the 1950s was the last war in which Australian wool was still seen as a vital commodity. At this time wool was still being used to make socks but this time, instead of the dreaded 'trench foot' caused by the atrocious conditions in the trenches, soldiers suffered from 'rice paddy feet'. It was a similar condition but caused by the soldiers' feet being immersed in water or snow for prolonged periods of time. During the Korean War soldiers took to wearing two pairs of socks, and sometimes two pairs of trousers, in the hope that the extra layers would alleviate some of the suffering caused by the conditions.

The wool sent to Korea was of poor quality and when it was used to produce uniforms, the fabric was rough and scratchy and caused serious skin irritation which sometimes left a lasting impression. The wool industry took a pounding and it took many years for it to regain its former reputation for a quality product.

Korea also saw the wearing of 'health vests' or as they were more commonly known as the string vest. These were issued by the army and knitted by women at home. They were recommended by the medical profession as they not only kept you warm in the winter but also cool in the summer by wicking the sweat away from the body. Twilley's No. 1 Health Vest Cotton was produced for use by the home knitter.

Read what a doctor had to say on the subject:

BEFORE TWILLEY'S HEALTH VEST COTTON WAS INTRODUCED:
"When bronchitics wear heavy cotton next to their skin and spend their money on a light, loose woollen overcoat, they will send for doctors half as often.

It takes a lot of argument to convince such people that vests made of dishcloth cotton on the same needles as knitters use for dishcloths are cheap, easy to wash, as warm as wool, softer than wool and dry. For the price of a set of woollies, you can get three or four, and change really often.

Why do we wear woollen underclothes? They are expensive, difficult to wash and are water-repellent, so that when we move with any energy at all, we sweat and stay wet and itchy and smelly for the rest of the day.

There are many makers of light cellular cotton for Summer. But so far as I know, there is no maker of heavy cotton underclothes, so they have to be knitted."

The pattern went on to say:

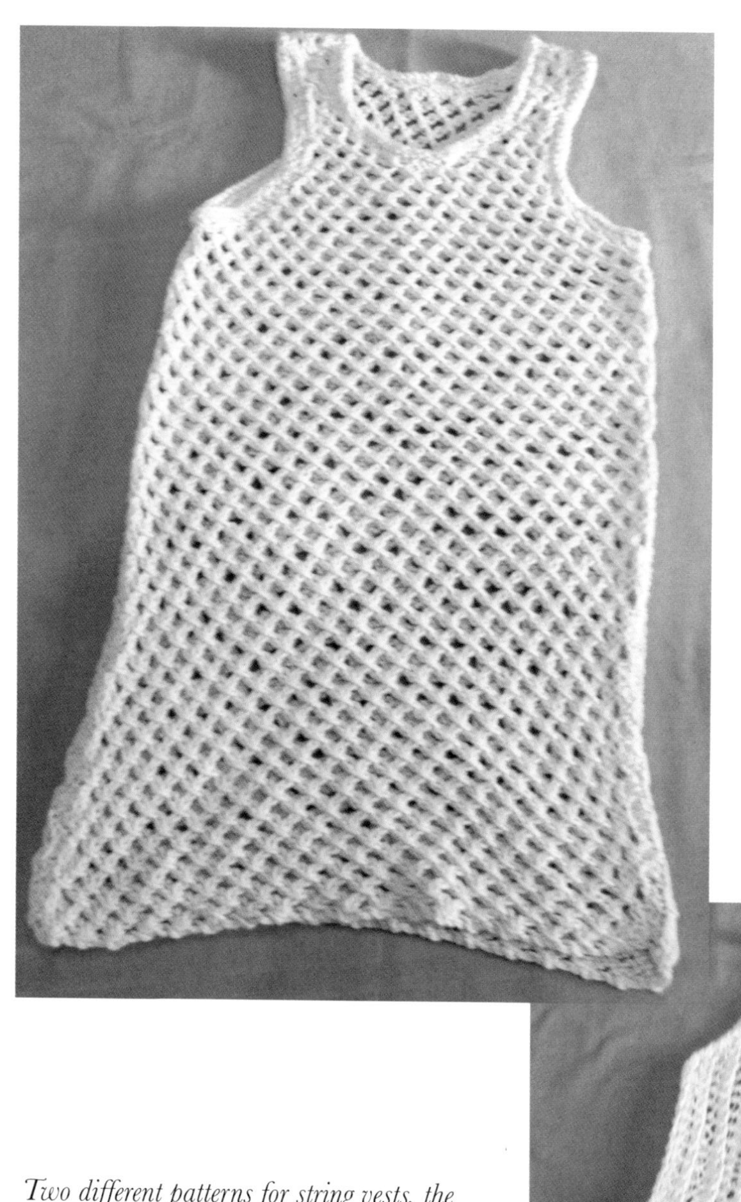

The Twilley Health Vest principle is no 'gimmick'. It has been proved on the Everest, Arctic and Antarctic expeditions, and by the Armed Forces in the severe climate of Korea. Why not benefit yourself?

Two different patterns for string vests, the top one was made from unbleached ecru cotton while the bottom one was made from bleached white cotton.

There were many patterns printed by the cotton producers in the UK – Strutts, Twilleys and Patons. The No. 1 cotton had a note on the ball band stating: "This is the type of vest that was used by members of the Everest expedition and by our troops in Korea."

Below is a pattern book published to make items for Rhodesian soldiers during the conflict. The book includes patterns for a balaclava helmet, fingerless gloves, neck warmer, socks, scarf and mittens.

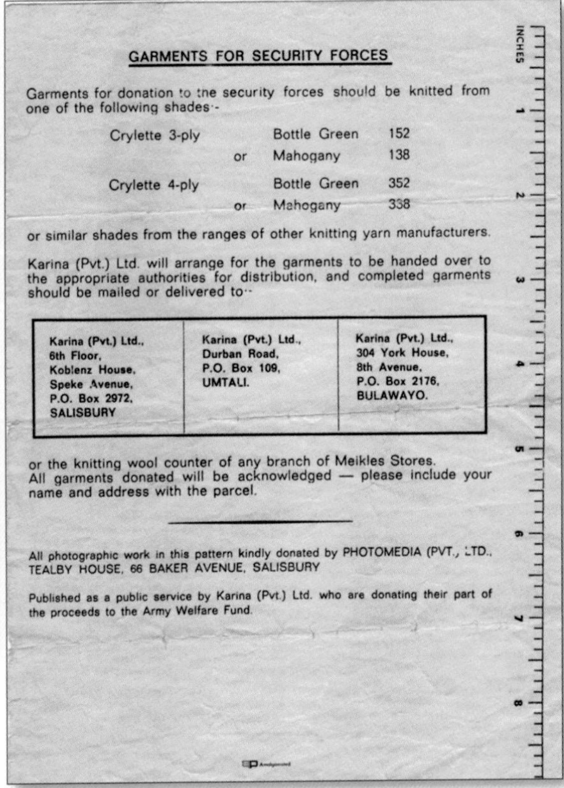

GARMENTS FOR SECURITY FORCES

Garments for donation to the security forces should be knitted from one of the following shades:-

Crylette 3-ply		Bottle Green	152
	or	Mahogany	138
Crylette 4-ply		Bottle Green	352
	or	Mahogany	338

or similar shades from the ranges of other knitting yarn manufacturers.

Karina (Pvt.) Ltd. will arrange for the garments to be handed over to the appropriate authorities for distribution, and completed garments should be mailed or delivered to:-

Karina (Pvt.) Ltd., 6th Floor, Koblenz House, Speke Avenue, P.O. Box 2972, SALISBURY	Karina (Pvt.) Ltd., Durban Road, P.O. Box 109, UMTALI.	Karina (Pvt.) Ltd., 304 York House, 8th Avenue, P.O. Box 2176, BULAWAYO.

or the knitting wool counter of any branch of Meikles Stores.
All garments donated will be acknowledged — please include your name and address with the parcel.

All photographic work in this pattern kindly donated by PHOTOMEDIA (PVT.) LTD., TEALBY HOUSE, 66 BAKER AVENUE, SALISBURY

Published as a public service by Karina (Pvt.) Ltd. who are donating their part of the proceeds to the Army Welfare Fund.

THE FALKLANDS

During this war issued uniform was found to be wanting. The boots were not suitable for the local terrain and, combined with the socks, trench foot became prevalent.

These socks were made of Nylon and did not allow for the evaporation of sweat. One hundred per cent wool, or a high wool content, socks were much healthier for anyone who does a large amount of walking or are unable to change their socks on a regular basis.

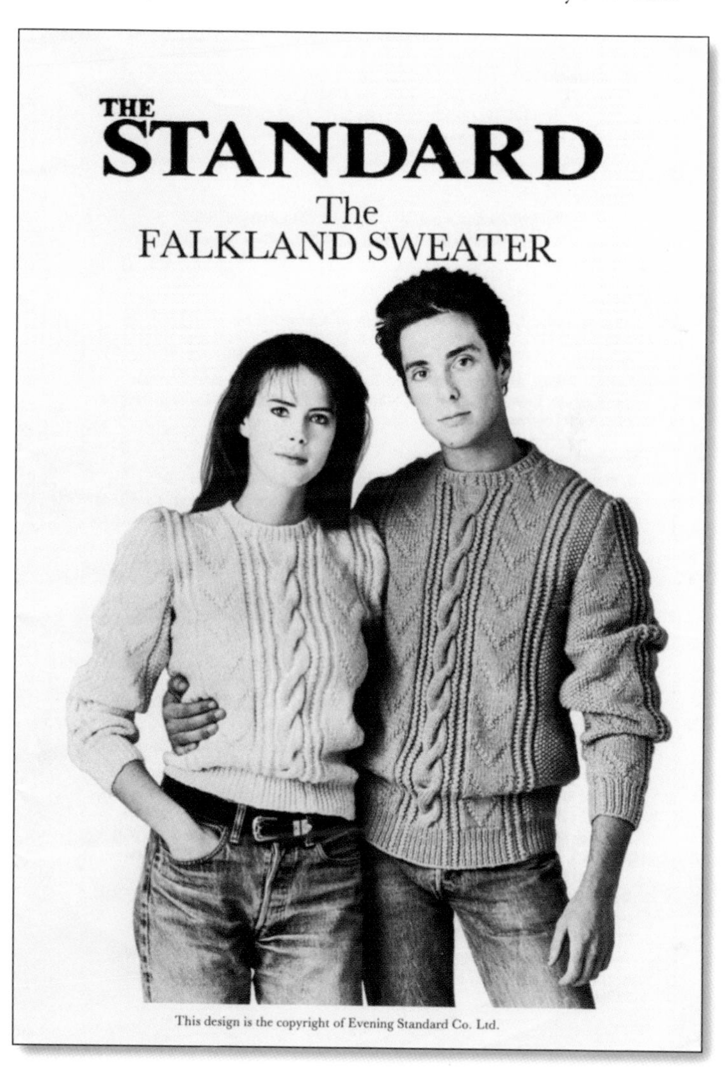

It is quite sad that this problem re-emerged when it had already been noticed by the Army in 1915. Foot inspection and the changing of socks helped to prevent trench foot and this became part of the general orders of the day.

During the Falklands War the *Evening Standard* produced a pattern to encourage the British public to knit an Aran-style adult jumper using knitting wool produced in the Islands. There were patterns printed so that you could have a home-knit jumper to use when going shooting, fishing or any other outside activity.

THE GUERNSEY GOES TO WAR

Traditional knitted garments have been made on Guernsey in the British Channel Islands for centuries. The jumper, which became known as 'the Guernsey', gave its name to the classic square-shaped wool sweater, which was designed with a straight neck so that it could be worn reversed. Until the invention of knitting machines, most industries were small-scale and made by hand; a garment much favoured by fishermen as they were virtually windproof and waterproof. Although the classic Guernsey sweater was plain, some of the parishes on the island did vary the pattern allowing more elaborate stitches to be included in the original pattern. Every soldier that went to the Falklands was issued with a Guernsey.

The Guernsey as worn by 7th Armoured Division Desert Rats

IRAQ & AFGHANISTAN

If anyone is still under the illusion that knitting is only for little old ladies, Staff Sergeant John Sorich is here to prove that they're sadly mistaken. Just look at all these rough and tough American soldiers knitting in Baghdad, Iraq!

Sergeant Sorich is on the far right, closest to the camera. In 2014 he wrote to me: "There ended up being ten of us that knit in our group. Our group was also given a very masculine and Army name... 'Knit Shit.' Sorry for the language but the name stuck. Ha ha." Who cares about the language? I think it's awesome! Especially as these knitters not only kick butt, they're doing it with vintage patterns!

John Sorich, aged 26, served for a year with the Army Reserves' 401st Bridge Engineer Company, stationed at Victory Base Camp in Baghdad. Instead of letting the stress and horror of war get to him, he faced it in a creative way: stockinette stitches. There is no doubt he certainly knows his way around a knitting needle as he has made winter caps, gloves, socks and even a pouch for his M4 rifle which, by the way, he ingeniously made by using parachute cord.

He wasn't alone in his craft, as he passed his skill on to a number of bemused fellow troops who stopped ribbing him and started knitting. At one point, ten soldiers, all male with the exception of one, joined him in an occasional knitting circle. They sent many of their creations home to surprised loved ones at Christmas.

John Sorich is now safely back from Iraq, but his knitting is far from over. He continues his

Left: John and his 'Knit Shit' group while still in Iraq

craft as a member of the Historical Re-enactment Society at Historic Fort Snelling. When he arrived home he had with him ten knitted caps which he had made for his friends, two wristlets and the world's longest sock – a total of 62,000 stitches and countless kudos. He ran out of time to make the second one.

You might wonder how John managed to obtain the wool for making his garments, well most of it arrived in Iraq thanks to his sister, Naomi. She made regular trips to Needlework Unlimited in Minneapolis, buying skeins of a replicated olive-coloured yarn that is modelled after an original World War II glove made by members of the American Red Cross.

A long-time friend of John's, Joe Torkildson, aged 29, watched in amazement when his buddy picked up a pair of knitting needles and actually produced a garment whilst on deployment. Instead of ridiculing his friend he said, "I've gotta learn this."

The first thing Joe made was a scarf for his wife, Kendel, although the first attempt was a disaster. He ended up unpicking the garment which he referred to as "ridiculously ugly". The second attempt was better and he said that once it was worn round his wife's neck it would look "pretty cool."

HATS FOR HEROES

Tina Selby set up the 'Hats for Heroes' campaign because she was concerned about our troops getting cold on the front line. She was awarded a British Empire Medal after sending 13,000 colourful woolly hats to our soldiers serving overseas.

Her original plan was to send about 500 colourful beanie hats to servicemen stationed in Afghanistan, after reading that a soldier's morale can be boosted after receiving a gift from home. However, after starting the hats in 2009, Tina found she was unable to stop making the hats and ended up recruiting a small army of knitters to help her complete her task.

Tina surrounded by the wool an just a few of the colourful hats she has knitted

As the beanie hats are only when the soldiers are off duty, Tina says it doesn't matter what colour they are, although she was advised not to use white or fluorescent wool for safety reasons. Although the summers are hot, winters in Afghanistan can be particularly harsh, with temperatures sometimes dropping to −20°C, making her knitting hats an essential accessory for both men and women.

Depending on the style in which the hat is knitted, it takes around one or two balls of wool to make each one at a cost of between £5–£10 depending on the choice of yarn. It cannot be understated just what a comfort these hats are to men stranded away from home.

THE SHIPS PROJECT

The Ships Project was founded in October 2001, when a female sailor on board USS *Bataan* responded to an 'Any Sailor' letter which was sent out by the founder, Ellen Harpin. In the letter Ellen mentioned her love of knitting which prompted one of the sailors to joke that perhaps because she was so fond of knitting she could send her a pair of knitted slippers to keep her feet warm.

From that tiny beginning the Ships Project has grown considerably and also earned the respect and support of the military. Although the USS *Bataan* has long since returned home, the knitters continue to send packages to sailors and marines as well as the Army, Marine and Air Force units on the ground.

The Ships Project now sends hats, slippers, cool-ties and cool-heads to servicemen and women around the world who are still fighting the War on Terror. It is recognised that it is very important for the troops to receive 'Hugs from Home' from time to time if they are to keep up morale and continue the fight for our safety.

Here is what one of the recipients had to say:

January 10 – "A couple of months ago my company was called on very short notice to fly to the northern portion of Afghanistan. No one told us that we were going to conduct operations in mountains southeast of Bagram. Basically we packed for three days – imagine our surprise to learn that we would be there for three weeks and the temperature at 8,000 feet was falling below zero every night. Coincidentally, I had our mail clerks forward the mail with us and it just so happened that three of your boxes arrived the first night the temperature dropped. I swear the whole company was wearing some variety of knitted product … It was quite a scene. The thought of these hardened men fighting over a pair of brightly coloured 'booties' brings a smile to my face every time I think of it."

Above: Airborne electricians at Kandahar *Below: A selection of Ellen Harpin beanie hats*

LEARNING TO CROCHET IN AFGHANISTAN

David Muir, originally from Easton, Maryland, joined the Army because of the 'adventure' and to get to use some 'awesome toys'. But of course the true meaning of being in the Army was much greater than that. He made many great friends, but as many of his buddies got moved to different units, the adventure didn't seem the same somehow after ten years of service.

When asked why he learned to crochet while he was stationed in Afghanistan he explained there were two reasons. The first because he was unable to find an afghan (a US name for a blanket) he felt was fit to adorn his walls back home and secondly he wanted something to keep his two Boston Terriers warm, both of whom hated the cold.

One day he found a book online about making clothes for dogs and he thought, "I can do that." He also wanted to make something very special for the love of his life, Krista, so to make it more personal he decided to start crocheting.

David's sister-in-law, Christina, was the inspiration behind his new hobby and gave him the idea for crocheting while serving his country. He chose the Lion Brand of yarn to make his first afghan because they offered online patterns and instructions, which he thought was a good place to start. Having learned the various different stitches, David said the hardest part was waiting for the yarn to arrive at his base in Afghanistan.

SOME PATTERNS NEVER CHANGE

Patterns for military style coats, jackets and cardigans have been produced for the last thirty to forty years and are still popular today. These are mainly for women and many look very glamorous.

However, there are also patterns to make military garments for children. The one above is from the late 1970s and has instructions to make a Guard's uniform and the green shoulder tab and padded elbow jumper. Military themed jumpers for little boys still continue to be produced with Prince George's little sleeveless, V-neck top (see opposite page).

Son of the Duke and Duchess of Cambridge, Prince George, wearing his military knitted tank top. (Getty Images)

SECTION FOUR
Anti-War and Peace Movement in Knitting

YARNSTORMING

Yarnstorming, also known as yarnbombing, is the art of enhancing a public place or object with graffiti knitting. Most yarnstormers meet in secret and, although they living ordinary lives as every day people, they usually meet and knit under assumed names.

Unlike real graffiti, yarn installations can be easily removed and are not designed to last a lifetime. Also it is not seen as a form of vandalism, rather an expressive, decorative art which can brighten up cold, public places, although some do send strong messages.

The art of yarnstorming is believed to have originated in the United States, when a group of Texas knitters wanted to find a creative way of using their leftover yarn. Since then it has spread worldwide.

In the 1990s an artist from Houston called Bill Davenport, started creating and exhibiting crochet-covered objects and today the art has spread throughout the world. In 2015, a group of nameless knitters have brightened up the old red post boxes of South Essex with bright Christmas scenes, and people love the fact that these scenes brighten the grey December days.

REMEMBRANCE POPPIES

Remembrance Day is a major focus in the UK and is also observed by other countries throughout Europe and the Commonwealth during November. Many of us will buy and wear British Legion poppies in memory of service personnel who fought and died in the line of duty, while others will be inspirational and knit their own versions.

INSTRUCTIONS FOR KNITTED BARBED WIRE AND POPPIES

Using 4-ply grey wool or yarn and a French knitting, hand-held machine, make double the length you require. Fold in half and twist to give it that wire look. To make the barbs, just make short lengths of grey French knitting and wrap around the twisted knitting and attach by sewing in place.

The pattern below gives a ribbed knitted poppy and is easy for beginners. The ply of the yarn does not matter but if, for instance, you are using 8-ply then try a 4mm needle.

Colour A 1 ball of red yarn (one ball will make a number of poppies)
1 black button (for centre of poppy)

Body of Poppy

Using Col A cast on 60 sts.
Row 1–10 K2 P2 to end of row
Row 11 K2 tog across the row.
Row 12 Sl 1, K2 tog, psso across the row.
Break off yarn with a long tail and thread
back through the remaining stitches and pull tight.
Join edges with mattress stitch.

Finishing

Attach the black button using black yarn or thread to make the centre of the poppy.

KNITTING FOR NOTHING

A former prisoner of war, who spent more than eighteen months in a prisoner of war camp in Germany during the Second World War, not only survived interrogations, torture and appalling conditions, but succeeded in knitting a valuable war artefact.

Jim Simpson had no wool and no knitting needles, but did this hinder him, not at all. He used pot handles as needles and simply unpicked old knitted garments and set about his massive task. What he achieved was a knitted woollen blanket which measures 1.83 x 1.8 metres, featuring the map of Australia and the Coat of Arms.

"I knitted it with straightened handles from the camp's cooking pots," said Jim, "they looked like pieces of number eight wire. The cook agreed to give them to me if I knitted him a pair of socks."

Jim's rug has been beautifully preserved and is arguably Australia's most valuable war artefact, outside of a museum.

KNIT YOUR OWN SOLDIER

A knit your own soldier book was published in 2014 after charities realised the urgent need to support military families. Over five thousand of these books have been handed out to regiments across the country to try and help the children of serving soldiers.

It was launched by the Royal Navy and Royal Marines Children's Fund and has been heralded as a vital step in trying to get children to understand the changes in family life when a parent returns from deployment overseas.

After a decade of intense fighting in the Middle East, more and more soldiers are returning to their families but are finding it hard to adjust. They suffer from post traumatic stress disorder, depression and other mental health issues which result from the horrors they have witnessed and are often contributed to adjustment to civilian life following such an intense experience. As many as one in five soldiers is finding it hard to reintegrate into normal family and working life.

One little eleven-year-old girl wrote:

"When I see my dad's bag I know he's going away."

Of her own volition she wrote a series of notes, cards and letters and hid them between his clothes so that he would find them when he unpacked his kit.

SUBVERSIVE KNITTING

Primarily a feminine pastime or hobby, knitting does have a rich history of political subversion. A fine example of this is during the 1760s when Britain levied higher and higher taxes on its colonies. Americans wanted to demonstrate their displeasure and did so by weaning themselves off British imported goods and by 1769 British imports were officially banned.

In addition to the banning of British tea, resulting in the Boston Tea Party revolt in 1773, Americans were reliant upon the import of British textiles to clothe themselves. Women would have clandestine meetings under the guise of 'spinning meetings' or 'spinning bees' where they could partake in political debates while spinning yarn and thread, sewing or knitting items to clothe their families in the absence of British fabric.

Because women would normally be excluded from what were considered primarily masculine topics, these 'spinning bees' expanded and eventually included men. They developed into spectator sporting events with good-natured competitions taking place between church congregations, married and unmarried women, towns and cities and there was no age limit whatsoever – young and old were welcome. These industrious women were attributed the slogan 'Freedom, Liberty and Frugality' as they used their own initiative to clothe their families in homespun and recycled garments.

DEFEATING THE ENEMY!

Because women had become accustomed to clothing their own families, it was a short transition to providing uniforms for their men when they were called up to fight in the Revolutionary War (1775–1783). The Army's needs were enormous and the duty fell to the towns and cities who published the names of knitters and how much they could produce. Some industrious women even added their own embellishment to the socks by knitting the date '1776' into their socks. The American poster below uses a play on words to remind people that knitting was just one of the ways to defeat the enemy!

When reports reached back home that some of their men were having to go naked due to shortage of clothing, the women all rallied and started to gather old blankets, yarn and clothing which they would either unpick and reknit, or simply darn and patch and make into new stockings, shirts, breeches and blankets, actually transporting the items themselves to the front line. Seen as harmless and innocent women they could easily slip past the British guards. It was these women's patriotism that saw no bounds and because of them knitting has lasted through the centuries.

With each war knitting enjoyed a resurgence and there probably isn't a single soldier who hasn't benefited from the ingenuity of the knitter back home.

Marianne Joergensen made a pink blanket to cover a combat tank to protest against Denmark's involvement in the Iraq war in 2006.

Each square was knitted or crocheted by volunteers from Denmark, the United Kingdom, the United States and several other countries. Joergensen writes:

> *"Unsimilar to a war, knitting signals home, care, closeness and time for reflection. Ever since Denmark became involved in the war in Iraq I have made different variations of pink tanks and I intend to keep doing that until the war ends..."*

SECTION FIVE
Knitting Pattern Examples

KNITTING PATTERN EXAMPLES

This section includes patterns from the various eras that have been adapted or altered to fit modern body shapes and sizes.

KNITTED MUFFLER (CRIMEAN WAR)

MATERIALS:
1 pair of knitting needles size: 3¾ mm (UK 9) (US 5)

3 x 50 g Tartan Green New Lanark Mills DK
1 x 50 g ball Black
1 x 50 g ball Milano
1 x 50 g ball Ecru
1 x 50 g ball Cherry
1 x 50 g ball Ochre

INSTRUCTIONS:
Cast on 74 stitches using black wool.

1st row: Wrap wool round right hand needle to make a stitch. The wool is now at the front of the work. Slip 1 purlwise. Purl 2 stitches together. Repeat this to the last 2 stitches of the row. Make a stitch as before then purl 2 together.

2nd row: Wrap wool round right hand needle to make a stitch. The wool is now at the front of the work. Purl 2 together. * Wrap wool round right hand needle to make a stitch. Slip 1 purlwise. Purl 2 stitches together. Work from * to end of row.

All further rows are now worked as 2nd row only.

COLOUR PATTERN:

Work: 4 rows – Black (This is called 1 stripe pattern)
4 rows – Milano
4 rows – Ecru
4 rows – Cherry
4 rows – Ochre

4 rows – Black
4 rows – Ochre
4 rows – Cherry
4 rows – Ecru
4 rows – Milano
4 rows – Black

Work 20 rows in Tartan Green.

Repeat Stripe pattern once.

Work 33 rows in Tartan Green.

Work 1 Stripe pattern.

Work 20 rows in Tartan Green

Work 1 Stripe pattern.

Then cast off in Black.

Make a fringe for both ends of Comforter using Tartan Green.

SLEEPING HELMET (BOER WAR)

MATERIALS:
Set of 5 double pins size: 3¼ mm (UK 10) (US 3)
1 pair of knitting needles size: 3¼ mm (UK 10) (US 3)
1 40 cm circular knitting needle size: 3¼ mm (UK 10) (US 3)
1 keep pin
1 marker

3 x 50 g balls Pebble 100% wool DK
1 x 50 g ball Cherry New Lanark Mill

INSTRUCTIONS:
Using Pebble colour cast on 6 stitches using 3¼mm double point needles.
2 stitches on each of 3 needles.

1st and every alternate round for 30 rounds knit plain stitch.

2nd round: * Make a stitch by lifting a loop from the previous round and knitting it.
(Make one is always done this way throughout the pattern)
Knit 1, make 1, knit 1, repeat from * twice more.

Place marker at beginning of the round.

4th round: * Make 1, knit 2, make 1, knit 2, repeat from * twice more.

6th round: * Make 1, knit 1, purl 2, repeat from * to end of round.

8th round: * Make 1, knit 2, purl 2, repeat from * to end of round.

10th round: * Make 1, purl 1, knit 2, purl 2, repeat from * to end of round.

12th round: * Make 1, purl 2, knit 2, purl 2, repeat from * to end of round.

14th round: * Make 1, knit 1, purl 2, knit 2, purl 2, repeat from * to end of round.

16th round: * Make 1, knit 2, purl 2, knit 2, purl 2, repeat from * to end of round.

18th round: * Make 1, purl 1, knit 2, purl 2, knit 2, purl 2, repeat from * to end of round.

20th round: * Make 1, purl 2, knit 2, purl 2, knit 2, purl 2, repeat from * to end of round.

22nd round: * Make 1, knit 1, purl 2, knit 2, purl 2, knit 2, purl 2, repeat from repeat from * to end of round.

24th round: * Make 1, knit 2, purl 2, knit 2, purl 2, knit 2, purl 2, repeat from * to end of round.

26th round: * Make 1, purl 1, knit 2, purl 2, knit 2, purl 2, knit 2, purl 2, repeat from * to end of round.

28th round: * Make 1, purl 2, knit 2, purl 2, knit 2, purl 2, knit 2, purl 2, repeat from * to end of round.

30th round: * Make 1, knit 1, purl 2, knit 2, purl 2, knit 2, purl 2, knit 2, purl 2, repeat from * to end of round.

31st round: Knit 2, make 1 * knit 4, make 1, repeat from * ending with knit 2.

You should now have 40 stitches on each of the 3 needles.

32nd round: Knit 3, purl 2, repeat this ribbing for 6 more rounds.

39th round: Knit plain with Cherry wool.

40th round: Cherry rib as 32nd round.

41st round: With grey knit plain.

42nd round: Grey rib as 32nd round.

43rd round: With red knit plain.

44th round: Red rib as 32nd round.

45th round: With grey knit plain.

46th round: Grey rib as 32nd round.

47th round: With red knit plain.

48th round: With grey knit 30 stitches on to one needle and put these stitches on to the keep pin.
Knit the remaining stitches of the round (90) onto normal needle.
On these 90 stitches knit in rows backwards and forwards as follows:
7 rows of ribbing in grey
* 1 plain and 1 ribbed row in red.
1 plain and 1 ribbed row in grey.
1 plain and 1 ribbed row in red.
1 plain and 1 ribbed row in grey.

1 plain and 1 ribbed row in red.
1 plain and 1 ribbed row in grey. *

Repeat from * to * for 18 rows in knitting and colour pattern once.
Then, continuing in the rib pattern work 2 red, 2 grey, 2 red, 2 grey, 2 red rows, 1 plain, 2 ribbed rows in grey.

Cast on 30 stitches for the lower edge of the face opening to match with the 30 stitches left at the top of the opening.

Continue knitting rounds as the pattern (18 rounds) until 6 sets of stripes have been worked. There should be 113 rounds below the face opening to form the muffler.
Cast off loosely in pattern.

FACE OPENING FINISHING
Using grey wool pick up 30 stitches along the right hand side of the opening. Pick up and knit across the top 30 stitches. Pick up 30 stitches down the left hand side of the face. Now knit along the bottom 30 stitches.

You now have 120 stitches on 4 double point needles. Using the 5th needle knit as follows:
4 grey ribbing rounds.

1 plain and 1 ribbed round in red.

1 plain and 1 ribbed round in grey.

1 plain and 1 ribbed round in red.

Cast off moderately tightly.

ARMLETS OR ARM WARMERS (FIRST WORLD WAR)

MATERIALS:
1 set double point knitting needles 4 mm (UK 8) (US 6)
1 set double point knitting needles 3 mm (UK 11) (US 2)

3 x 50 g balls DK, Sandstone, New Lanark Mills, 100% wool

INSTRUCTIONS:
Cast on – not too tightly – 72 stitches over size 4 mm needles.

24 stitches on each of the three needles.

Works rounds in knit 2, purl 2 rib for 9 inches (23 cm). Place marker at the beginning of the 1st round.

Change to 3 mm needles and work a further 8 inches (20 cm).

This gives the armlet all the shaping to fit the arm.

Cast off loosely and sew in any ends on the inside of the armlet.

KNITTED CHEST PROTECTOR (FIRST WORLD WAR)

MATERIALS:
1 crochet hook 3¾ mm (UK 9) (US 5)
1 pair of 3¾ mm (UK 9) (US 5) knitting needles
1 stitch keep pin

2 x 50 g balls DK Sandstone 100% wool
1 x 50 g ball DK Black, New Lanark Mills
1 x 50 g ball DK Ecru
2 buttons

INSTRUCTIONS:
Cast on 80 stitches in chequer board colours – 10 white, 10 black stitches – 4 times.

The front is work using the intarsia technique, small balls of each colour.

Working in stocking stitch – 1 row knit, 1 row purl – keep the coast on colours for 10 rows.

Change the colours to 10 black, 10 white stitches, 4 times.

Continue as before working 10 rows.

Work these 20 rows another 3 times. This should give you a chequer board effect.

Break off all colours and with Sandstone knit 4 rows in garter stitch – all knit.

NECK SHAPING:
Knit 30 stitches. Cast off 20 stitches. Knit 30 stitches.

Working on one set of 30 stitches, knit 53 rows in garter stitch.

Leave these stitches on the keep pin, break off yarn.

54th row: Knit to inside edge and cast on 20 stitches and knit across the other 30 stitches from keep pin.

You should now have 80 stitches on your needle.

Now working in garter stitch, all knit, work 84 rows and then cast off.

Single crochet round the outside edge of the garment to stabilise the edge.

Using 3¾ mm needles pick up 10 stitches along the front side 2 rows up from the cast on edge.

Working in Sandstone work 30 rows in garter stitch, all knit.

Make a buttonhole, knit 4 stitches, cast off 2 stitches, knit 4 stitches.

Knit 4 stitches, cast on 2 stitches, knit 4 stitches.
Work a further 6 rows in garter stitch and cast off.

Make another side strap to match on the other side of the front.

Sew button each side of the back so the side straps can be closed around the body.

Sew in any ends of yarn to complete the garment.

STUMP WARMER (SECOND WORLD WAR) (AMPUTATION LEG COVER)

MATERIALS:

1 set 4 double point needles size 4½ mm (UK 7) (US 7)

1 set 4 double point needles size 4 mm (UK 8) (US 6)

1 marker

2 x 50 g White Woolly Merino wool DMC, Colour 01

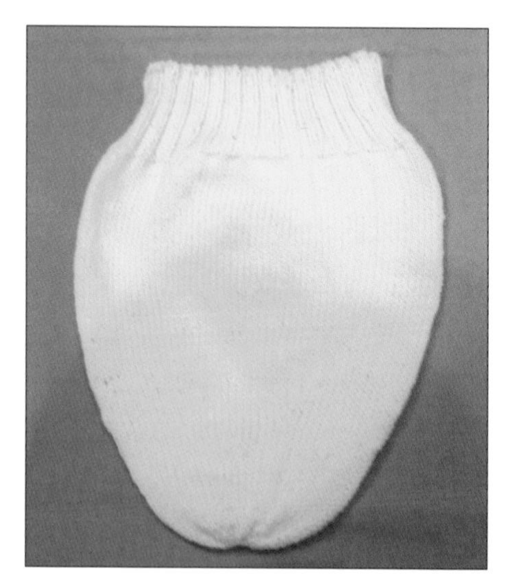

INSTRUCTIONS:

Using 4½ mm needles cast on 116 stitches. 36 stitches on 1st needle and 40 stitches on 2nd and 3rd needles.

Work 8 cm (3 in) in knit 2, purl 2 rib.

Remember to place a marker at the beginning of the round.

Work 6 cm (2½ in) in stocking stitch.

Change to 4mm needles and continue in stocking stitch until the work measures 18 cm (7 in) from the cast on edge.

Decreasing to shape the cover to fit the stump.

The decreasing rows are spaced unevenly so that ridges are not formed. The article must not have any ridges of any kind as this can cause pressure and sores on the fragile skin.

1st decrease round: * Knit 12, knit 2 together * repeat to last 4 stitches, knit 4.

Knit 6 rounds

2nd decrease round: Knit 4 * knit 11, knit 2 together * repeat from * to end of round.

Knit 6 rounds

3rd decrease round: * Knit 9, knit 2 together, repeat from * to end of round.

Knit 3 rounds

5th decrease round: Knit 1 * Knit 12, knit 2 together, repeat from * to end of round.

Knit 6 rounds

6th decrease round: * Knit 11, knit 2 together, repeat from * to last stitch, knit 1.

Knit 4 rounds

7th decrease round: Knit 3 * knit 12, knit 2 together, repeat from * to end of round.

Knit 2 rounds

8th decrease round: Knit 3 * knit 2 together, knit 11 to end of round.

9th decrease round: * Knit 10, knit 2 together, repeat from * to end of round.

10th decrease round: Knit 3 * knit 2 together, knit 2, repeat from * to end of round.

11th decrease round: Knit 3 * knit 2 together, knit 2, repeat from * to end of round.

12th decrease round: Knit 3 * knit 1, knit 2 together, repeat from * to end of round.

Knit 1 round

Last round: Knit 1 * knit 2 together, repeat from * to end of round.

Break off the wool and run the yarn through the last stitches and fasten off securely.

This finishing must be flat to prevent rubbing on the wound.

ODDMENT KNEE BLANKET (SECOND WORLD WAR)

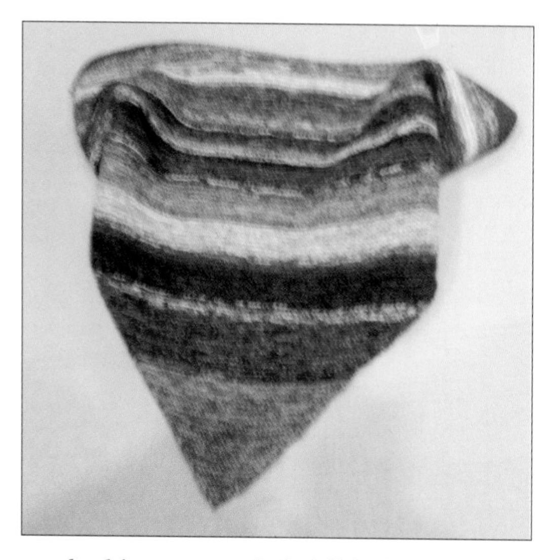

MATERIALS:
1 x 150 cm circular needle size 4 mm (UK 8) (US 6)

Oddments of 4 ply and double knit wool/yarn.

During the Second World War women were told not to throw away any piece of yarn that was 6 inches long or longer, as it could always be used to make something. This blanket is made with any colour or type of yarn and worked in garter stitch (all knit). It is great to see what you end up with, colour and texture wise.

INSTRUCTIONS:
Cast on 3 stitches and knit 1 row, working in yarn weight made up to double knitting.

Increase 1 stitch at the beginning of next row, 4 stitches on the needle and knit all stitches.

Continue increasing 1 stitch at the beginning of each row until you reach your required width of blanket.

Knit 1 row across all stitches.

Now decrease 1 stitch at the beginning of each row by knitting 2 stitches together until you have 3 stitches left. Knit these 3 stitches together and fasten off.

Sew in any ends left on the blanket.

RHODESIAN SCARF (UDI 1964–1965)

MATERIALS:
1 ball WI soft and silky 4-ply

1 pair knitting needles size 4 mm (UK 8) (US 6)
1 pair knitting needles size 3¼ mm (UK 10) (US 3)
1 keep pin

INSTRUCTIONS:
Using 4 mm needles cast on 1 stitch.

Increase 1 stitch at the beginning of next 2 rows.

You now have 3 stitches on the needle. Work in garter stitch – all knit.

1st row: Slip 1 stitch, increase in next stitch by knitting into front and back of stitch, knit 1 stitch.

2nd row: Slip 1 stitch, increase in the next stitch as in 1st increase row. Knit to end of row.

Continue to increase at the beginning of each row as set above until there are 40 stitches on the needle.

Now work 40 rows, slipping the 1st stitch at the beginning of each row.

Change to 3¼ mm needles and work 24 rows in knit 2, purl 2 rib.

Change back to 4 mm needles and work 120 rows in garter stitch – all knit.

Change to 3¼ mm needles and work 2 rows in knit 2, purl 2 rib.

1st row: Knit 20 stitches, continue working only on these stitches, leave the other 20 stitches on a keep pin.

Continue in knit 2, purl 2 rib for 20 rows. Cut yarn and place these stitches on to a keep pin.

Place the other 20 stitches back onto the 3¼ mm needles. Rejoin the yarn and work 20 rows in set pattern.

Continue by working the next row in rib pattern and knit across the other 20 stitches in rib pattern.

Work 2 rows in knit 2, purl 2 rib.

Change to 4 mm needles and work in garter stitch for 4o rows, slipping the 1st stitch at the beginning of each row.

Work the decrease row, reversing the increase rows.

Work to last 3 stitches, knit together.

Cut yarn and secure the last stitch.

MODERN SERVICES BEANIE HAT

MATERIALS:
1 set double point pins size 3½ mm (US 4)

1 ball each	Ochre	100% wool
	Tartan Green	Double Knit
	Autumn	New Lanark Mills

INSTRUCTIONS:
Cast on 112 stitches using Tartan Green.
Put 37 stitches on the 1st and 2nd needles and 38 stitches on the 3rd needle.

Place marker at the beginning of 1st row.

Work in the round in knit 4, purl 4 rib for 32 rounds.

Continue in 4 x 4 rib in Autumn colour for 28 rounds.

Change to Ochre colour wool and work 16 rounds in 4 x 4 rib.

Continue in Ochre colour and on next round commence the decrease for top of beanie.

1st round: Knit 1, knit 2 together, knit 1, purl 4. Continue to end of round.

2nd round: Knit 3, purl 4 to end of round.

3rd round: Knit 3, purl 1, purl 2 together, purl 1. Continue to end of round.

4th round: Knit 3, purl 3, to end of round.

5th round: Knit 1, knit 2 together. Continue to end of round.

6th round: Knit 2, purl 3, to end of round.

7th round: Knit 2, purl 1, purl 2 together. Continue to end of round.

8th round: Knit 2, purl 2, to end of round.

9th round: Knit 2 together, purl 2 to end of round.

10th round: Knit 1, purl 2, to end of round.

11th round: Knit 1, purl 2 together, to end of round.

12th round: Knit 1, purl 1, to end of round.

Cut wool, leaving a 10 cm tail, and thread through the remaining stitches and pull the top opening closed.

Fasten off and secure the top. Sew in any ends on the inside of the beanie.